Deeds and Words

Gendering Politics after Joni Lovenduski

Edited by
Rosie Campbell and Sarah Childs

First published by the ECPR Press in 2014

The ECPR Press is the publishing imprint of the European Consortium for Political Research (ECPR), a scholarly association, which supports and encourages the training, research and cross-national cooperation of political scientists in institutions throughout Europe and beyond.

ECPR Press
University of Essex
Wivenhoe Park
Colchester
CO4 3SQ
UK

Typeset by ECPR Press

Printed and bound by Lightning Source

British Library Cataloguing in Publication Data

A catalogue record for this book is available from the British Library

Hardback ISBN: 978-1-907301-52-0
Paperback ISBN: 978-1-910259-45-0
PDF ISBN: 978-1-910-259-31-3

www.ecpr.eu/ecprpress

Series Editors:
Dario Castiglione (University of Exeter)
Peter Kennealy (European University Institute)
Alexandra Segerberg (Stockholm University)
Peter Triantafillou (Roskilde University)

ECPR – *Studies in European Political Science* is a series of high-quality edited volumes on topics at the cutting edge of current political science and political thought. All volumes are research-based offering new perspectives in the study of politics with contributions from leading scholars working in the relevant fields. Most of the volumes originate from ECPR events including the Joint Sessions of Workshops, the Research Sessions, and the General Conferences.
Books in this series:

A Political Sociology of Transnational Europe
ISBN: 9781907301346
Edited by Niilo Kauppi

Between Election Democracy
ISBN: 9781907301988
Edited by Hanne Marthe Narud and Peter Esaiasson

Deliberative Mini-Publics: Involving Citizens in the Democratic Process
ISBN: 9781907301322
Edited by Kimmo Grönlund, André Bächtiger and Maija Setälä

Europeanisation and Party Politics
ISBN: 9781907301223
Edited by Erol Külahci

Great Expectations, Slow Transformations: Incremental Change in Post-Crisis Regulation
ISBN: 9781907301544
Edited by Manuela Moschella and Eleni Tsingou

Growing into Politics
ISBN: 9781907301421
Edited by Simone Abendschön

Interactive Policy Making, Metagovernance and Democracy
ISBN: 9781907301131
Edited by Jacob Torfing and Peter Triantafillou

Matching Voters with Parties and Candidates: Voting Advice Applications in a Comparative Perspective
ISBN: 9781907301735
Edited by Diego Garzia and Stefan Marschall

New Nation States
ISBN: 9781907301360
Edited by Julien Danero Iglesias, Nenad Stojanović and Sharon Weinblum

Perceptions of Europe
ISBN: 9781907301155
Edited by Daniel Gaxie, Jay Rowell and Nicolas Hubé

Personal Representation: The Neglected Dimension of Electoral Systems
ISBN: 9781907301162
Edited by Josep Colomer

Political Participation in France and Germany
ISBN: 9781907301315
Oscar Gabriel, Silke Keil, and Eric Kerrouche

Political Trust: Why Context Matters
ISBN: 9781907301230
Edited by Sonja Zmerli and Marc Hooghe

Practices of Interparliamentary Coordination in International Politics: The European Union and Beyond
ISBN: 9781907301308
Edited by Ben Crum and John Erik Fossum

Spreading Protest: Social Movements in Times of Crisis
ISBN: 9781910259207
Edited by Donatella della Porta and Alice Mattoni

The Political Ecology of the Metropolis
ISBN: 9781907301377
Edited by Jefferey M Sellers, Daniel Kübler, R. Alan Walks and Melanie Walter-Rogg

Please visit www.ecpr.eu/ecprpress for up-to-date information about new publications.

Contents

List of Figures, Tables and Boxes

Figures

Tables

Boxes

List of Abbreviations

AWS	All Women Shortlists
BC	British Columbia
EOC	Equal Opportunities Commission, UK
RNGS	Research Network on Gender, Politics and the State
UN	United Nations

Contributors

PETER ALLEN is a Lecturer in British Politics at Queen Mary, University of London. His research focuses on political behaviour and representation, and he has published work in journals including *Political Studies*, *Parliamentary Affairs* and *The Political Quarterly*.

FAITH ARMITAGE is a Research Associate on the ERC-funded programme, Understanding Institutional Change: A Gender Perspective at Manchester University. Faith uses the expenses and debating regimes in the parliaments of the United Kingdom and South Africa to explore these concepts. This work builds on previous research that Faith has conducted on ceremony and ritual in parliaments.

ROSIE CAMPBELL is a reader in politics at Birkbeck, University of London. She has written widely on gender and British politics. Her book *Gender and the Vote in Britain* was published in 2006 and she has recently written on the politics of diversity, women voters' responses to public spending cuts and what voters want from their parliamentary candidates, published in the *British Journal of Political Science*, *Party Politics* and *Political Studies*. Rosie is Vice Chair of the Political Studies Association of the UK and a member of the 2015 British Election Study's advisory board.

KAREN CELIS is research professor at the Department of Political Science, and affiliated to RHEA (Centre for Gender and Diversity) of the Vrije Universiteit Brussel. From 2007 till 2013 she was Co-convenor of the Standing Group on Gender and Politics of the European Consortium for Political Research. She is co-editor (with Georgina Waylen, Johanna Kantola and Laurel Weldon) of the *The Oxford Handbook on Gender and Politics* (Oxford University Press, 2013).

SARAH CHILDS is Professor of Politics and Gender at the University of Bristol. Books include *Sex, Gender and the Conservative Party* (2012); *Gender and British Party Politics* (2008). Articles on women MPs, representation, critical mass, and conservatism, and gender and representation, have been published in *Political Studies*, *Politics and Gender*, *Parliamentary Affairs* and *Party Politics*. She is currently researching gendered institutions with the UK Parliament and political parties. In 2009–10 she was Special Adviser to the UK Parliament's 'Speaker's Conference' on representation and in 2014 to the APPG Women in Parliament Inquiry.

DRUDE DAHLERUP is Professor of Political Science, University of Stockholm, Sweden and graduated from University of Aarhus in Denmark. She has written extensively on gender and politics, the history of the women's movements and gender equality policies. She has worked as a consultant for international organisations to countries on how to empower women in politics, on quota systems and electoral systems (in Sierra Leone, Cambodia, Tunisia, Kosovo, China, Egypt, Bhutan). Among her recent publications are *Women, Quotas and Politics* (ed. Routledge, 2006), and *Breaking Male Dominance in Old Democracies* (with Monique Leyenaar, Oxford University Press, 2013). Drude Dahlerup is one of the 20 members of the UN Global Civil Society Advisory Group to the executive director of UN Women.

ANA ESPÍRITO-SANTO (PhD, European University Institute, 2011) is an invited assistant professor at ISCTE-IUL (Lisbon University Institute), Department of Political Science & Public Policies. Her main current research interests are gender and politics and comparative politics. She is the co-author of several book chapters and an article in *West European Politics* (2012).

YVONNE GALLIGAN is Professor of Comparative Politics at Queen's University Belfast where she is also the founding Director of the Centre for Advancement of Women in Politics. Among her publications are *States of Democracy: Gender and Politics in the European Union* (ed. Routledge, 2015), *Politics and Gender in Ireland* (ed. with Fiona Buckley, Taylor and Francis, 2014), *Gender Politics and Democracy in Post-Socialist Europe* (with Sara Clavero and Marina Calloni, Barbara Budrich Publishers, 2007), and *Sharing Power: Women, Parliament, Democracy* (ed. with Manon Tremblay, Ashgate, 2006).

MERYL KENNY is Lecturer in Government and Politics in the Department of Politics and International Relations at the University of Leicester. Her research focuses on gender and political recruitment, and feminist institutionalism. Recent publications include *Gender and Political Recruitment: Theorizing Institutional Change* (Palgrave, 2013).

MONA LENA KROOK is Associate Professor of Political Science at Rutgers University. Her first book, *Quotas for Women in Politics: Gender and Candidate Selection Reform Worldwide* (Oxford University Press, 2009), received the American Political Science Association Victoria Schuck Award for the Best Book on Women and Politics in 2010. She is also co-editor of *The Impact of Gender Quotas* (Oxford University Press, 2012), exploring the impact of quotas beyond numbers in Western Europe, Latin America, Asia/theMiddle East, and Sub-Saharan Africa.

FIONA MACKAY is Professor of Politics and Dean of the School of Social and Political Science at the University of Edinburgh. Her research interests include women's political representation, and gender and institutions. She founded and co-directs FIIN: Feminism and Institutionalism International Network (www.femfiin.com). Her most recent book is *Gender, Politics and Institutions: Towards a Feminist Institutionalism* (co-edited with Mona Lena Krook, Palgrave Macmillan, 2011).

ROSA MALLEY did her doctorate at the University of Bristol as part of the Gendered Ceremony and Ritual in Parliaments research project. Her thesis looked at parliamentary culture at Westminster and the Scottish Parliament and the substantive representation of women.

AMY G. MAZUR is Professor of Political Science at Washington State University and an Associate Researcher at SciencesPo, Paris. Her recent books include: *Politics, Gender and Concepts* (editor with Gary Goertz, Cambridge University Press, 2008); and *The Politics of State Feminism: Innovation in Comparative Research* (with Dorothy McBride, Temple University Press, 2010). She is currently co convener (with Joni Lovenduski) of the Gender Equality Policy in Practice Project.

DOROTHY E. MCBRIDE is professor emerita of political science at Florida Atlantic University. With Amy Mazur, she was co-director of the Research Network on Gender, Politics and the State (RNGS) and co-author of *The Politics of State Feminism: Innovation in Comparative Research* (Temple University Press, 2010). She is co-author with Janine Parry of the forthcoming *Women's Rights in the USA: Policy Conflicts and Gender Role*s 5th Ed.

RAINBOW MURRAY is Reader (Associate Professor) in Politics at Queen Mary University of London. Her research on gender, politics and representation has been published in journals such as the *American Political Science Review*, *Political Research Quarterly*, *European Journal of Political Research* and *Politics & Gender*. She is the author of *Parties, Gender Quotas and Candidate Selection in France* (Palgrave, 2010) and the editor of Cracking the *Highest Glass Ceiling: A Global Comparison of Women's Campaigns for Executive Office* (Praeger, 2010).

PIPPA NORRIS is the McGuire Lecturer in Comparative Politics at the John F. Kennedy School of Government, Harvard University, ARC Laureate Fellow and Professor of Government and International Relations at the University of Sydney, and Director of the Electoral Integrity Project. Honors include the Johan Skytte and the Karl Deutsch awards. She has published more than 45 books in comparative politics (many in translation). Those for Cambridge University Press include *Political Representation* (with Joni Lovenduski, 1995), as well as *Why Electoral Integrity Matters* (2014), *Making Democratic Governance Work* (2012), *Democratic Deficits* (2011), *Cosmopolitan Communications* (with Inglehart, 2009), *Driving Democracy* (2008), *Radical Right* (2005), *Sacred and Secular* (with Inglehart, 2004, 2010, winner of the 2005 Virginia Hodgkinson Research Prize), *Electoral Engineering* (2004), *Rising Tide* (with Inglehart, 2003), *Democratic Phoenix* (2002), *Digital Divide* (2001), and *A Virtuous Circle* (2000) (winner of the 2006 Doris A. Graber prize for the best book in political communications). Details: www.pippanorris.com

JOYCE OUTSHOORN is Professor Emeritus of Women's Studies at the University of Leiden, where she is affiliated to the Institute of Political Science. She is editor of *The Politics of Prostitution* (2004), *Changing State Feminism* (2007) (with Johanna Kantola), *European Women's Movements and Body Politics* (forthcoming). Her work has been published in Public Administration Review, *Social Politics, Acta Politica, Journal of Comparative Public Policy, European Journal of Women's Studies and Sexual Research* and *Social Policy*. She was co-convenor of the Research Network on Gender, Politics and the State (RNGS) and one of the project leaders of the Feminism and Citizenship (FEMCIT) project. Her research interests are women's movements, women's equality policy, and body politics, notably abortion and prostitution.

VICKY RANDALL is Emeritus Professor of Government at the University of Essex. She has published widely on gender-related issues in politics, with books including *Women and Politics*, *Women in Contemporary British Politics* (with Joni Lovenduski) and *The Politics of Child Daycare in Britain*. Her current research focuses on older people's political participation but with a continuing interest in relevant gender differences.

JENNIFER RUBIN is vice president of RAND Europe and director of the division's Communities, Safety & Justice research programme. While at RAND Rubin has led research with and for a range of EU, British, and wider European institutions, agencies, departments, and foundations. In addition to leading research, Rubin has served as social scientific advisor to projects funded by European foundations; has been invited to contribute to Dutch, British, and US home affairs policy papers; and has contributed to TEDx events, consultations, and roundtables in the UK, US, and EU.

Acknowledgements

We would like to thank Judith Squires for first suggesting this project to us and for helping us to develop the idea and bring it to fruition.

Alan Ware was, as always, generous with his time and full of useful suggestions. Thanks also to Anne Philips and Joyce Outshoorn – the other two members of the advisory board – for their suggestions and support.

Recruiting contributors to this project – from both the academic and practitioner world – was a painless exercise; as all were keen to celebrate Joni Lovenduski's contribution to political science and political life, and we are very grateful to them for making this project such a rewarding experience.

The ECPR Press have been incredibly helpful and encouraging and have enabled us to put together a *Festschrift* that we hope will be a useful text for researchers and students, as well as a fitting tribute to an esteemed scholar and dear friend.

Rosie Campbell and Sarah Childs
London, UK
September 2014

Foreword

Albert Weale

People sometimes deny that political science should be value-free because they think it should be value-relevant. But this is to confuse two quite different things. Value-relevance is the principle that the topics worth studying are those that are important. Value-freedom is the principle that, when studying important topics, we should not allow wishful thinking to interfere with our understanding. Identifying the causes of political processes and outcomes is to be guided by the best evidence available, not by what we hope or expect to be true in advance of research.

Among her many virtues, Joni Lovenduski has never confused value-relevance and value-freedom. She has been responsible for producing some of the best political science we have on the subject of women and politics, exemplifying the principle of value-relevance. Yet she has pursued her understanding even when the results show the facts to be more complicated than at first sight we might think. For example, she once showed that female candidate non-selection in UK constituencies is at least as much a function of supply – of women excluding themselves – than of demand – of bias against women by constituency parties. For many it would have been more convenient to have discovered the crucial role of prejudice on the demand side rather than reluctance on the supply side. Joni stuck with the evidence, just as she helped uncover the fact that younger women were less sympathetic to descriptive political representation than older women, despite their also rejecting traditional feminine roles. With further research, she later came to a different view about the relative importance of supply, but the change reflected the evidence.

A commitment to value-relevance also means a commitment to work for practical improvement. At a time when the academy is being urged to make an impact on the quality of social and public life, Joni stands as an exemplar of what it means to bring the results of one's research to bear on fundamental political questions, for no one can deny the importance of political representation. In this volume a number of women who have been active in politics witness to the esteem in which she is held in the world of practice just as her academic colleagues witness to her role in the world of scholarly research.

In seeking to understand the barriers that have existed to women securing political office, Joni has not avoided the hard work of comparative inquiry, using cross-national evidence to explore the relationship between political institutions and gender politics. She has never been content with reciting generalities, but has explored how debates about gender in politics interact with dominant ideologies of the state and to what effect.

Good comparative empirical work requires good team work. Had Joni been born in an earlier generation, I sense that she might have been an activist in the US garment workers' union, with its slogan: 'organise, organise!' In modern political science cross-national comparative work means organisation, with its need for a careful definition of problems, an ability to raise funds, insistence on deadlines being met by collaborators and the knack of seeing how the whole can become more than the sum of its parts. Joni would be the first to acknowledge that without her international network she could not have accomplished what she has; in this volume the members of her network honour her for her role in making their combined work possible.

The same qualities of cooperation and commitment to the cause of political science have led people on many occasions and in many contexts always to insist on including Joni on important committees – whether as an Executive member of the U.K.'s Political Studies Association or of the European Consortium of Political Research or whether as a panel member in the UK's Research Assessment Exercise. In all these important roles she has displayed that most valuable of combinations, independence of mind together with a willingness to work with others to find common solutions to pressing problems.

Listing these qualities makes it seem as though Joni embodies only the austere and puritanical virtues – commitment to a cause, intellectual integrity in research and administrative ability in organisation. Yet is there another political scientist who so evidently takes such pleasure in the senses, whether in the complex tastes of Italian cooking (always to be accompanied by fine wine) or the sights and smells of the garden or the back and forth of conversation? To hear her speak of how to cook a joint of meat is to understand how much intelligence enhances pleasure. To talk face to face with her is to understand how conversation can move from intellectual rigour to political engagement and then to the intimacies of personal friendship that is rooted in trust and good judgement. To contribute to this volume is to mark the achievements of a fine scholar but also the personal qualities of the warmest of friends.

Introduction: Deeds and Words

Rosie Campbell and Sarah Childs

This edited collection could have taken the standard scholarly framework – a series of discrete but nonetheless linked chapters that provide a 'state of the art' review of the sub-discipline of gender and politics. It would in this format, at least in our view, have done a valuable job for students of gender and politics, and would have been a fine tribute to Professor Joni Lovenduski, the pioneering gender and politics scholar in whose honour this book (a kind of *Festschrift*) is published. In so doing, it would also show how gender and politics scholarship speaks to the rest of political science, revealing that (male) gender has always been present in political science, and demonstrating how a re-gendering (feminising) of the discipline changes both what is studied and how it is studied; transforming our understanding of 'the political'. But feminist gender and politics research, whilst about these and other things, is also about more than academic outputs; it is about changing the world; about being 'of use' beyond academia. As such the overarching narrative of *Deeds and Words* is the crucial role played by critical actors and ideas in politics and political science, and in feminising politics. It is for this reason that each academic contributor has been asked to reflect on the interaction between academic research and the practice of politics in the individual chapters. It is also why we have invited a series of leading practitioners of politics – whether Members of Parliaments, party professionals, political actors in civil society or the state, and gender activists – to reflect on how their activities, strategies and, or campaigns, have benefited from interaction with gender and politics scholarship and scholars. Our reasoning is straightforward; whilst the British Suffragettes and suffragists in the early 20th century demanded 'deeds' (for their words had failed to persuade the male political establishment to give them the vote); 'deeds' and 'words' very much went together in the late 20th century and should continue to do so in the 21st. We think this for two reasons: first feminist academics frequently are, and seek to be, both scholars and activists; secondly, as understandings of gender relations have become more sophisticated, addressing for example, issues of intersectionality and the complexity of power and its variation across space and time, feminist praxis demands engagement with ideas and debates.

Feminising politics

Feminising politics refers both to the (1) integration of women and (2) women's concerns into politics (Lovenduski 2005). The former refers to the presence of women's bodies in our institutions, whether these are political organisations, movements or parliaments. The latter refers to the inclusion on the political agenda of women's perspectives, issues and interests, noting that these are contested concepts.[1] In both its dimensions feminisation reveals the gendered (read: masculinised) nature of politics: that men are nearly everywhere (all bar two lower houses in the world) over-represented in our formal political institutions (Murray 2012; www.ipu.org), and that the political agenda largely reflects men's perspectives and concerns, and or fails to acknowledge that women may well have different attitudes even when they share concerns with men. In this book authors consider how electoral politics has been feminised over the last few decades. Vicky Randall (Chapter One) charts the development of the sub-discipline of gender and politics over the last couple of decades.

We do not seek to reproduce Randall's analysis here. However we reiterate the claim that whilst gender and politics research started with the 'simple counting' of women's bodies in our electoral institutions, today gender and politics scholars are also very much focused on a wider range of foci: women's substantive representation (when representatives act for women), and albeit to a lesser and more recent extent, symbolic representation (Campbell and Wolbrecht 2006; Celis *et al.* 2007; Childs and Lovenduski 2012; Dovi 2007; Dovi 2010; Lovenduski *et al.* 2005; Meier and Lombardo 2012). In addressing the descriptive, substantive and symbolic representation of women, Chapter authors frequently emphasise the importance of context – spatial and temporal. A comparative approach importantly permits a more comprehensive understanding of what is going on and why. And even when scholarship is of a single case a comparative perspective throws more light, revealing causal and mediating factors. Many of our contributors, in common with much contemporary gender and politics research, also employ new institutional and, or feminist institutional approaches (Krook and MacKay 2010; Lovenduski 1998). These investigate institutional rules and norms, architecture and spaces, conventions and practices, and explore how changing gender relations can re-gender institutions (Lovenduski 1998).

Making a difference: The feminist imperative[2]

In addition to presenting the latest research on gender and politics, *Deeds and Words*, examines how feminist academics have influenced the 'real' world of politics – impact that is frequently overlooked within the wider academy. Universities in the UK became an important site for feminist politics after the peak of the second wave of feminism in the 1970s. Indeed, in the face of spending cuts in the 1980s, and alongside a depressingly successful media backlash, feminist academics in British university departments worked with the women's movement to keep women's issues on the political agenda. Pioneering feminist political scientists including Joni Lovenduski, Judith Evans, Annie Phizacklea,

1. What constitutes women's issues and interests has generated extensive debate, *see* 'Critical perspectives', Politics and Gender, 2012 for recent contributions.
2. This section draws on Campbell and Childs 2013.

Vicky Randall, Margherita Rendel, Jean Woodall, later joined by Jill Hills, Elizabeth Meehan and Pippa Norris, put gender and politics onto the politics curriculum in the UK. They also importantly created a forum for women within the discipline: the Political Studies Association (PSA) Women and Politics group (http://psawomenpolitics.wordpress.com/). These women also worked with, and created networks of, scholars across Europe (the women and politics standing group of the European Consortium of Political Research, http://www.ecpr.eu/StandingGroups/StandingGroupHome.aspx?ID=8),[3] and globally, not least with the American Political Science Association women's groups (http://www.apsanet.org/sections/sectionDetail.cfm?section=Sec16). In all this they were feminist institution building within the discipline.

In feminising the university and its curriculum, these women in turn raised a new generation of women and politics researchers some of whom – like ourselves – remain in the universities. Our foremothers were consciously and generously concerned with ensuring the success of the next generation; investing in mentoring younger academics and those from less established places and seeking to ensure that their legacy was taken forward. In this we, the younger generation, have very much benefitted from their battles to extinguish the dinosaurs (Lovenduski 2012), though of course some appear free to roam still.[4] Nevertheless we believe that being a gender and politics scholar, or even just a woman political scientist, is much easier now that it was for them.

As gender and politics scholars took on the academic dinosaurs, women party members were attempting to tame the macho beasts that were their political parties – in the UK from the 1970s and 1980s onwards. Many of the leading gender and politics scholars were intimately involved in this fight too, both as party members and activists and through their academic research. Arguments for the feminisation of the UK Labour Party were, for example, supported by Lovenduski and Norris's research on political recruitment, identifying supply- and demand-side obstacles (Norris and Lovenduski 1995); Lovenduski notably wrote a Fabian pamphlet, (co-authored with a woman who later became a Labour MP), bolstering the efforts of Labour party women as they made demands of their leaders (Eagle and Lovenduski 1998; Harman and Mattinson 2000); she also co-authored a Fawcett Society report, helping to arm women in civil society with facts and arguments, and who mobilised to raise the issue up the political agenda (Shepherd-Robinson and Lovenduski 2002); and behind the scenes Lovenduski has acted as an informal advisor and consultant to parties and government throughout her career. As such, Lovenduski exemplifies the critical actions of a number of high profile feminist academics internationally. They act on the basis of their own feminist politics; they have a shared goal of enhancing women's political representation with their

3. For six years Joni was the founding convenor of the ECPR gender and politics standing group.

4. Battles remain. In the current British Research Excellent Framework (REF) assessment, the mobilisation of women was necessary to ensure that those having had maternity leave were treated fairly.

activist sisters. (They also, to be fair, sometimes seek out other actors who may not identify as feminist). They do so because they recognise that that robust empirical evidence in combination with the political savvy employed by activists is a powerful force for change.

Academic 'impact' is currently a hot topic in the UK – as scholars debate the relevance of political science (*Political Studies Review* 2013), and the government demands evidence of impact beyond the academy (www.ref.ac.uk). It is our personal view that that being relevant and influencing change is something that political scientists *should* do (Campbell and Childs 2013). It is also our view – although this may not be universally appreciated – that feminist political research has always sought to have an 'impact'. There is, we believe, little point continuing to produce masses of research every year if it is only shared between ourselves. We are strongly of the belief too that the notion of the academic 'ivory tower' never accurately captured what many feminist scholars – including feminist political scientists – were, and are, doing. In sum, because *they are feminists*, feminist political scientists want to change, as well as observe the world. Accordingly, feminist researchers frequently engage with practitioners and the subjects of their research, beginning at an early stage of their research, and allowing for genuine knowledge exchange. Such an approach fits well with feminist perspectives on the researcher–research subject relationship, which challenges the sometimes hierarchical power relations that position the researcher above the researched. The value of interviewing, observing, and frequently co-producing knowledge with political practitioners is widely accepted by researchers.

Feminist academics relationship with the 'real world' of politics is, importantly, not a one way street. As gender and politics research thrives on the interaction with, and insights from feminist and other political actors (Campbell and Childs 2013), this interaction also makes for better and more effective political activity. Indeed, it is for this reason that each of the academic chapters – which provide an authoritative survey of the existing literature – is complemented by 'vignettes' written by a variety of political actors. These detail transformative political moments and ideas, and are reflections of where feminist academic scholarship on politics has impacted politics on the ground. Many of the women who engage in our research, report our findings, and elicit our views, are 'sisters' in the feminist sense of the word. A shared political project which, at the minimum, values the presence of women and women's perspectives in politics, facilitates considerable cooperation

Professor Lovenduski's career embodies this theme of *Deeds and Words*: the interaction between gender and politics scholarship and real world politics. There is no doubt as a pioneer scholar she's had a real impact in both academia and formal politics. Her writing (individually and with other women academics of her generation) is widely acknowledged to have transformed the way political science is done; she has ensured a second (and, indeed, third) generation of gender and politics scholars, and crucially she has also ensured that her research findings have reached a wide audience within political science and beyond the academy. She has, in this respect, worked with politicians and other political actors over the decades, and of different political hues, to refine arguments about, and mechanisms for, the greater and better representation of women in politics.

Our consideration of feminist academics' interventions and impact on practical politics in *Deeds and Words*, brings the study of gender and politics 'to life'. We think it also makes this book unique; revealing the links between the academic study of gender and politics, feminist political scientists, and political practice. In our view, without foregrounding the interactions between scholarship, scholars and activists (recognising that at times these may well be the same individuals) would be to miss a significant part of the story of feminising politics in the academy and beyond.

Chapter One: Gendering political science – Vicky Randall

This chapter provides a narrative account of feminist academics' influence on the discipline of politics. It charts the increase in the numbers of women in political science, and the development of feminist approaches to the study of politics, documenting new approaches and methods (feminist/comparative) advanced by gender and politics scholars, and the ways in which these have challenged, and transformed (to some degree) the mainstream, in terms of what it studies and how this is studied.

Within feminist political science, Randall discusses the following developments of the sub-discipline: (1) The 'add women in and stir' approach; its critique and yet continuing relevance; (2) redefining/widening concepts of what constitutes political participation and the political; (3) the New Right and the theories of the state; (4) the concept and practice of representation, including critical mass, quotas, gender machinery; (5) gender and democratisation; (6) gender, women and masculinity; (7) gendering political institutions; (8) state feminism and policy; (9) intersectionality. The chapter concludes by reflecting on how feminist political science has changed, what is being emphasised now, and what new developments we might like to see, and what impact it has had on the mainstream (uneven and contested).

Chapter Two: The comparative study of politics and gender – Yvonne Galligan

Comparative political science has a long history, and in this chapter Galligan sets out to show how feminists have offered a critique of traditional comparative political science's assumptions and methods. It also presents a summary of the current 'state of play' in the comparative study of politics and gender. Studies of political behaviour are shown to frequently be underpinned by gendered assumptions about women and politics, for example, that women are less interested in, and undertake fewer, political acts than men, whereas feminist scholarship has revealed that women and men often participate differently. Turning to political institutions, Galligan introduces comparative work on women's descriptive representation in parliaments, noting the role of electoral systems and gender quotas. She also provides an introduction to notions of feminist institutionalism which draws attention to the ways in which gender is embedded and constituted in political institutions (discussed in full by Mackay *et al*'s Chapter Five).The chapter then introduces the comparative study of policy (discussed in addition by Mazur and McBride in Chapter Six). The chapter closes with a discussion of two challenges that Galligan identifies in the literature. First, how to embrace and incorporate the interrogation of how feminine and masculine identities are constructed in democratic politics into our research designs. Second, how to develop empirically testable theories of gendered political behaviour that can inform scholarship in the wider comparative politics field.

Chapter Three: Gendering representation – Karen Celis

Entitled 'Gendering Representation', Celis' chapter provides a comprehensive overview of traditional conceptions of political representation and an account of feminist engagement with the concept. The chapter opens with a discussion of the definition and use of the concept over time. Representation is then introduced as a concept with multiple dimensions: formalistic, descriptive, substantive and symbolic. Each dimension is described in turn. And each is shown to be gendered. Formalistic representation focuses on the arrangement that bestows the representative with their representative function; descriptive representation focuses on the characteristics of representatives. A descriptively representative chamber should 'look like' the represented; hence, a parliament that is under-representative of women would be found wanting. Symbolic representation is found not to rely upon a congruency between the sex of the represented and representative – at least in traditional conceptions. However, feminist contributions suggest the gendered nature of symbolic representation is more complex. Turning to substantive representation, Celis examines the assumption that there is a link between this dimension and descriptive representation – and holds that the nature of this link is ultimately an empirical question. Another section of the chapter summarises some of the empirical research undertaken by feminist scholars. Critically, Celis introduces her arguments relating to 'good' representation, and discusses ideas regarding both creative accounts of representation, and questions of feminism, gender and political representation.

Chapter Four: Party politics – Sarah Childs and Rainbow Murray

Childs and Murray's chapter reflects on the ground-breaking contribution of Joni Lovenduski and Pippa Norris' 1993 edited collection, *Gender and Party Politics* (Lovenduski and Norris 1993). Conceptually it established the key concerns of gender and party politics scholarship: women's participation in parties; the feminisation of party policy; and gendered institutions within parties and parliaments. And yet today there is still too little known about women's participation as ordinary party members, as party activists and as actors in the higher echelons of political parties, especially when compared what is known of women elected representatives. In the first part of Chapter Four, a feminist reading of recent changes to party organisation is introduced, including debates about the extension of intra-party democracy (IPD) which currently characterises the comparative parties literature. IPD, as currently conceived, has frequently failed to speak to issues of gender, and might be thought to conflict with women's descriptive representation. A case for a feminist IPD which involves both a transfer of power from men to women, and between the party leadership and party members is made. The second section examines the case of France, and the adoption of sex quotas – a mechanism that would be considered antithetical to traditional conceptions of IPD. French parity legislation compels all political parties to field an equal number of male and female candidates to most elections. France's political parties responded, however, in different ways to the legislation and with different outcomes, for a variety of ideological, party management, party organisational and electoral competition reasons.

Chapter Five: Political institutions – Fiona Mackay, Faith Armitage and Rosa Malley

In their chapter, Fiona Mackay, Faith Armitage and Rosa Malley consider the contribution made by feminist institutionalists to answering some of the most important questions that concern feminist academics and practitioners alike; such as 'in what ways are Parliaments, political parties and governments gendered?'. Two case studies of feminist institutionalist research in practice are used to illustrate the strengths of the approach: Armitage's work on the Speaker of the UK House of Commons, and Malley's comparative study of cultures in the UK and Scottish parliaments. Mackay *et al*'s chapter chart, then, how feminist institutionalists have made explicit the processes whereby gendered norms and practices structure everyday interactions within institutions and masculinist ideologies come to dominate (Lovenduski 1998); and how these processes interact with other social divisions such as race/ethnicity, class and sexuality. New institutionalism is used to explain how institutions can act as both a constraint on and a resource for feminist political actors. The chapter draws on a wide range of international research including studies of emerging democracies, the international criminal court and western democracies. More specifically, Armitage considers gendered norms of dress and behaviour in the British Parliament, how they have changed over time and what they represent, highlighting the continuing significance of informal rules and procedures. Malley compares parliamentary cultures at Westminster and the Scottish Parliament and argues that the origins of political rituals matter, and crucially the presence of women representatives in the Scottish Parliament, from the outset, has had a substantial impact on its norms and practices. The chapter concludes by stating that an overly narrow focus on women representatives or gender equality policy initiatives can lead feminist political scientists to overlook the question of 'how and with what effect state and political institutions are gendered'.

Chapter Six: Women and the state – Amy Mazur and Dorothy McBride

Amy Mazur and Dorothy McBride use the Research Network on Gender, Politics and the State (RNGS) project to examine the impact made by state women's policy agencies. This impressive and extensive international collaboration (running for 17 years and including 13 nation states) combined the best of feminist political science: (1) the use of cutting edge scientific methods and research designs; (2) alongside engagement with feminist practitioners (femocrats, feminist politicians and feminist activists); an integrated feminist approach. The research sought to disentangle the complex relationship between women's movements, women's policy agencies and the state which required a rigorous, systematic and, above all, a genuinely comparative approach. The RNGS project understood the state as a multilayered structure that advocates for gender equality might access at different junctures and with varying degrees of success. They sought to establish whether the state would change in response to these interactions. They found that the most successful women's policy agencies were insiders with strong links to movement actors; where positive change was identified women's interests became part of the main business of government. However, they also found many barriers to women's policy agencies and transforming the dominant discourse and allies inside the state were crucial for achieving real change. Key structural factors facilitating change varied by policy area with closed policy subsystems requiring the intervention of women legislators for change to occur. Many of the RNGS researchers worked with women's policy agencies; a two-way process of disseminating the lessons drawn from the research findings and learning more about how agencies operate on the ground. The convenors of RNGS actively engaged with policy makers at many levels of governance, including transnational as well as national levels. As such the RNGS research project provides an exemplar of how the words generated by systematic research can sometimes contribute to the deeds of political actors.

Chapter Seven: Critical mass theory in public and scholarly debates – Drude Dahlerup

Drude Dahlerup revisits critical mass, a concept drawn from physics that has been extensively applied to the study of gender and politics and has popular purchase around the world. In her story of critical mass, which includes an account of Moss Kanter's work, Dahlerup notes that the 'theory' is used both to highlight the importance of increasing the descriptive representation of women and to defend women from critics who contend that they have failed to make a difference in politics once present. She draws attention moreover to the possibility, as more countries reach the UN's 30 per cent level of women's descriptive representation, to undertake empirical research investigating what she terms the 'critical mass' hypothesis. At the same time, Dahlerup stresses the importance of the concept in shifting the focus from women's alleged lack of qualifications in politics to a critique of the conditions women face when present in politics. She also rightly emphasises feminist scholarly criticism of the concept and draws attention to the importance of *critical acts* rather than critical mass, a point that she first made in her highly significant 1988 article. Three selected dimensions of 'change' are identified, and the latter part of the chapter explores these in some depth: changes in workplace culture; in substantive representation – where she draws out a distinction between (1) women's ability and (2) their commitment to make change; and the question of acceleration in women's descriptive representation. She concludes that there is no 'tipping point', and stresses the importance of critical actors and critical acts over critical mass. The chapter closes with a brief but important discussion of quotas on company boards.

Chapter Eight: Gender and political recruitment – Meryl Kenny

According to Norris and Lovenduski's ground-breaking book, *Political Recruitment*, legislative recruitment 'refers specifically to the critical step as individuals move from lower levels into parliamentary careers' (Norris and Lovenduski 1995). The dominant framework for understanding the outcomes and processes of legislative recruitment is the 'supply and demand' model. Norris and Lovenduski's analysis derived from an extensive empirical study of UK political parties' selection processes and a candidate survey in advance of the 1992 general election. Meryl Kenny provides both a comprehensive account of the supply and demand framework in her chapter – noting the interaction between the two 'sides' of the model, and showing how political parties privilege masculine characteristics and how gendered socialisation and societal structures are likely to leave women with fewer resources than male candidates – and a critical take on this approach. Kenny queries the emphasis placed on supply side factors as the key to explaining the UK case study, noting how demand explanations have had greater purchase in subsequent research. Indeed, she suggests that gender is underestimated in the model, and arguably more so in subsequent secondary accounts; that 'gender norms shape and distort the dynamics of supply and demand'. Indeed, more recent work places greater emphasis on the 'multiple directions of causality' in the political recruitment process as well as the multiple institutions (she discusses Krook's 2009 systemic, practical and normative institutions) that configure in different combinations to produce variation in women's political recruitment and descriptive representation (Krook 2009).

Chapter Nine: Political recruitment beyond quotas – Pippa Norris and Mona Lena Krook

Pippa Norris and Mona Lena Krook's chapter acts as a companion piece to Chapter Eight by Meryl Kenny. Here, one of the original authors of *Political Recruitment* undertakes a new analysis of the legislative recruitment process informed by recent developments that have transformed the process of candidate selection in a good number of cases: the adoption of gender quotas and gender-sensitive party regulation of legislative recruitment. In their chapter, Norris and Krook theorise the implementation of gender quotas as informal institutional rules, and contend that they have the potential to impact on both the supply of women, and party demand for women. In respect of the former, quotas may encourage women to put themselves forward as candidates and become more confident that they will face a fair chance of being selected; in the latter, party gatekeepers are exhorted and encouraged to find and select women. Using data from a European Parliamentary election study in 2009, Norris and Krook find that women candidates perceived largely similar gatekeeper encouragement, and had slightly more financial resources for campaign spending; women candidates also had similar or marginally greater political experience; and men and women were equally politically ambitious. Comparing countries with no quotas, party quotas, and legal quotas, they conclude that gender quotas importantly 'shape' party demand. Hence selectors encourage women to stand for selection. And, where there are gender quotas, Norris and Krook find that the women coming forward for selection are sufficiently qualified.

Chapter Ten: Policy – Jennifer Rubin and Joyce Outshoorn

Joyce Outshoorn and Jennifer Rubin consider the contribution feminist scholarship has made to the study of public policy. Joyce Outshoorn explores the problem of classifying women's issues using the topic of 'body issues' to illuminate the terrain. Outshoorn argues that in order to understand gender policy and its outcomes researchers must concentrate their efforts on the policy sub-system. She discusses Lowi's classic typology alongside four classifications from the feminist public policy field, looking specifically into how they deal with 'body issues'. She argues that this sophisticated approach is useful to feminist practitioners as it helps us to identify strategies which are likely to be attractive to policy makers in the field. Jennifer Rubin draws on examples from her experience working for RAND Europe to demonstrate how employing a gendered lens improves policy analysis. She traces the impact of formal gender mainstreaming on EU policy analysis, looking particularly at migration research. Together, Outshoorn and Rubin's contributions illustrate how detailed theoretical work can provide nuanced tools for policy analysis and how such tools are used in practice.

Chapter Eleven: Measuring women's political interests – Peter Allen, Rosie Campbell and Ana Espírito-Santo

Peter Allen, Rosie Campbell and Ana Espírito-Santo assess the contribution that quantitative studies of public opinion and political behaviour have made to our understanding of gender and politics, with a focus on their relevance to public debates about the representation of women's interests. They trace the tensions between presenting sex differences in public opinion as they are currently manifested and attempting to understand the processes that generate them. They demonstrate that although describing women's interests is notoriously slippery there is good quantitative evidence of gender differences in political preferences, albeit ones that are subject to change over time and space. The chapter summarises the current literature on gender and political interest, knowledge, social capital and voting behaviour illustrating the depth and breadth of gender scholarship in these areas. The international evidence of a declining traditional gender gap, with women more often voting for parties of the right than men, and the trend towards a modern gender gap, where women are to the left of men, is described. The decline in the gender gap in political participation is juxtaposed against the resilient gender gap in political interest and knowledge. Mixed evidence for role model effects, where women politicians stimulate the political attitudes and behaviour of others, is set out showing that in certain contexts women leaders play a key role in motivating women and making politics feel relevant. Allen *et al.* contend that although the demands for the representation of women's interests should not be predicated on quantitative evidence of sex differences in public opinion alone, the sophisticated and nuanced research in this area provides genuinely useful evidence for practitioners.

Afterword

Deeds and Words closes with a summary of the thoughts and reflections of a wider group of academics who have worked with, been inspired by, and known Joni Lovenduski over the last few decades. They include some of her co-authors, but it also includes the comments of the very many individuals whose work and lives have been changed by Joni's work and presence in the academy.

References

Campbell, D. and Wolbrecht, C. (2006) 'See Jane run: women politicians as role models for adoclescents', *The Journal of Politics* 68 (2): 233–47.

Campbell, R. and Childs, S. (2013) 'The impact imperative: here come the women', *Political Studies Review* 11:182–89.

Celis, K., Childs, S., Kantola, J. and Krook, M. (2007) 'Rethinking Women's Substantive Representation', Paper presented at the 2007 ECPR Joint Sessions, Helsinki.

Childs, S. and Lovenduski, J. (2012) 'Representation', in G. Waylen, K. Celis, J. Kantola, and L. Weldon (eds) *Oxford Handbook of Gender and Politics*, Oxford: Oxford University Press.

Dovi, S. (2007) 'Theorizing women's representation in the United States', *Politics and Gender* 3 (3) : 297–319.

— (2010) 'Measuring representation: rethinking the role of exclusion', in *APSA,* Washington.

Eagle, M. and Lovenduski, J. (1998) 'High time or high tide for Labour women?', London: Fabian Society.

Harman, H. and Mattinson, D. (2000) 'Winning for women', London: Fabian Society.

Krook, M. (2009) *Quotas for Women in Politics,* New York: Oxford University Press.

Krook, M. and MacKay, F. (eds) (2010) *Gender, Politics and Institutions,* Houndmills, Basingstoke: Palgrave Macmillan.

Lovenduski, J. (1998) 'Gendering research in political science', *Annual Review of Political Science* 1 (333–56).

— (2005) *Feminizing Politics,* Cambridge: Polity Press.

— (2012) 'Feminising *British Politics' The Political Quarterly* 83 (4): 697–702.

Lovenduski, J. and Norris, P. (eds) (1993) *Gender and Party Politics,* London: Sage.

Lovenduski, J., Baudino, C., Guadagnini, M., Meier, P. and Sainsbury, D. (2005) *State Feminism and Political Representation,* Cambridge: Cambridge University Press.

Meier, P. and Lombardo, E. (2012) 'Towards a new theory on the symbolic representation of women', *APSA*.

Murray, R. (2012) 'Quotas for men? Reframing gender quotas as a means of quality control' in *APSA*.

Norris, P. and Lovenduski, J. (1995) *Political Recruitment*, Cambridge: Cambridge University Press.

Shepherd-Robinson, L. and Lovenduski, J. (2002) 'Women and candidate selection in British political parties', London: Fawcett.

Chapter One

Gendering Political Science

Vicky Randall

Introduction

Over the last three to four decades feminist political scientists have largely transformed our understanding of the role of women, and gender, in politics, hugely extending our knowledge and providing increasingly sophisticated analyses. This chapter provides an overview of that process, including the part played by individual scholars.[1] A central theme in this survey of the 'gendering' of political science is the sheer scale and range of what has been achieved in what has become an increasingly international undertaking. As a result, the relevant field and literature are vast and multi-faceted and there is no way in which they can be fully done justice in a single chapter. Instead the intention is to develop particular arguments, inevitably focusing on just a selection of the key texts.

It should further be noted that, although our subject is 'political science', one of the issues raised both by feminists and in attempts to 'gender' the discipline, concerns where the boundaries of this field are located. Many of the conceptual puzzles and substantive issues that emerge in these attempts can hardly be contained within the purview of a single conventionally defined academic discipline. On the one hand many topics straddle the traditional boundary with other social sciences and with history. On the other the distinctions that have become institutionally embedded between political science, political theory or philosophy and international relations obscure important continuities of insight and debate. Accordingly an account of the gendering of political science cannot be too rigidly confined within one disciplinary perspective.

The discussion will proceed fairly chronologically, beginning in the 1970s with the attempts of a new generation of feminism-influenced women political scientists to counter the latent sexism of the discipline, its marginalisation of women as serious political actors and, associated with these, its limited conception of the scope and nature of politics. Thereafter, from the 1980s, and reflecting developments in the real political world as well as women's changing position

1. Although in a sense this has been a collective endeavour, with ideas and arguments honed in debate and collaboration, certain contributions stand out and, incidentally, none more so than the work of Joni Lovenduski, in advancing our understanding on so many different fronts.

within the discipline, there was growing focus on the state or central political institutions, both women's political representation and the gendered character of the institutions themselves. This general focus has persisted but a further section considers two additional recent trends – a response to the question of diversity as well as much greater concern with questions of methodology. The final section, in summarising this history, considers how far and in what sense(s) the project of gendering political science has been accomplished.

Early days

The field of political science, as it consolidated its presence in the early post WW2 years, was resolutely masculine as was the world of public politics it studied. There were few women academics and few questions asked about what we would now call gender differences. Arguably what changed all this was in the first instance the revival of feminism in the 1960s, itself a complex development whose social and political roots cannot be fully examined here, but which included the growing numbers of women in higher education and New-Left inspired student politics.

What was retrospectively identified as a feminist movement was in fact extremely diverse, generating all kinds of internal conflicts and arguments. Radical, Marxist and liberal feminists, amongst others, had different agendas, almost different languages. But what they shared was a questioning of the status quo as either natural or acceptable. A new generation of women political scientists was exposed to these ideas and many sought to apply them to their discipline.

Actually this probably began in the US with the commentaries of Bourque and Grossholtz (1974) and Iglitzin (1974). Gradually a critique emerged of the 'sexism' of existing political science, through which women were either disregarded, subsumed under universal categories, considered only in terms of their relationship to (political) men or portrayed according to traditional stereotypes. Accordingly an early priority for such scholars was simply to focus directly on women, and add to the very limited stock of knowledge concerning their political participation. This involved, for instance, finding out more about those women who had made it into public politics – how had they succeeded, what obstacles did they face? (Vallance 1979).

Although this process of 'adding women in' was subsequently disparaged by some feminist scholars as conceptually limited and insufficiently critical, it has continued to constitute one very important aspect of the task of gendering political science. In fact it has repeatedly been necessary to lay this groundwork of information wherever women remain marginalised in analysis and in political reality. This has been the case, for instance, in the context of studying the politics of successive regions of the developing and post-Soviet world. Thus it is only in recent years that systematic research has focused on women in African politics (Goetz and Hassim, 2003; Bauer and Britton, 2005) whilst scholarly sources on women's political participation in Arab countries still remain hard to find. It has also been necessary in situations when some new concept or approach becomes particularly influential in the discipline, as in the case of the notion of 'social capital' (Lowndes 2004) or the 'new institutionalism' (*see* Chapter Five of this volume).

Besides adding women in, it was also necessary to revisit and revise the facile, often sexist, generalisations about women's political participation that already existed in the literature (Goot and Reid 1975). This was especially the case concerning women's voting behaviour. Prevailing accounts for instance suggested – rather contradictorily – that women voted as directed by their menfolk and that they voted for conservative parties. Feminist scholarship examined voting behaviour and attitudes more systematically, looking at differences amongst groups of women and over time. It investigated the existence of a 'gender gap', originally conceived as a greater propensity for women to support conservative parties but later seen, in the US, in stronger support amongst women than men for Democrat candidates. This area of research has continued to be a central element of feminist political science (Campbell 2006; Carroll and Fox 2005).

As has been emphasised, women were highly marginalised within the reality of conventional, mainstream politics at this time. Thus in the UK House of Commons, following the 1964 General Election, the percentage of women MPs rose to its highest level so far at 4.6 per cent. In the 87th US Congress, 1961–3, women constituted only 3.7 per cent. So in addition to providing fuller, more reliable information about women's political participation conventionally understood, feminist scholarship also sought to challenge and widen notions of political participation. There was interest in women's participation in different forms of 'community' politics (Mayo 1977). In particular this was the era of the emerging 'new social movements' including, besides the feminist movement, those dedicated to peace, the environment and combating racism. The 1970s and 1980s saw considerable interest in women's participation in social movements but especially in feminist movement politics (Dahlerup 1986; Lovenduski and Randall 1993).

Scholarly interest in women's participation in unconventional forms of politics, most of all their involvement in social movements, has continued over the years. It was a major theme, for instance, in the context of Latin American transitions from authoritarian to more democratic systems of rule, with studies considering not only women's part in feminist organisations and in 'progressive' or pro-democracy movements but also their role in conservative movements, such as the pro-Pinochet women banging on their pots in the streets of Santiago (Waylen 1992). With the 'reconfiguration' of the developed democratic state from the 1990s, scholars also examined how women's movements responded to such changes as increased delegation to transnational organisations and the private sector (Banaszak, Beckwith and Rucht 2003).

Implicit in this broadened notion of participation was a questioning of conventional understandings of the scope of politics and what should be the proper subject-matter of political science. Although political science has always included a variety of perspectives and analytic approaches, it would be fair to say the prevalent focus was on processes and institutions associated with the constitution and activities of central government. This was restrictive for those scholars who wanted to understand what women did do politically as well as what they did not do, and who wanted to explain why women's mainstream political presence was so limited. They appealed to a broader conception of politics as being to do with relations of power that were embodied in everyday structures including the family as well as actively created through the political process.

Related to this was a critique of the range of issues that tended to be recognised as political in character and appropriate for political analysis. Conventional political science largely disregarded many issues it categorised as either private (domestic) or at least social rather than political. Challenging this blinkered approach, feminist political theorists such as Okin (1991) perceptively interrogated traditional distinctions between public and private spheres, whilst other scholars expanded the subjects of political analysis to include issues like women's reproductive rights, beginning with abortion (Lovenduski and Outshoorn 1986), and sexual violence.

This insistence on the political character of issues previously regarded as private or domestic has continued to be a feature of gendered political science. Questions of reproductive rights and sexual violence do not go away and have been revisited in numerous recent studies. Where sexual violence is concerned, there has been more recent scholarly work on prostitution and trafficking (Outshoorn 2004). On the other hand interest in patterns of women's paid employment led to a new concern with the issue of child day care (Randall 2000).

Vital groundwork, then, was laid in the 1970s. The process of gendering political science was effectively launched and the agenda adumbrated at that point has in many ways continued to inform scholarship in this area. The constant need to ensure that women are part of the picture and that factors affecting their political behaviour, including their absence, are properly studied remains with us. The critique of traditional, conventional understandings of politics, including the public-private divide, continues to be deeply relevant.

From the 1980s: Gender, state and representation

Despite its roots in the 1970s, and important continuities, there are ways in which the project of gendering political science has arguably and perhaps inevitably changed over time. Already in the 1980s these shifts were in evidence. They reflected a number of important contextual changes.

First, the numbers and confidence of women political scientists were beginning to grow and whilst many continued to identify strongly with the feminist movement and to justify their research interests, and even their research methods, in its terms, they were also increasingly caught up in the imperatives of political science as a discipline and indeed as a career path. At the same time and to the extent that they did look to feminism for inspiration they were able to draw upon developments in feminist theory which allowed both for more subtle and for more state-centred analysis than previously. Within mainstream political science, also, new themes and emphases successively emerged. And these intellectual trends to some degree reflected changes in the real world of politics that tended to reaffirm the relative autonomy and importance of the state or government and to underline both the need and the possibility for women to play a more prominent political role. Finally, given these convergent developments, many of the findings and frameworks of gendered political science also fed back into the strategies and rhetoric of feminist activism, especially with regard to women's political representation.

It was in the 1980s that the shift began in political science from talking about sex differences to using the language of 'gender'. The distinction between sex and gender was originally emphasised by Marxist feminists, seeking to highlight the extent to which 'gender' is socially constructed. Within political science, gender terminology has been taken up in different ways. In many cases it is just used as a new, more fashionable means of referring to differences between men and women, with the emphasis very much on women's experience. But some scholars have reflected more deeply on the significance of the distinction and what the use of 'gender' offers political analysis (Beckwith 2005).

If gender is to a degree socially constructed, rather than biologically determined, there is the implication that the content of specific gender identities and differences is historically and culturally extremely variable, thus requiring careful examination and delineation. Additionally, as Beckwith notes, there has been more recent use of the term 'gender' as a verb or a process, meaning 'behaviours, practices and dynamics engaged in by individuals, organisations, movements, institutions and nations' (2005: 132). For example, we have seen a growing literature investigating how particular legislative institutions and procedures are 'gendered' (*see* Chapter Five in this volume). A focus on gender rather than just women is also sometimes seen to require more consideration of the relationship between masculine and feminine genders. And then more recently there has been the growing scholarly interest directly in masculinity – including 'hypermasculinity' and the distinction between dominant and subordinate forms of masculinity – and its various manifestations in politics (Connell 1995).

At the same time as this move to the language of gender, feminist political scientists found increasing acceptance within the feminist movement itself of the need both to understand and to engage with the state. Revolutionary forms of feminism, whether Radical or Marxist, had tended to depict the state in heavily reductionist terms as an apparatus of male and/or class power. They stressed the necessity for autonomous organisation, and whilst still for the most part making the state the target of their campaigns, they were dismissive of liberal feminist concerns with increasing women's presence within governing institutions. Now developments in Marxist thinking about the state, but above all, actual political developments – in Britain first the election of a woman, Margaret Thatcher, as Prime Minister in 1979 and then, under Right-wing governments, the threat to welfare state provisions feminists had already criticised as inadequate – pointed to the need, and also perhaps the enhanced feasibility of feminists getting into mainstream politics. This debate amongst feminists about whether or how far to engage with the state, or political parties, incidentally proceeded to play out in many different national arenas – for instance feminism in Peru saw a split between *independientes* and *politicas* (Lievesley 1996).

Growing feminist acceptance of the need to engage the state gave new impetus to feminist political scientists focusing on the interrelated questions of women's representation and of the state, including as time went on, state feminism and gendered institutions. And it is in this context that they produced some of their most significant work which has impacted both on political science as a discipline and on political activism and practice.

Representation

On the one hand feminist scholarship was increasingly taken up with the question of the political representation of women. Drawing on the earlier work of Pitkin (1967), Phillips (1995) reflected on the nature of political representation, focusing in particular on the difference between descriptive, substantive and symbolic forms. Pitkin had argued that substantive representation, regardless of the descriptive attributes of the representative, was what really mattered but Phillips argued against dismissing too readily the importance of descriptive representation, developing instead her thesis of 'the politics of presence'. This fruitful set of ideas has been extensively developed and applied in subsequent studies. For instance Puwar (2004) has written about the somatic disruption caused by the presence of women's bodies, or the 'space invaders', in the House of Commons. These insights, and especially the arguments encapsulated in the 'politics of presence' concept, have been highly influential beyond the sphere of gender politics, within the wider political science discipline, as for instance in Williams' study (1998) of the representation of marginalised groups in the US.

Related to this is the empirical question of whether women do in fact represent women, in the sense of standing for their interests. This is however difficult to research, let alone make generalisations about. One impressive study is by Wängnerud (2000), looking at members of Sweden's Riksdag. She found that in response to a series of questions more than half the women, but only 10 per cent of the men, believed they had an important duty to advance women's interests. This finding may partly reflect the particular circumstances of Swedish politics and not all scholars would agree. Vincent (2001: 78) for instance points out that 'in Africa research has shown that women MPs have consistently failed to place women's issues on national agendas'.

Alternatively it could be that women are only able effectively to represent women if their numbers reach a certain 'critical mass' (Childs and Krook 2008; *see also* the discussion by Dahlerup in this volume). For a time there was considerable popular convergence around the figure of 30 per cent as constituting the magic threshold, and this was given additional authority when it was adopted as a target for women's parliamentary representation by the UN Fourth World Conference of Women in Beijing, 1995. But whilst this became a valuable campaigning argument for feminist activists, feminist political scientists were soon striking a more cautious note. The 30 per cent figure was criticised as overly mechanistic and insufficiently sensitive to contextual variation (for instance in Grey's study (2002) of the House of Representatives in New Zealand). In the most recent literature the emphasis has in fact been more on the role of individual 'critical actors' than on a critical mass of women (Childs and Krook 2006).

The answer to the question as to whether women can and should 'act for women' at least partially depends on our concept of gender, as a social construct or an essential difference between men and women. A strand of Radical feminist thinking has tended to depict women, if not as the superior sex, at least imbued with particular nurturing and caring qualities. Feminist scholars like Gilligan (1982) have developed these suggestions in the more contingent notion of a woman's 'standpoint'. Without endorsing such arguments, feminist political scientists have considered whether and how far, in addition to forwarding women's interests, women make a distinctive – and implicitly superior – contribution to political life in terms of promoting peace (Regan and Paskeviciute 2003), resisting corruption (Goetz 2007, who is however very sceptical), or simply conducting themselves in a more 'feminine', consensual, inclusive fashion (for instance, Childs 2004).

All this research and argument, if at times perhaps drawn on rather selectively, has helped to provide feminist activists with effective justifications for higher rates of women's political representation. This has especially been the case in countries experiencing democratic transition, where the critical mass thesis, despite the reservations that scholars have voiced in more recent years, has continued to hold a particular appeal. But if feminist political science has been used to justify increasing women's political representation, it has also addressed the question of how to achieve such an increase.

As Chapter Eight discusses, early feminist political analysis distinguished between supply and demand aspects of the women's political recruitment. On the demand side there was particular interest, which persists, in the impact of the electoral system, with the general observation that proportional list systems were especially favourable (Rule 1987; Norris 2006). Focusing more specifically on the key role played by political parties, Lovenduski (1993, 2005) pinpointed three different ways that party leaders could encourage women candidates – equality rhetoric (pronouncements), equality promotion (such as training) and quality guarantees (such as quotas). Gender quotas had first been adopted in Norway in the 1970s. In Britain by the 1990s they were being advocated both by feminist scholars and Labour Party activists as the only realistic solution (Short 1996) and implementation of the reform prior to the 1997 General Election contributed to a substantial increase in the number of Labour women MPs from to 37 to 101.

A sizeable political science literature both reflecting and stimulating the spread of gender quotas has developed from the 1990s (*see* Chapter Nine by Pippa Norris and Mona Lena Krook in this volume). The Inter-Parliamentary Union and IDEA have further sponsored a Global Database of Quotas for Women, drawing in part on this literature. Initially interest focused on the experience of parties adopting candidate quotas in Western European countries, generally the consequence of a protracted activist campaign. But from the mid-1990s and in association with measures of democratisation, they were taken up in a succession of Latin American and African countries, so that today more than 100 countries have gender quotas in some form (Tripp and Kang 2007; Krook 2010). These more recent quotas are more likely to be 'imposed', rather than 'voluntary'; in Dahlerup and Friedenwall's influential typology (2005), they are 'fast track'. Feminist political scientists, in addition to distinguishing between the different forms and trajectories of gender quotas, have sought to explain their cross-national diffusion (Krook 2010). They have debated how far in practice they have actually led to an increase in women's political representation and specifically their legislative presence (Tripp and Kang 2007), and which forms of quotas and in what circumstances were they most likely to be effective.

The 'state', gendered institutions and state feminism

Complementing this major scholarly focus on issues associated with women's political representation, feminist political scientists from the 1980s also submitted the state, its institutions and policies to sustained scrutiny. As more women entered politics it became increasingly urgent to trace the kinds of embedded masculinity and resistance within state institutions, the better to understand obstacles and opportunities for feminist agendas. Early Marxist and Radical feminist accounts of the state tended to depict it in quite crude and reductionist terms, as embodying capitalist rule and male dominance (patriarchy), although over time the analyses became more sophisticated. As feminist political scientists began to grapple with these questions they tended to use less 'statist' language but still took on board the notion of patriarchy. One very influential analysis of the patriarchal state by the political theorist Carole Pateman (1988), argued that rather than literally a patriarchal state or state ruled by fathers, the modern democratic state, as in Australia, was more like a 'fraternal state' in which a new equality had been created amongst men, part of which however continued to be a 'sexual contract' which subordinated women.

Feminist political scientists also drew on, and contributed to, a substantial emerging literature concerning the gendered character and impact of the welfare state. Taking issue with Esping-Andersen's three-fold typology of welfare states (1990) for neglecting the gender dimension, this literature produced alternative categories, such as the male-breadwinner (Lewis 1997) and later reflected on the gender implications of welfare state restructuring. But the only systematic attempt to produce a gendered 'theory of the state' as such was Connell (1990). He suggested that each state could be regarded as constituting a particular, historically influenced, 'gender regime'. This regime included a gender division of labour within its own staff, a gender hierarchy, and also an associated structure of emotional attachments. In turn the state's internal gender regime impacted on the wider gender order, through regulating gender relations and in the process helping to reconstitute gender categories.

In the UK, another important text in the development of this approach was Savage and Witz's edited volume of essays (1992) dealing with gender in organisations and bureaucracy. This included an excellent analysis of the problems encountered by pioneering women's officers and women's committees in British local government authorities and what they revealed about the gendered character of such institutions (Halford 1992). Cockburn's revealing study (1991) of the various forms of male obstructionism within four organisations also deserves mention in this context.

But a further major influence from within the discipline itself was the rise of the so-called 'new institutionalism', generally dated back to the publication of the article under that name of March and Olsen (1984, *see also* Chapter Five by Mackay *et al.* in this volume). Though clearly rooted in a long tradition of institutional approaches to political analysis, this was considered 'new' on a number of grounds including its emphasis on rules as opposed to organisations and its interest in informal as well as formal aspects. As such it gave new impetus to the study of political institutions and inspired feminist political scientists to produce their own gendered accounts.

In her much-cited review article identifying this trend, Kenney (1996) considered four examples in the US. One of these, Thomas (1995), looked at the experience of women legislators in the federal and state-level assemblies. The other three concerned the legal profession, the press and the foreign service respectively. Another extremely influential research project has been Kathlene's study (1995) study of US state legislative committees.

Elsewhere there has been much scholarly interest in the gendered implications and opportunities of constitutional reform (Dobrowolsky and Hart 2003). For instance the process and consequences of creating devolved parliaments and assemblies in Scotland, Wales and Northern Ireland in the 1990s were keenly scrutinised (*see* Vignette by Alice Brown in this volume, and Brown *et al.* 2002). In the UK, recent work also centres on the core executive as a gendered institution (Annesley and Gains, 2010), whilst a larger comparative research project on ceremony and ritual in parliaments has focused on the more informal, cultural dimensions of legislatures as gendered institutions (*see* Rai's introduction and the special issue of *The Journal of Legislative Studies*, 2010). This partly picks up on the emphasis on informal processes which is characteristic of the 'new institutionalism'.

Over time, gendered institutionalism has become a more self-conscious and theoretically defined project (Krook and Mackay 2011). The 'new institutionalism' is itself not a unified approach but notably contains three divergent strands – rational-choice institutionalism as well as sociological-come-cultural, and historical forms. Feminist political scientists have not always agreed about which of these is most compatible with a gender perspective (*see* the symposium on 'Critical Perspectives on Gender and Politics' in *Politics and Gender* June 2009), and some have advocated a further, discursive, form (Kulawik 2009). Related to this has been the question of whether they should aspire to a new 'feminist institutionalism', which would of course mean surmounting some of these internal differences. At the same time, fears have been expressed lest such a close fusion with mainstream institutionalism should prove too restrictive, more like a strait-jacket than enabling (Kenny and Mackay 2009).

A related strand of scholarship has been concerned with what is loosely termed 'state feminism' (*see* Chapter Six by Mazur and McBride in this volume). It reflects the growing, if gradual, impact of feminist campaigning on government policies and structures. The term itself originated in Scandinavia in the 1970s and was later defined as 'activities of government structures that are formally charged with furthering women's status and rights' (Stetson and Mazur 1995: 1–2). In practice the concept has tended to embrace both feminists, or 'femocrats', an initially derogatory term by conservative critics of feminist influence in government, but which came to be embraced to refer to feminists who inhabited positions of influence within state bureaucracies, and state policies designed to improve women's position. Another term often used in this context is 'women's policy machineries'.

Within the UK, this firstly entailed a focus on the work of the Equal Opportunities Commission, established following the 1975 Sex Discrimination Act (Lovenduski 1995). Although already facing cutbacks in the early 1980s, it became increasingly effective until in 2007 it was merged in the new Equality and Human Rights Commission. It also entailed consideration of the body, originally set up as the Women's Unit in 1997, placed within the Department of Social Security but expected to be an agent of 'mainstreaming' gender equality policy. This has undergone numerous changes in form, location and nomenclature (Squires and Wickham-Jones 2004) and has recently merged into the Government Equalities Office within the Home Office.

Feminist research on this topic from twelve developed world countries was brought together in the important comparative volume edited by Stetson and Mazur (1995). Reflecting on these very varied experiences, Stetson and Mazur considered how different instances of state feminism should be evaluated and in what circumstances state feminism was most likely to be successful. In the conclusion they suggested that prospects were best where the prevailing ideology was compatible (generally meaning Left or social democratic), where there was a relatively positive attitude to state intervention and where there was an active but supportive women's movement. They also discussed the most conducive organisational forms and strategies.

Although initially associated with developed countries, the idea of women's national machinery was soon taken up in parts of the developing world and within various UN bodies, receiving a strong endorsement at the 1995 Beijing Women's Conference, which saw this as the means 'to support government-wide mainstreaming of a gender-equality perspective in all policy areas' (cited Rai 2003: 2). The UN's Division for the Advancement of Women threw its weight behind this strategy, incidentally facilitating the emergence of the comparative study edited by Rai (2003). In addition to developed countries, this included case studies of Ecuador, India, the Philippines and Uganda. One conclusion emphasised by Rai was the importance of an enabling political environment and specifically of political will in rendering the machinery effective.

Research into state feminism has continued, with new themes and questions emerging more recently. Following up on their first comparative volume, Stetson and Mazur, together with three other feminist scholars – Lovenduski, Outshoorn and Guadagnini – acted as coordinators for an extensive Research Network on Gender, Politics and the State (RNGS) which included 43 researchers from 16 developed countries and brought out subsequent volumes relating state feminism to job training (Mazur 2001), abortion (Stetson 2001), prostitution (Outshoorn 2004), representation (Lovenduski 2005) and globalisation (Haussman and Sauer 2007). In 2012 RNGS declared its work completed but interest in the topic of state feminism persists. Outshoorn and Kantola's edited volume (2007) reflects on how state feminism is changing as a result both of changing women's movement politics and changes in the developed democratic state. It looks at the impact of multi-level governance, notably the EU together with regionalisation and decentralisation within states; of welfare state restructuring and the incorporation of principles of (market-oriented) New Public Management into state bureaucracy; and of the move towards gender 'mainstreaming'. In their conclusion, whilst noting the very varied experiences of the countries under study, the editors observe that gender mainstreaming has been adopted in all but the USA and they have all been affected in different ways by the emerging issue of diversity, (discussed more fully in the following section). They conclude that despite all the challenges, state feminism has actually grown stronger in at least half the case study countries. However, Kantola and Squires (2012) also reflect on whether, given the trend towards neo-liberal market reform, the term 'state feminism' should perhaps be giving way to 'market feminism' (as manifest for instance in political consumerism, working with corporations and especially engagement with the new market-oriented forms of governance).

Recent developments

The account so far has demonstrated the heroic extent to which feminist scholars have taken on the mission of 'gendering' political science. From the 1980s the focus of that enterprise came especially, though never exclusively, to rest on the representation of women within, and the gendered character of, political institutions. This project continues forward and there have been no obvious major shifts of emphasis in recent years. However within this perspective one can identify two rather different recent trends, one to do with subject-matter and the other to do with methodology.

The first has already been alluded to and concerns responses to the increasing salience of differences or 'diversity' amongst women, and indeed across gender. Within second wave feminism itself this had soon surfaced as a crucial but difficult issue. In Britain the Women's Liberation Movement, formed around the notion of women's common oppression, began to fragment almost from its inception (Lovenduski and Randall 1993) with the first conflicts arising over sexuality and race. The sheer intellectual challenge for feminism of accommodating the different emerging forms of gendered identity is one reason for the appeal to many feminist thinkers of post-structural analysis with its rejection of 'essentialism' and insistence on the contingent nature of identity (Butler 1992).

The question of diversity complicates the already problematic task of defining central analytical concepts such as 'women's issues' and 'women's interests' (*see* Chapter Eleven by Campbell *et al.* in this volume). These terms have sometimes been used quite lazily without recognising the extent to which they are open-ended or contentious. Lovenduski (1997) argued that women's issues should be understood in a fairly objective sense as those which mainly affect women, whether for biological or social reasons. 'Women's interests' is a more subjective notion, to some extent constructed in the very process of political representation itself. Many find useful Wängnerud's suggestion (2000) that policies promoting women's interests are those which increase their autonomy. Nonetheless, the strong possibility remains that interests so defined could differ or indeed conflict between different groups of women.

In a rather more practical context, new challenges arose where there was a pressing need for different kinds of women's organisations to collaborate on issues where they shared a common goal. Originating in the Bologna women's movement in Italy, the notion of 'transversalism' was seen as one way to think about this kind of alliance. Yuval-Davis (1999) describes this as building on feminist standpoint theory, and thereby avoiding both the essentialism of identity politics and the exclusionary character of 'universalist', Leftist approaches which denied the relevance of difference. It entailed recognition of the rootedness of identity but also of the possibility of 'shifting' or putting yourself in another's place.

The concept of transversalism was probably taken up more enthusiastically in the context of international relations than in political science traditionally understood. At any rate its appeal has been rapidly overtaken, as reflected in the work of Yuval-Davis herself, by the notion of 'intersectionality'. This was initially associated with American sociologist Crenshaw (1991) examining the position of black women, at the intersection of race and gender, and arguing that it could be reduced to neither. The theme of intersectionality has been deployed in many different policy and disciplinary fields, including areas of political science. Kantola and Nousiainen (2009 260), who define intersectionality as the 'ways in which different inequalities intersect leading to unique forms of discrimination', use it as a framework with which to critically review developments in EU equality policy. They argue that presently such policy tends to address multiple discrimination – an additive model – rather than considering the ways that different bases of discrimination interact to form new types of inequality. Squires (2009) in the same special issue of *International Feminist Journal of Politics*, looks specifically at how far there has been progress in institutionalising intersectionality in Britain. As noted earlier, by 2007 the Equal Opportunities Commission (EOC) had been merged in the Equality and Human Rights Commission while the Women and Equality Unit was merged in a Government Equalities Office. In the preceding period while these changes were being debated, the EOC was generally supportive, believing in particular that they would be beneficial for 'minority' women, although there were also fears that gender equality issues could be marginalised or could indeed clash with ethnic minority or religious rights. Squires' conclusion is cautious: single equality bodies may be necessary but are insufficient means of successfully institutionalising intersectionality.

So, one trend evident in the recent literature has been an attempt to think through the conceptual and practical conundrums posed by gender diversity. But a second apparent tendency has more to do with the style or process of political research and consists of a much stronger emphasis on methodological awareness and justification. This reflects, in particular, developments in political science as a discipline; there is a growing demand for methodological rigour as part of the case for being a (social) science and in the competition for research funding. But it is also perhaps related to the position and outlook of women political scientists.

Early on it would be fair to say that there was relatively little reflection in feminist political science concerning research methodology. Some feminist social researchers raised issues about the power relationship between researcher and researched, stressing the importance of not abusing this relationship and of allowing the voices of those being studied to be distinctly heard. But on the whole, feminist political scientists did not significantly engage with such questions. It was really with the 'methodological turn' in mainstream political science that they began to reflect on their own methodological assumptions and practices. This was partly because of their position within the profession, an understandable concern with career progression and the wish for their research to be taken seriously. But there was also interest in the particular methodological questions that might be raised in studying gender and politics.

What has been most evident in gendered political science is increasing explicit discussion and justification of methods of research and analysis used. In keeping with the broad character of mainstream political science, and as noted by Krook and Squires (2006), post-positivist or discourse analysis approaches have played little part in UK scholarship, in contrast with the situation in international relations where forms of constructivism have been widely employed. Otherwise there has been considerable methodological versatility, with a range of quantitative and qualitative methods deployed singly or in combination. Comparative approaches have been used to great effect, as in the RNGS state feminism project discussed earlier (and discussed further in Chapter Six in this volume), gender quota studies (Tripp and Kang 2007; Krook 2010), Waylen's study *Engendering Transitions* (2007) which includes case studies set in south America, eastern Europe and South Africa and Weldon's study (2002) of policies concerning violence against women. The one staple political science approach that has not been enthusiastically taken up is rational choice. This is partly a consequence of the assumptions, and also silences, associated with the notion of the (disembodied, autonomous) 'rational' actor, which have been an ongoing problem for feminism. Recently Driscoll and Krook (2009) have argued that this largely mutual antipathy between feminism and rational choice theorists is regrettable and based on insufficient recognition of what they have in common. Using gender quota analysis to illustrate their case, they maintain that a synthesis of the two perspectives could be very fruitful.

Apart from suspicion of rational-choice thinking, there remains the question of what has been distinctive about the methodology of feminist political science.

There is some consensus that this is first and foremost a function of the topic, both that it is informed to some extent by a feminist perspective and that its character will then largely determine the selection of research method(s). Beyond this, we have seen that feminist political science tends to be flexible in its choice of research methods, with the possible exclusion of those based upon rational-choice thinking. In a recent textbook, Ackerly and True (2010), also suggest that it is governed by a 'feminist research ethic'. This entails an awareness and sense of responsibility about the implications of how the research is conducted and disseminated, particularly from a power perspective, together with 'a normative commitment to transforming the social order'. Even if such an approach is not always to the fore in feminist political science scholarship, it is good to feel that this is being passed on as part of 'best practice' to future researchers.

Conclusion

This opening chapter has traced the emergence of a gendered political science beginning in the 1970s with the influx of women influenced by second-wave feminism into the discipline, who questioned its sexist assumptions about women's political behaviour, conducted their own research to bring women more realistically into focus and, in the process, critiqued prevailing conceptions of the nature and scope of politics and political issues. From the 1980s, whilst building on these endeavours, feminist political scientists turned their attention more squarely on the state, or political institutions, taking up the questions of representation on the one hand and the gendered nature of institutions, including women's policy machinery, on the other. That focus remains central but in recent years it has been accompanied first, by an increasing preoccupation with the issue of diversity and second, by growing methodological awareness and rigour.

Influencing these changes of emphasis several factors have been at work. First, whilst there is still a long way to go, women have made undoubted advances within the discipline. By 2001 in the USA they constituted 24 per cent of full-time faculty (APSA Workshop 2005) whilst a very recent study in the UK (Bates *et al.* 2012) finds that women make up 31 per cent of political scientists (though only 15 per cent of professors). There is inevitably a tendency and an incentive for such women (I include myself) to absorb and work with the conventions, and fashions, within the mainstream discipline – although it must also, in fairness, be said that the 'mainstream' itself is quite an elusive entity (Hay 2001). At the same time feminism as a movement or movements has also changed; in its old heartland as its influence has seeped into the dominant culture and institutional framework it has tended to decline as a radical, autonomous force. So there is less sense of an ongoing dialogue between feminist political scientists and radical forms of feminism.

Last but not least, the real world of politics has been changing; most notably, within much of the developed world at least, women's presence within central political institutions has grown significantly. Of course they are not all necessarily committed to furthering 'women's interests' – whatever these may be – but still, as noted by Lovenduski (2005) the political process is being increasingly 'feminised', raising all kinds of questions about what such women could do, should do and actually do in office, for feminist political scientists to explore.

When it comes to assessing what has been achieved, it is difficult not to be impressed by the energy, ingenuity and range of gendered political science scholarship. As we have seen, in certain research fields, such as women's political representation (especially gender quotas), state feminism and gender mainstreaming, there has been significant dialogue and collaboration with feminist activists. There has undoubtedly also been considerable impact on 'mainstream' political science, although judgements will differ as to how great and there certainly remain 'some indicators of continued marginality' (Childs and Krook 2006: 25). In practice there will be marked variation from one sub-field to another, and in respect of specific arguments and concepts: feminist political science thinking about representation has been especially influential, but attempts to widen conceptions of what is considered a political issue probably much less so.

There are inevitably areas of inquiry where more work could be done. The whole question of 'masculinity', its manifestations, dimensions, and consequences in political life, remains underexplored in comparison, say, to feminist research in international relations. But in any case the task of gendering political science will never be complete. Besides extending its scope to cover the remaining neglected regions of the world, it will always be necessary to respond to new developments in politics and in political science, to remain vigilant.

References

Ackerly, B. and True, J. (2010) *Doing Feminist Research in Political and Social Science*, Basingstoke: Palgrave Macmillan.

Annesley, C. and Gains, F. (2011) 'The core executive: gender, power and change', *Political Studies*, 58: 909–29.

APSA Workshop on the Advancement of Women in Academic Political Science in the United States (2005) *Women's Advancement in Political Science*, (Washington DC : American Political science Association).

Banaszak, L. A., Beckwith, K. and Rucht, D. (eds) (2003) *Women's Movements Facing the Reconfigured State*, Cambridge: Cambridge University Press.

Bates, S., Jenkins, L. and Pflaeger, Z. (2012) 'Women in the profession: the composition of UK Political Science departments by sex', Politics, 32 (3): 139–52.

Bauer, G., and Britton, H. E. (eds) (2005) *Women in African Parliaments*, Boulder, Co: Lynne Rienner.

Beckwith, K. (2005) 'A common language of gender?', *Politics and Gender*, 1 (1): 128–137.

Bourque, S. C. and Grossholtz, J. (1974) 'Politics an unnatural practice: political science looks at female participation', *Politics and Society* 4 (4): 225–66.

Brown, A., Donaghy, T. B., Mackay, F. and Meehan, E. (2002) 'Women and constitutional change in Scotland and Northern Ireland', *Parliamentary Affairs*, 55 (1): 71–84.

Butler, J. (1992) 'Contingent foundations: feminism and the question of "postmodernism"', in J. Butler and J. W. Scott (eds) *Feminists Theorize the Political*, London: Routledge.

Campbell, R. (2006) *Gender and the Vote in Britain: Beyond the gender gap?*, Colchester: ECPR Press.

Carroll, S. J. and Fox, R. J. (eds) (2005) *Gender and Elections: Shaping the future of American politics*, Cambridge: Cambridge University Press.

Childs, S. (2004) 'A feminised style of politics? Women MPs in the House of Commons', *British Journal of Politics and International Relations* 6: 3–19.

Childs, S. and Krook, M. L. (2006) 'Gender and politics: the state of the art', *Politics*, 26 (1): 18–28.

— (2008) 'Critical mass theory and women's political representation', *Political Studies* 56 (3): 725–36.

Cockburn, C. (1991) *In the Way of Women: Men's resistance to sex equality in organizations*, ILR Press.

Connell, R. W. (1990) 'The state, gender and sexual politics: theory and appraisal', *Theory and Society*, 19: 507–544.

— (1995) *Masculinities*, London: Polity.

Crenshaw, K. (1991) 'Mapping the margins: intersectionality, identity politics and violence against women of colour', *Stanford Law Review* 43 (6): 1241–99.

Dahlerup, D. (ed.) (1986) *The New Women's Movement: Feminism and political power in Europe and the USA*, London: Sage.

Dahlerup, D. and Friedenwall, L. (2005) 'Quotas as a 'fast track' to equal representation for women', *International Feminist Journal of Politics*, 7 (1): 26–48.

Dobrowolsky, A. and Hart, V. (eds) (2003) *Women Making Constitutions*, London: Palgrave.

Driscoll, A. and Krook, M. L. (2009) 'Can there be a feminist rational choice institutionalism?', *Politics and Gender* 5 (2): 238–45.

Esping-Andersen, G. (1990) *The Three Worlds of Welfare Capitalism*, Princeton, NJ: Princeton University Press.

Gilligan, C. (1982) *In a Different Voice: Psychological theory and women's development*, Cambridge, Mass: Harvard University Press.

Goetz, A. M. (2007) 'Political cleaners: women as the new anti-corruption force?', *Development and Change* 38 (1): 87–105.

Goetz, A. M. and Hassim, S. (eds) (2003) *No Shortcuts to Power: African women in politics and policy making*, London: Zed Books.

Goot, M. and Reid, E. (1975) *Women and Voting Studies: Mindless matrons or sexist scientism?*, Contemporary Political Sociology Series, London: Sage.

Grey, S. (2002) 'Does size matter? Critical mass and New Zealand's women MPs', *Parliamentary Affairs* 55, 19–29.

Halford, S. (1992) 'Feminist change in a patriarchal organisation: the experience of women's initiatives in local government and the implications for feminist perspectives on the state' in M. Savage and A. Witz (eds) *Gender and Bureaucracy*, Oxford: Blackwell.

Haussman, M. and Sauer, B. (eds) (2007) *Gendering the State in the Age of Globalization: Women's Movements and State Feminism in Post-Industrial Democracies*, Rowman and Littlefield Press.

Hay, C. (2001) 'British politics today: towards a new political science of British politics?', in C. Hay (ed.) *British Politics Today*, Cambridge: Polity.

Iglitzin, L. B. (1974) 'The making of apolitical woman: femininity and sex-stereotyping in girls' in J. Jacquette (ed.) *Women in Politics*, New York: John Wiley.

Kantola, J. and Nousiainen, K. (2009) 'Institutionalizing intersectionality in Europe: introducing the theme', *International Feminist Journal of Politics* 11 (4): 459–77.

Kantola, J. and Squires, J. (2012) 'From state feminism to market feminism?', *International Political Science Review* 33 (4): 382–400.

Kathlene, L. (1995) 'Position Power Versus Gender Power: Who holds the Floor?' in G. Duerst-Lahti and R. M. Kelly (eds) *Gender Power, Leadership and Governance*, Ann Arbor, MI: University of Michigan Press, pp. 167–94.

Kenney, S. J. (1996) 'New research on gendered political institutions', *Political Research Quarterly* 49: 445–66.

Kenny, M. and Mackay, F. (2009) 'Already doin' it for ourselves? Skeptical notes on feminism and institutionalism', *Politics and Gender* 5 (2): 271–80.

Krook, M. L. (2010) *Women in Politics: Gender and candidate selection reform worldwide*, Oxford: Oxford University Press.

Krook, M. L. and Mackay, F. (2011) 'Gender, Politics and Institutions: Setting the agenda', in M. L. Krook and F. Mackay (eds) *Gender, Politics and Institutions: Towards a Feminist Institutionalism*, New York: Palgrave, pp. 1–20.

Krook, M. L. and Squires, J. (2006) 'Gender quotas in British politics: multiple approaches and methods in feminist research', *British Politics* 1: 44–66.

Kulawik, T. (2009) 'Staking the frame of a feminist discursive institutionalism', *Politics and Gender* 5 (2): 262–71.

Lewis, J. (1997) 'Gender and welfare regimes: further thoughts', *Social Politics* 4 (2): 160–77.

Lievesley, G. (1996) 'Stages of growth? Women dealing with the state and each other in Peru', in S. Rai and G. Lievesley (eds) *Women and the State: International perspectives*, London: Taylor and Francis.

Lovenduski, J. (1993) 'Introduction: the dynamics of gender and party' in J. Lovenduski and P. Norris (eds) *Gender and Party Politics*, London: Sage.

— (1995) 'An emerging advocate: The equal opportunities commission in Great Britain', in D. M. Stetson and A. Mazur (eds) *Comparative State Feminism*, London: Sage.

— (1997) 'Gender politics: a breakthrough for women?', *Parliamentary Affairs* 50 (4): 708–719.

— (2005) *Feminizing Politics*, Cambridge: Polity.

Lovenduski, J. and Randall, V. (1993) *Contemporary Feminist Politics: Women and power in Britain*, Oxford: Oxford University Press.

Lovenduski, J. and Outshoorn, J. (eds) (1986) *The New Politics of Abortion*, London: Sage.

Lovenduski, J. (ed.) (2005) *State Feminism and Political Representation*, Cambridge: Cambridge University Press.

Lowndes, V. (2004) 'Getting on or getting by? Women, social capital and political participation', *British Journal of Politics and International Relations*, 6 (1): 45–64.

McBride Stetson, D. (ed.) (2001) *Abortion Politics, Women's Movement and the Democratic State: A comparative study of state feminism*, Oxford: Oxford University Press.

McBride Stetson, D. and Mazur, A. G. (eds) (1995) *Comparative State Feminism*, London: Sage.

March, J. G. and J. P. Olsen (2004) 'The New Institutionalism: organizational factors in political life', *American Political Science Review*, 78 (3): 734–49.

Mayo, M. (ed.) (1977) *Women in the Community*, London: Routledge and Kegan Paul.

— (ed.) (2001) *State Feminism, Women's Movements and Job Training: Making Democracies Work in the Global Economy*, New York and London: Routledge.

Norris, P. (2006) 'The impact of electoral reform on women's representation', *Acta Politica*, 41 (2): 197–213.

Okin, S. Moller (1991) 'Gender, the Public and the Private' in D. Held (ed.) *Political Theory Today*, Cambridge: Polity Press.

Outshoorn, J. (ed.) (2004) *The Politics of Prostitution: Women's movements, democratic states and the globalisation of sex commerce*, Cambridge: Cambridge University Press.

Outshoorn, J. and Kantola, J. (eds) (2007) Changing State Feminism, London: Palgrave Macmillan.

Pateman, C. (1988) *The Sexual Contract*, Stanford University Press.

Phillips, A. (1995) *The Politics of Presence*, Oxford: Oxford University Press.

Pitkin, H. F. (1967) *The Concept of Representation*, Oakland CA: University of California Press.

Puwar, N. (2004) *Space Invaders: Race, gender and bodies out of place*, Oxford: Berg.

Rai, S. (2010) 'Analysing ceremony and ritual in parliament', *The Journal of Legislative Studies*, 16 (3): 284–97.

— (ed.) (2003) *Mainstreaming Gender: Democratizing the state? Institutional mechanisms for the advancement of women*, Manchester: Manchester University Press.

Randall, V. (2000) *The Politics of Child Daycare in Britain*, Oxford: Oxford University Press.

Regan, P. M. and Paskeviciute, A. (2003) 'Women's access to politics and peaceful states', *Journal of Peace Research*, 40 (3): 287–302.

Rule, W. (1987) 'Electoral systems, contextual factors and women's opportunity for election to parliament in twenty-three democracies', *Western Political Quarterly* 40: 477–98.

Savage, M. and Witz, A. (eds) (1992) *Gender and Bureaucracy*, Oxford: Blackwell.

Short, C. (1996) 'Women and the Labour Party', *Parliamentary Affairs* 49 (1): 17–25.

Squires, J. (2009) 'Intersecting inequalities: Britain's equality review', *International Feminist Journal of Politics* 11 (4): 496–512.

Squires, J. and Wickham-Jones, M. (2004) 'New Labour, gender mainstreaming and the Women and Equality Unit', *British Journal of Politics and International Relations* 6 (1): 81–98.

Thomas, S. (1995) *How Women Legislate*, Oxford: Oxford University Press.

Tripp, A. M. and Kang, A. (2007) 'The global impact of quotas: on the fast track to increased female legislative representation', *Comparative Political Studies* 41 (3): 338–361.

Vallance, E. (1979) *Women in the House*, London: Athlone Press.

Vincent, L. (2001) 'A Question of Interest: Women as opposition' in R. Southall (ed.) *Opposition and Democracy in South Africa*, London: Frank Cass.

Wängnerud, L. (2000) 'Testing the politics of presence: women's representation in the Swedish Riksdag', *Scandinavian Political Studies* 23 (1): 67–91.

Waylen, G. (1992) 'Rethinking women's political participation and protest: Chile 1970–1990', *Political Studies* 40 (2): 299–314.

— (2007) *Engendering Transitions: Women's mobilization, institutions and gender outcomes*, Oxford: Oxford University Press.

Weldon, L. (2002) *Protest, Policy and the Problem of Violence against Women: A cross-national comparison*, Pittsburgh, PA: University of Pittsburgh Press.

Williams, M. S. (1998) *Voice, Trust and Memory: Marginalized groups and the failings of liberal representation*, Princeton: Princeton University Press.

Yuval-Davis, N. (1999) 'What is "Transversal Politics"?', *Soundings* 12: 94–8.

Chapter Two

The Comparative Study of Politics and Gender

Yvonne Galligan

Introduction

In 1986 Joni Lovenduski published *Women and European Politics: Contemporary Feminism and Public Policy*. This comparative study, whose geographical reach extended from Britain to Russia and its allied states, addressed three themes that are today major sub-fields in the comparative study of politics and gender: women's political behaviour, women's representation in political institutions, and sex equality policies. Around the same time, Pippa Norris (1987) assessed the impact of social democratic politics on progress towards gender equality, Wilma Rule (1987) compared women's opportunities for election in 23 democracies, while Elina Haavio-Mannila and other feminist scholars (1985) compared the role of women in Nordic politics. Taken together, this body of research marked a seismic shift in the study of women and politics. The false universalities of women's political behaviour (such as, because women were less politically knowledgeable than men, they were devoid of political opinions, Bourque and Grossholtz 1984: 118) prevalent in mainstream comparative studies were challenged by this generation of feminist scholars. Lovenduski's (1986: 4) observation of the paucity of comparative accounts of European women's political engagement invited feminist scholars of politics to explore this emerging field.[1] In the course of this journey, the focus on women has been nuanced by the conceptual development of the notion of gender, underscoring the relational character of power, politics and the public sphere.

This chapter assesses the extent to which this shift in approach has taken place in the major comparative areas of gender politics (identified by Lovenduski in 1986): political behaviour, institutions, and public policy. It suggests that while sex and gender have been subject to extensive political theorising, and while there

1. In 2005, two decades later, Lovenduski was still to the fore in breaking new comparative ground, in *State Feminism and Political Representation*, with other scholars from the Research Network on Gender, Politics and the State (RNGS) consortium. In the intervening period marked by these two publications, she played a leading role in developing feminist comparative politics in Europe from a comparative politics *and* women/gender orientation, and towards a comparative politics of gender.

is a flourishing comparative research agenda underway in Europe, there is more to be done in integrating this knowledge into feminist and mainstream empirical research. In some areas, questions of women's inclusion are the focus of attention, implying that men and male behaviour is the norm and that women's participation and presence needs to be explained. In other areas, comparative studies of gender and politics continue to rely on single country or issue case studies in collections of essays prefaced with integrative introductory chapters. But in other aspects of gender politics, notably new feminist institutionalism and public policy, conceptual and empirical breakthroughs have provided the tools for a comparative politics of gender to emerge. This scholarship is identified by its interrogation of 'the extent to which gender is a major and primary constitutive element of political power' (Beckwith 2010: 160). There is still some way to go, though, before the theoretical, methodological and empirical richness of feminist scholarship is integrated into mainstream comparative politics.

Comparative political behaviour

The study of political behaviour has a long tradition in comparative politics, dating back to the 1930s (Cantril with Strunk 1951; Barnes and Kaase 1979), and has had a formative influence on the discipline of political science. An embedded assumption – and indeed finding – in much of this research is that women are less interested in politics than men. This deduction is based on women's higher 'Don't Know' response rate to the questions asked in public opinion surveys. It has coloured perceptions of women's citizenship, their role as political actors, and assessments of the quality of women's political agency. In 1955, French political scientist Maurice Duverger analysed women's voting patterns, candidatures, legislative representation, party involvement and pressure group engagement in four European countries in the first half of the twentieth century. This was the first cross-national and longitudinal study of women's political behaviour, and its findings did not challenge the emerging view in political science of women's subordinate political behaviour. In brief, Duverger found that women were somewhat less likely to vote than men, were slightly more conservative, and that married couples tended to vote similarly. His analysis, along with that of many other comparative scholars at the time and thereafter, was handicapped by an inability to theorise political behaviour in a way that distinguished between sex and gender. His explanations were grounded in an essentialist view of gendered political behaviour: men were innately warlike, and women were predisposed to being subordinate to men. In an early critique of this reductionist view of women's political behaviour, Susan Bourque and Jean Grossholtz (1984: 119) argued 'It is clear that the assumptions being made here exclude those interests about which women are most concerned'. Yet three decades on, the extensive literature on political behaviour in its many forms treats sex as but one of many variables; survey questions seldom explore male-female differences in policy orientations; and gender as a relational concept in interpreting political behaviour is absent from analytical discussion. Indeed, in reviewing the state of comparative research from a feminist standpoint, Lisa Baldez (2010: 199) comments that even today overviews of the field ignore, or dismiss, a gender-focused analysis. Thus, while feminist comparativists frame their research in terms of the gaps, omissions and oversights in the mainstream literature, the mainstream field with rare exceptions (e.g. Inglehart 1981; Mayer and Smith 1985; Banaszak and Plutzer 1993; Hayes *et al.* 2000) continues to ignore gender, treating sex as an 'add women and stir' variable (Weldon 2006: 246).

The continued resistance of comparative political behaviour specialists to incorporating a gendered analysis into their work, despite the efforts of feminist political scientists, is disappointing. Nonetheless, feminist scholars continue to forge ahead, identifying the gaps in mainstream research and designing questions that seek to uncover the gendered nature of political behaviour. A recent contribution in this vein is that of Hilde Coffé and Catherine Bolzendahl (2010) who investigated gender gaps in political participation for 18 advanced Western democracies, using linear and logistic regression models. They provide evidence to show that recent research on political participation offers too narrow a conceptualisation of political engagement, returning to Bourque and Grossholtz (1984) and others who had earlier pointed out that 'women do not participate less, but rather, participate differently' (2010: 320). Their task was to identify and explain these gender differences in political participation. They found that women were much more likely than men to engage in private activism (i.e. sign petitions, boycott products for political reasons) because such participation could be most readily accommodated to the pattern of women's lives. They also questioned received wisdom of women's and men's electoral behaviour which holds that women and men generally have the same propensity to vote. Their analysis showed that when attitudinal positions were controlled, women were in fact more likely to vote than men. Finally, they found that controlling for attitudinal characteristics significantly decreased the gender gap in party membership, collective activism, and in their contact of, and with, politicians. In explaining the remaining gender differences in political activity, they offered a nuance on the accepted economic, socialisation and family-based explanations: private activism was boosted by labour force participation; collective activism was heavily dependent on time resources; while differences in political contact flowed from the different socialisation processes to which women and men are subject. Coffé and Bolzendahl, then, bring to the fore new questions about the gender gap in political behaviour, with consequences for politics, political outcomes, and gender equality.

In a study of women's economic, social and political position in western democracies, Pippa Norris (1987) sought to assess the impact of Left-wing and socialist parties on progress toward sexual equality. As a comparative study, it highlighted women's exclusion from economic and political power and at the time opened cross-national research on the interaction of sex, gender and political institutions. However, its under-theorisation of sex and gender meant that it provided a relatively weak explanatory framework in which to situate observed country differences. Later, electoral studies undertaken by feminist researchers offered more fine-grained analyses of gender differences (e.g. Giger 2009) based on, or influenced by, the developmental theory of gender realignment developed by Inglehart and Norris (2000, 2003). This theory suggested that as a society modernised, the female electorate would be inclined to shift support from conservative to left and/or green parties in line with their greater labour force participation and interest in social welfare matters. Using Eurobarometer data from 1977–2000, Giger (2009: 480) found evidence to support this theory, but with more fluctuation over time and variation among European countries than the linear progression implied by Inglehart and Norris. She explains this leftward shift among women voters as being partly caused by women's greater labour force participation. She also identifies different views held by women and men on campaign issues as contributing to women's left-party orientation, and links this with current explanations of voter choice in electoral studies literature. This study illustrates the active theory-testing by feminist comparative researchers and the growing orientation of comparative electoral studies to gender differences in voter behaviour.

Comparative institutions

Closely related to the study of political behaviour is the enduring feminist interest in political institutions and processes. Two major research strands characterise this field of comparative gender politics: gendered patterns of representation in legislatures and feminist revisiting of political structures through 'new institutionalism' (*See* Chapter Five in this volume). In the field of representation, comparative feminist inquiries into the persistent exclusion of women from parliament has been a dominant theme, with studies including a European component in their design (Rule 1987; Paxton 1997), focusing on two or more European cases (Beckwith 1992; Towns 2003; Kittilson 2006). Much of this research has focused on the interaction of electoral systems with gendered outcomes, and is generally treated in single case essay collections that include a range of European country studies (e.g. Tremblay 2012) though some gender-based comparative electoral studies are beginning to emerge (Squires and Wickham Jones 2001; Schwindt-Bayer *et al.* 2010; Górecki and Kukołowicz 2013; Millard, Popescu and Toka 2013). Critical feminist attention also has been paid to electoral system differences, party gatekeeping roles, and aspiring candidates' acquisition of political capital. New comparative ground in this area was broken by Mercedes Mateo-Díaz (2005) through employing a systematic comparative approach to the descriptive and substantive representation of women (*See* Chapter Three by Celis in this volume) in west European parliaments. Its central research questions provide continued scope for comparative research on gender and parliaments: what affects the presence of women in parliament; does the number of women in parliament have an effect; and do women in parliament represent ('act for') women. Theories of women's representation also underpinned a comparative country study of women in post-communist politics, adding diversity and richness to the west European literature (Matland and Montgomery 2003). The crafting of a theoretically-derived framework for investigating country cases leading to a comparative conclusion is now an established research strategy that seeks to link empirical theory with qualitative investigations (e.g. Galligan and Tremblay 2005). The boundaries of comparative research are constantly being pushed in newer research. In a study of the gender balance of parliamentary representatives returned for 57 west European political parties during the late 1980s, Lilliefeldt (2012) identified a range of conditions for women's equal entry to parliament with men, including the presence of candidate gender quotas and leftist party policy, party size, and egalitarian social structures. This is a rare example of the use of the fuzzy-set qualitative comparative analysis method, a particularly rigorous form of investigation designed to provide robust results for small and medium-sized 'n' studies.

While the comparative study of women's under-representation in politics continues, feminist research attention has today moved to analysing the measures adopted to redress the embodied gender imbalance in legislatures, mainly through analysis of quota arrangements (as discussed by Norris and Krook in Chapter Nine). Indeed, the proliferation of political gender quotas of various types has attracted a growing analytical literature though its comparative study in Western Europe, as elsewhere, is still relatively under-developed in terms of the gendered effects of gender quotas. In a study of gender quotas worldwide, Krook (2009) compares party quotas in Sweden and the UK, uncovering the institutional configurations helping or hindering quota adoption in both countries. She also compares the conditions governing the adoption of legislative quotas in Argentina and France, highlighting through detailed descriptive analysis the integrative nature of the Argentinian law compared to the competitive, disjointed effect of the French reforms. In later work, Krook along with Lovenduski and Squires (2009) examine how three models of citizenship – consociational/corporatist, liberal, and republican – facilitate or hinder particular forms of gender quota adoption in seven instances across Western Europe, North America, Australia and New Zealand. Their findings confirm Dahlerup's (2006: 305) conclusion that quotas can act to bring a feminist agenda into political life once certain factors are present: 'an active and critical women's movement, women politicians open to feminist agenda, strong public equal opportunity units, and an extended and critical public debate on gender'. Both Dahlerup (2006) and Krook (2009) suggest that the effect of gender quotas on legislative outcomes, women's empowerment, and public policy change will only be known in time. However, a recent study by Chen (2010) provides robust comparative evidence that increases in women parliamentarians has the effect of increasing public spending on health and social welfare, and gender quota systems are seen as contributing significantly to women's expanded legislative seat-holding. This article brings a political economy approach to the study of gender politics and points feminist political science in new comparative research directions.

The sustained focus on comparative representation has also led to a renewed interest in interrogating the gendered nature of political institutions. This research agenda is influenced by North American and Australian feminist analysis of how political institutions are structured, and the scope for women politicians to make a distinctive mark on the rules and procedures, as well as policies and practices, of legislatures (Acker 1992; Chappell 2006; Kenny 2007). Grounded in mainstream new institutionalism, feminist institutionalism (*see* Chapter Five in this volume) provides a well-articulated theoretical research framework for understanding the gendered nature of political institutions. As with the study of representation, the challenge for feminist research is to develop comparative projects that utilise the strong theoretical insights on the intersection between gender and political institutions that this research field has to offer. New feminist scholarship is addressing this challenge, in the area of comparative political agenda-setting (Annesley, Engeli and Gains, 2013). Working with new datasets that map government attention to policy issues, they seek to identify the causal linkages between women's increasing representation in legislatures and government attention to gender equality issues in five European countries. This project is an example of gender politics scholars integrating their work in mainstream policy and institutional comparative studies.

Comparative policy

If new feminist institutionalism offers a means of developing a comparative politics of gender and institutions in western Europe (and elsewhere), studies in comparative public policy offer important feminist insights into democratic policy-making processes in Europe. Crucially, too, a comparative study of public policy allows for a consideration of the role played by non-state actors, such as women's movements, women's and feminist policy advocates, and how these civil society groups interact with and influence the policy and political agenda (*see* Chapter Nine in this volume). Much of this research has focused on single-issue case studies, usually at national level, with the comparative element consisting of an integrative chapter or article binding the collection together. Their focus is to explore the efforts of women in civil society to mitigate, counter, and influence public policy that holds implications for gender equality and the status of women in society. Early studies in this field placed more of an emphasis on description than on theory – which is not surprising given the extensive work required in mapping the outlines of women's relationship to the state in under-researched areas. The different ways in which women in European countries interacted with national political institutions was an early matter of investigation (Rendel 1991; Bystydzienski 1992; Funk and Mueller 1993). The politics of issues central to women's movements also loomed large, with abortion, work, and equal opportunities becoming important research foci (Meehan 1985; Dahlerup 1986; Lovenduski and Outshoorn 1986; Meehan and Sevenhuijsen 1991; Allison 1994; Stetson 1994). The complexity of public policy drew the attention of feminist political scientists, sociologists, and lawyers while the gendered nature of welfare states also drew scholarly attention (Dominelli 1991; Lewis 1992; Sainsbury 1999). The long-running RNGS (Research Network on Gender, Politics and the State) project, led by Dorothy McBride and Amy Mazur, developed a rigorous comparative methodology in a range of issue areas across 16 advanced democracies. In this project, the relationship between women's movements and the state were explored, bringing new insights – not least in respect of political participation on the working of democratic politics to light (McBride *et al.* 2010). Today's public policy research agenda is rich and wide, incorporating the politics of gender relations and their intersection with other public policy fields violence against women, prostitution, trafficking, and care (Outshoorn 2004, 2005; Mayes and Thomson 2012).

Political developments on the continent of Europe attracted the attention of feminist comparativists – the development of the European Union gender equality agenda in particular yielding a rich research stream, introducing a thematic approach that contrasted with the largely country-case focus of other comparative collections (e.g. Buckley and Anderson 1988). Later, the fall of communism and European Union enlargement gave renewed impetus to comparative public policy research in the new Europe (Gal and Kligman 2000; Pascall and Lewis 2004; Pascall and Kwak 2005; Einhorn 2006). Over time, this comparative approach has strengthened, providing a significant body of critical scholarship on the influence of the European Union on member state gender equality policies (Liebert 2003; Falkner *et al.* 2005; Guerrina 2005; Galligan and Clavero 2007; Masselot 2007; Smith and Williams 2007; van der Vleuten 2007; Velutti and Beveridge 2008; Kantola 2010; Abels and Mushaben 2012; Galligan 2015). It has also, explicitly or indirectly, contributed to the study of multi-level governance in Europe and has led to a renewed interest in exploring how gender politics is played out between the sub-national and supra-national levels, bypassing the nation state. Along with broadening and deepening the policy dimensions of politics, European studies have also interrogated the construction, and performance, of gender in the political and public spheres through the examination of specific policy or cultural practices. The VEIL research project, led by Birgit Sauer and Sieglinde Rosenberger (2011), for example, examined the renegotiation and reconstruction of collective gender and religious identities in Europe through the prism of Muslim women's headscarf-wearing. The FEMCIT project, directed by Beatrice Haalsa (Haalsa, Roseneil and Sümer 2012), took an interdisciplinary comparative approach to the gendered nature of citizenship in multi-cultural Europe, assessing how contemporary women's movements shaped citizenship politics. In these studies, the notion of the political was extended to encompass the public sphere, and the notion of political action incorporated cultural forms of the political. The MAGEEQ and QUING projects, led by Mieke Verloo over a decade examined the conceptualisation of gender equality in formal policies seeking to promote women's rights (Verloo 2006; Lombardo, Meier and Verloo 2009). It has contributed a new methodological tool to comparative political science – critical frame analysis – that allows for a critical deconstruction of the gendered imprint embedded in policy documents (Verloo 2007). Along with the VEIL and FEMCIT, the research projects MAGEEQ and QUING closely interrogated the meanings and manifestations of gender in a comparative European context.

While this review only begins to touch on the extensive comparative public policy research engaged in by feminist political scientists in Europe, it follows a similar theoretical and conceptual trajectory to the scholarship on political institutions. Beginning with studies that takes the relationship between women and the state as the central category of analysis, it has evolved to a critique of the differential impacts of state/European policies on women and men, contributing to the embedding of gender mainstreaming as a policy tool, policy process, and analytical concept (Rees 1998). The challenge of conducting comparative studies using qualitative methods is a significant one, though recent studies such as the VEIL and FEMCIT, along with MAGEEQ, QUING and others, approach this challenge by developing strong feminist theoretical frameworks and defined research methodologies (for a review of these and other recent large-scale comparative gender and policy projects in Europe, *see* Mazur 2009).

Future directions for a comparative politics of gender

The above review shows, if it was ever needed, that women and gender constitute important analytical categories for feminist comparative politics. Displaying a plurality of perspectives, approaches, and interdisciplinary connections, this sub-field of political science has blossomed since the 1980s in Western Europe and further afield. The eclecticism of the scholarship, however, is not without its challenges that need to be overcome if feminist comparative politics is to remain innovative, and fully exploit the potential of a comparative politics of gender. The challenge comes in two parts: one is to embrace and incorporate into research designs the interrogation of how feminine and masculine identities are constructed in democratic politics. The second is to develop empirically-testable theories of gendered political behaviour that can, in turn, inform scholarship in the wider comparative politics field.

While the study of women and politics has blossomed since the 1980s, the comparative study of gender politics has had a more patchy development. The large 'n' studies of political behaviour continue to base their analyses on sex differences and have not developed the means for interrogating relational gender behaviours. Sex remains a political variable, usually one of many independent variables. This constitutes sex as an aspect of individual identity, alongside other identities such as religion, class and ethnicity. Treated in this way in attitudinal surveys, sex becomes essentialised as a biological attribute, and not a relational concept with a profound effect on the organisation of society. The findings of research of this kind, then, cannot reflect the meaning of what it is to be a woman, or a man, across the societies surveyed. Of concern too is the inclination of cross-national studies to reference similar studies rather than incorporating insights from other branches of gender politics in developing hypotheses about attitudinal positions and behaviours. Perhaps an exploration of masculinities and femininities is a step too far for a positivist approach, (although *see* Winters unpublished PhD) though there is scope for work of this kind to be informed by the gendered nature of political agency that other aspects of the discipline have developed. This would lead to the identification of more nuanced research questions that can be explored with all of the analytical rigour that quantitative research can offer. Some feminist comparative research (eg Kronsell 2005; van der Vleuten 2007; Voorpostel and Coffé 2012) is already going down that path, placing sex-differences at the core of their research questions.

Much of the study of political institutions, including representative politics, rests on in-depth qualitative investigation of single case studies. Early feminist studies of political structures focused on the position of women within these institutions, and their relationship to the structures in question. Questions such as 'why so few' led to interrogations of the case-related barriers to women's participation, and thence on to the solution-driven 'what can be done' inquiry. These studies yielded rich insights, and contributed to comparative generalisations regarding women's positioning in relation to these political structures. The limited theoretical purchase of this approach became apparent as the hard work of mapping women's positions in relation to political structures yielded further insights and more complex questions. Thus, there was a move beyond collections of individual case studies to collaborative research with common questions and agreed methodologies for their investigation. As this form of comparative research has taken hold in Western Europe – and is particularly suited to taking account of the diverse country cases and research traditions in the European region – their contribution to a universal understanding of the gendered nature of political power, institutions, and representative politics has grown. Gender quotas for legislative office – now a global phenomenon – were trialled, and first compared for their effectiveness, in Europe. Comparative feminist political research of this kind employs rigorous, qualitative methodologies and produce robust findings. The understanding of what constitutes a 'case' is now interpreted more flexibly than the national focus of earlier research. Multi-level studies in single countries and longitudinal studies of how women interact at and with a specific level of sub-national and supra-national governance are becoming more common.

However, the conceptualisation of gender is not always clear in these studies. Often the analytical focus is on women, and women's agency within political systems and structures. Yet, quite often, the term 'gender' is used as a synonym for 'women' (Carver 1996). Treating women as an analytical category is valid, of course, but more attention needs to be paid to defining what is meant by 'gender' as a category rather than employing an easy elision of the two terms. Indeed, in this regard, Lovenduski's (1998: 348 quoted in Chappell 2006: 226) own reflections on the study of gender and institutions can serve to inform feminist comparative scholarship:

> that (1) Everyone in an institution has a sex and performs gender; (2) the experience of individuals in institutions varies by both sex and gender; (3) Sex and gender interact with other components of identity – for example, race, ethnicity – that also have implications for models of femininity and masculinity; and (4) Institutions have distinctive gendered cultures and are involved in processes of producing and reproducing gender.

Therefore, a more explicit definition of what meaning is attributed to gender in comparative cases can enable the exploration of the relational nature of gender politics, and the constructions and reconstructions that take place as a consequence of women's and feminist interventions in politics.

Finally, a comparative politics of gender is underway in a manner that promises to refresh the sub-field of comparative politics within the political science discipline. The heterogeneity of European countries presents ideal opportunities for the construction of research questions that examine the political interaction of masculine and feminine identities, the gendered nature of democratic processes, and evaluations of the quality of democratic institutions and practices in medium 'n' cases. In other words, utilising the concept of gender means addressing its two forms: as a category and as a process (Beckwith 2005). Indeed, concern for how gender is constructed and interpreted is something that is very much present in feminist comparative institutional research today. Current comparative feminist interest is moving beyond the traditionally-conceived 'political system' to that of the 'public sphere', where cultural politics and its gendered manifestations are played out. It is also bringing the cultural constructions of gender into the political system, through studies on the gendered cast of legislative forums. The state of the scholarship is vibrant, and influences from other disciplines continue to inform the theoretical and empirical research questions pursued in feminist comparative political science. The seeds sown by feminist academic pioneers in the 1980s have grown into an intellectually exciting, theoretically robust and methodologically diverse corpus of European research that is evolving into a distinctive comparative politics of gender.

References

Abels, G. and Mushaben, J. M. (eds) (*2012*) *Gendering the European Union: New approaches to old democratic deficits*, Basingstoke: Palgrave.

Acker, J. (1992) 'From sex roles to gendered institutions', *Contemporary Sociology* 21 (5) : 565–569.

Allison, M. (1994) 'The right to choose: abortion in France', *Parliamentary Affairs* 47 (2) : 222–237.

Annesley, C., Engeli, I. and Gains, F. (2013) 'Finding Gender on the Agenda: Using comparative agendas data to research gender equality policy change', Paper presented at PSA Annual Conference, Cardiff, 25–27 March.

Baldez, L. (2010) 'The gender lacuna in comparative politics', *Perspectives on Politics* 8 (1): 199–205.

Banaszak, L. A. and Plutzer, E. (1993) 'The social bases of feminism in the European Community', *Public Opinion Quarterly* 57: 29–53.

Barnes, S. H. and Kaase, M. *et al.* (1979) *Political Action: Mass participation in five western democracies*, London: Sage Publications.

Beckwith, K. (2010) 'Introduction: comparative politics and the logics of a comparative politics of gender', *Perspectives on Politics* 8 (1): 159–168.

— (2005) 'A common language of gender?', *Politics & Gender* 1 (1): 128–137.

— (1992) 'Comparative research and electoral systems: lessons from France and Italy', *Women and Politics* XII (2): 1–33.

Bourque, S. and Grossholtz, J. (1984) 'Politics an Unnatural Practice: Political science looks at female participation', in J. Siltanen and M. Stanworth (eds) *Women and the Public Sphere: A critique of sociology and politics*, London: Hutchinson, pp. 103–121.

Buckley, M. and Anderson, M. (eds) (1988) *Women, Equality and Europe*, Basingstoke: MacMillan Press.

Bystydzienski, J. M. (ed.) (1992) *Women Transforming Politics: Worldwide strategies for empowerment*, Indiana: Indiana University Press.

Cantril, H. and Strunk, M. (1951) *Public Opinion 1935–1946*, Princeton: Princeton Univeristy Press.

Carver, T. (1996) *Gender is not a Synonym for Women*, Boulder, Co: Lynne Reiner Publishers.

Chappell, L. (2006) 'Comparing political institutions: revealing the gendered "logic of appropriateness"', *Politics & Gender* 2 (2): 223–235.

Chen, L.-J. (2010) 'Do gender quotas influence women's representation and politics?', *The European Journal of Comparative Economics*, 7 (1): 13–60.

Coffé, H. and Bolzendahl, C. (2010) 'Same game, different rules? Gender differences in political participation', *Sex Roles* 62: 318–333.

Dahlerup, D. (1986) *The New Women's Movement: Feminism and political power in Europe and the USA*, London: Sage.

— (2006) *Women, Quotas and Politics*, London: Taylor & Francis.

Dominelli, L. (1991) *Women Across Continents: Feminist comparative social policy*, London: Harvester Wheatsheaf.

Duverger, M. (1955) *The Political Role of Women*, Geneva: UNESCO.

Einhorn, B. (2006) *Cinderella Goes to Market: Citizenship, gender and women's movements in East Central Europe,* London: Verso.

Falkner, G., Treib, O., Hartlapp, M. and Leiber, S. (2005) *Complying with Europe: EU harmonization and soft law in the member states*, Cambridge: Cambridge University Press.

Funk, N. and Mueller, M. (eds) (1993) *Gender Politics and Post Communism: Reflections from Eastern Europe and the former Soviet Union*, New York: Routledge.

Gal, S. and Kligman, G. (2000) *The Politics of Gender after Socialism*, Princeton: Princeton University Press.

Galligan, Y. (ed.) (2015) *States of Democracy: Gender and Politics in the European Union*, Abingdon: Routledge.

Galligan, Y. and Clavero, S. (2007) 'Gender equality and multi-level governance in East Central Europe', in J. de Bardeleben and A. Hurrelmann (eds) *Democratic Dilemmas of Multilevel Governance*, Basingstoke: Palgrave Macmillan, pp. 216–239.

Galligan, Y. and Tremblay, M. (2005) *Sharing Power: Women, parliament, democracy*, Aldershot: Ashgate.

Giger, N. (2009) 'Towards a modern gender gap in Europe? A comparative analysis of voting behaviour in 12 countries', *The Social Science Journal* 46: 474–492.

Górecki, M. A. and Kukołowicz, P. (2013) 'Gender Quotas, Candidate Background and the Election of Women: A paradox of gender quotas in open-list proportional representation systems', paper delivered at European Consortium for Political Research Joint Sessions of Workshops, Mainz, 12–16 March.

Gurerrina, R. (2005) *Mothering the Union: The politics of gender, equality and maternity rights in the European Union*, Manchester: Manchester University Press

Haalsa, B., Roseneil, S. and Sümer, S. (eds) (2012) *Remaking Citizenship in Multicultural Europe: Women's movements, gender and diversity*, Basingstoke: Palgrave Macmillan.

Haavio-Mannila, E. *et al.* (eds) (1985) *Unfinished Democracy: Women in Nordic politics*, trans. C. Badcock, Oxford: Pergamon Press.

Hayes, B. C., McAllister, I. and Studlar, D. T. (2000) 'Gender, postmaterialism and feminism in comparative perspective', *International Political Science Review* 21 (4): 425–439.

Inglehart, R. and Norris, P. (2000) 'The developmental theory of the gender gap: women's and men's voting behaviour in global perspective', *International Political Science Review* 21 (4): 441–463.

— (2003) *Rising Tide: Gender equality and cultural change*, Cambridge: Cambridge University Press.

Inglehart, M. (1981) 'Political interest in West European women: an historical and empirical comparative analysis', *Comparative Political Studies* 14: 299–326.

Kantola, J. (2010) *Gender and the European Union*, Basingstoke: Palgrave Macmillan.

Kenny, M. (2007) 'Gender, institutions and power: a critical review', *Politics* 27 (2): 91–100.

Kittilson, M. C. (2006) *Challenging Parties, Changing Parliaments: Women and elected office in contemporary Western Europe*, Ohio: Ohio State University Press.

Krook, M. L. (2009) *Quotas for Women in Politics: Gender and candidate selection reform worldwide*, New York: Oxford University Press.

Krook, M. L., Lovenduski, J. and Squires, J. (2009) 'Gender quotas and models of political citizenship', *British Journal of Political Science* 39 (4): 781–803.

Krook, M. L. and Mackay, F. (2011) *Gender, Politics and Institution: Towards a feminist institutionalism,* Basingstoke: Palgrave Macmillan.

Kronsell, A. (2005) 'Gendered practices in institutions of hegemonic masculinity', *International Feminist Journal of Politics* 7 (2): 280–298.

Lewis, J. (1992) 'Gender and the development of welfare regimes', *Journal of European Social Policy* 2 (3): 159–173.

Liebert, U. (2003) 'Gendering europeanisation: patterns and dynamics', in U. Liebert (ed.) *Gendering Europeanisation*, Brussels: Peter Lang, pp. 255–285.

Lilliefeldt, E. (2012) 'Party and gender in Western Europe revisited: a fuzzy-set qualitative comparative analysis of gender-balanced parliamentary parties', *Party Politics* 19 (2): 193–214.

Lombardo, E., Meier, P. and Verloo, M. (2009) *The Discursive Politics of Gender Equality: Stretching, bending and policy-making,* Abingdon: Routledge/ ECPR Studies in European Political Science.

Lovenduski, J. (ed.) (2005) *State Feminism and Political Representation*, Cambridge: Cambridge University Press.

— (1998) 'Gendering research in political science', *Annual Review of Political Science* 1: 333–356.

— (1986) *Women and European Politics: Contemporary feminism and public policy*, Amherst: University of Massachusetts Press.

Lovenduski, J. and Outshoorn, J. (1986) *The New Politics of Abortion*, London: Sage.

McBride, D. E. and Mazur, A. G., with Lovenduski, J., Outshoorn, J., Guadagnini, M., Sauer, B. and Sainsbury, D. (2010) *The Politics of State Feminism: Innovation in comparative research*, Philadelphia: Temple University Press.

Mackay, F., Kenny, M. and Chappell, L. (2010) 'New institutionalism through a gender lens: towards a feminist institutionalism?', *International Political Science Review* 31 (5): 573–588.

Masselot, A. (2007) 'The state of gender equality law in the European Union', *European Law Journal* 13 (2): 152–168.

Mateo-Díaz, M. (2005) *Representing Women? Female legislators in West European parliaments*, Essex: ECPR Press.

Matland, R. E and Montgomery, K. A. (eds) (2003) *Women's Access to Political Power in Post-Communist Europe*, Oxford: Oxford University Press.

Mayer, L. C. and Smith, R. E. (1985) 'Feminism and religiosity: female electoral behaviour in Western Europe', *West European Politics* 8 (4): 38–49.

Mayes, D. G. and Thomson, M. (eds) (2012) *The Costs of Children: Parenting and democracy in Contemporary Europe*, London: Edward Elgar.

Mazur, A. G. (2009) 'Comparative gender and policy projects in Europe: current trends in theory, method and research', *Comparative European Politics* 7 (1): 12–36.

Meehan, E. (1985) *Women's Rights At Work: Campaigns and policy in Britain and the United States,* Basingstoke: MacMillan Press.

Meehan, E. and Sevenhuijsen, S. (eds) (1991) *Equality Politics and Gender*, London: Sage.

Millard, F., Popescu, M. and Toka, G. (2013) 'The Impact of Preference Voting Systems on Women's Representation and the Legitimation of Quota-Based Nomination Results', paper delivered at European Consortium for Political Research Joint Sessions of Workshops, Mainz, 12–16 March.

Norris, P. (1987) *Politics and Sexual Equality: The comparative position of women in western democracies*, Boulder CO: Lynne Reiner.

Outshoorn, J. (2005) 'The political debates on prostitution and trafficking of women', *Social Politics: International Studies in Gender, State and Society* 12 (1): 141–155.

— (ed.) (2004) *The Politics of Prostitution: Women's movements, democratic states and the globalisation of sex commerce*, Cambridge: Cambridge University Press.

Pascall, G. and Kwak, A. (2005) *Gender Regimes in Transition in Central and Eastern Europe*, Bristol: Policy Press.

Pascall, G. and Lewis, J. (2004) 'Emerging gender regimes and policies for gender equality in a wider Europe', *Journal of Social Policy* 33 (3): 373–394.

Paxton, P. (1997) 'Women in national legislatures: a cross-national analysis', *Social Science Research* 26 (4): 442–464.

Rees, T. (1998) *Mainstreaming Equality in the European Union*, London: Routledge.

Rendel, M. (ed.) (1981) *Women, Power and Political Systems*, London: Croomhelm.

Rule, W. (1987) 'Electoral systems, contextual factors and women's opportunity for election to parliament in twenty-three democracies', *Western Political Quarterly* 40 (3): 477–498.

Sainsbury, D. (1999) *Gender and Welfare State Regimes*, Oxford: Oxford University Press.

Sauer, B. and Rosenberger, S. (eds) (2011) *Politics, Religion and Gender: Framing and regulating the veil*, New York: Routledge.

Schwindt-Bayer, L. A., Malecki, M. and Crisp, B. F. (2010) 'Candidate gender and electoral success in single transferable vote systems', *British Journal of Political Science* 40 (3): 179–197.

Smith, A. and Williams, D. R. (2007) 'Father-friendly legislation and paternal time across Europe', *Journal of Comparative Policy Analysis* 9(2): 175–192.

Squires, J. and Wickham-Jones, M. (2001) *Women in Parliament: A comparative analysis,* Equal Opportunities Commission: Manchester.

Stetson, D. McBride (1994) 'Abortion rights in Russia, the USA and France', in M. Githens, P. Norris and J. Lovenduski (eds) *Different Roles, Different Voices: Women and politics in the United States and Europe*, London: Longman, pp. 97–117.

Towns, A. (2003) 'Understanding the effects of larger ratios of women in national legislatures: proportions and gender differentiation in Sweden and Norway', *Women and Politics* 25 (1–2): 215–238.

Tremblay, M. (ed.) (2012) *Women and Legislative Representation: Electoral systems, political parties and sex quotas*, New York: Palgrave Macmillan.

van der Vleuten, A. (2007) *The Price of Gender Equality: Member states and governance in the European Union*, Aldershot: Ashgate.

Velluti, S. and Beveridge, F. (eds) (2008) *Gender and the Open Method of Coordination: Perspectives on law, governance and equality in the EU*, London: Routledge.

Verloo, M. (ed.) (2007) *Multiple Meanings of Gender Equality: A critical frame analysis of gender policies in Europe*, CEU Press: Budapest.

— (2006) 'Multiple inequalities, intersectionality and the European Union', *European Journal of Women's Studies* 3: 211–229.

Voorpostel, M. and Coffé, H. (2012) 'Transitions in partnership and parental status, gender, and political and civic participation', *European Sociological Review* 28 (1): 28–42.

Weldon, S. L. (2006) 'The structure of intersectionality: a comparative politics of gender', *Politics & Gender* 2 (2): 235–248.

Winters, K. (2009) 'Sex and gender as sources of heterogeneity in political attitudes and behaviours', Department of Government, University of Essex, PhD, http://ethos.bl.uk/OrderDetails.do?uin=uk.bl.ethos.504841.

Chapter Three

Representation[1]

Karen Celis

Introduction

The gendered dimension to political representation is first evident regarding the actors of representation; because the represented and the representatives by definition have a sex and a gender, representation is not immune to being structured by hierarchical relations between men and women. However, 'gendering representation' is not only concerned with the sex of the bodies being represented or doing the representing, but also focuses on the 'what' of representation and examines representatives' acts and claims using a gendered lens (*see also* Mazur and McBride 2008).

Besides taking into account the sex of the actors involved and the gendered character of representation, 'gendering representation' fundamentally questions the way this concept is conceived and formulates conditions for 'good' – i.e. truly representative-representation (Dovi 2007) and even for democracy as such (*see* Paxton 2008). A key contribution of feminist scholars is the rejection of a clear-cut separation of the dimensions of representation, as well as of the hierarchy between them. According to theorists of group representation, descriptive and substantive representation are intertwined, as the former is a prerequisite for the latter. Thereby, feminist analysis of representation complements mainstream political debates revolving around the questions 'what is to be represented?' and 'what is the relationship between the representative and the represented?'

The context of political representation

The concept of 'representation' has had different meanings at different times and in different contexts.[2] Etymologically, 'representation' derives from the Latin verb *repraesentare*: 'making present (again)'. Originally, the term was used most frequently for inanimate objects that were made present (again); for instance, by introducing them or presenting them. It was also applied in artistic settings

1. This is a slightly revised reprint of Celis, K. (2008) Gendering Representation. In: G. Goertz & A. Mazur, Politics, *Gender, and Concepts: Theory and Methodology*, Cambridge: Cambridge University Press, 71–93. The volume as a whole explores the methodology of concept construction and critique. In this particular chapter the concept of representation and its gendering are analysed thereby following the guidelines provided by the editors of the book.

2. Pitkin 1969: 1–5; *see also* McLean 1991, 1996; Eulau 1967; Thomassen 1994.

where actors or art (paintings or sculptures) represented characters, virtues, or ideas. Only later, in the Christian literature and practice of the Middle Ages, was the word used to refer to the embodiment of a collective by a person. In the same period, embryonic institutions of political representation emerged. In the seventeenth century, and more specifically during the English Civil War, representation was interpreted as 'acting for others' (agency) and representative institutions were linked with democratic practice and rights. The American and French revolutions that took place during the following century established representation as a universal, democratic right. The nineteenth century witnessed the institutionalisation of that right and from then on, much effort was devoted to an accurate formalisation of representation.

Although democracy can theoretically exist without representation, representation is firmly imbedded in western liberal democracies (Lijphart 1984; *see also* Paxton 2008). Representation and representatives are seen as indispensable for putting into practice the democratic principle of 'government by the people' (Beetham 1992: 41). This makes representation a core concept for political scientists. Additionally, its semantic neighbor 'representativeness' (cf. infra) is a central feature in recent debates concerning the democratic level of political institutions and processes (Guinier 1994; Paolino 1995). Nonetheless, there has been disagreement about its nature and definition: '"Representation" is one of the slippery core concepts of political theory' (McLean 1991: 172).

Gendering representation?

Gendering representation is a scientific activity that consists of describing, analysing, and explaining the gendered nature of the 'who' and the 'what' of political representation. Representatives, representation, and representativeness are and have always been gendered; gendering representation concerns the investigation of the gendered character of these concepts.

Gendering representation is more than mapping, analysing, and explaining inclusion and exclusion of sex and gender in (the praxis of) representation. It is also a feminist activity. Ultimately, gendering representation and representativeness aims at improving these concepts and their operationalisation; i.e. making them more inclusive and therefore more just and democratic (*see also* Paxton 2008). It adds gendered conditions to representation and representativeness as ideal types regarding the inclusion and exclusion of sex and gender. The underlying rationale is that representation is only successful when it is also representative in terms of sex and gender. It is evident that such critical examinations of representation should not be limited to the categories of sex and gender. For instance, similar investigations can be conducted regarding inclusion and exclusion on the basis of race, age, ethnic background, class, and sexual orientation.

Dimensions of political representation

Reduced to its essence, representation is the making present of something or someone (principal) who is not literally present through an intermediary (agent) (Pitkin 1969:16). This implies not only that the presence of the represented via the representative but also that their absence are necessary components of representation; inclusion and exclusion are inherent aspects of the concept (Judge 1999). Essential to political representation is that a mediating representative or assembly of representatives is set between the citizenry and political decision making, and therefore it is the antipodal of direct political decision making (Brennan and Hamlin 1999). Representativeness is an indication of the degree to which the representative (be it a person, an object, or an institution) succeeds in making the absent that is being represented present.

Although useful, this basic definition of representation is not sufficient. It does not give answers to important questions such as: Why is that mediating person or assembly 'representative'? Why are their presence and actions 'representation'? What constitutes representation and the representative? The answers to these pertinent questions refer to formal participation, the identity of the representatives, and their acts.

Who are the actors?

Representation as a formal participation and as 'standing for' – A first component of representation consists of a formal agreement between the representative and the represented (Pitkin 1969: 13; *see also* Griffiths 1960; Birch 1971 1993; Braud 1985). Thomas Hobbes' *Leviathan* is a representative because he is given that authority. The people are bound by the acts of the *Leviathan*. In this conception, there is no escape from representation (except for not belonging to the people). Others stress that neither the initial act of giving authority nor obedience is crucial in the formal relationship between the representative and the represented. What constitutes the representative and representation is the fact that, as a result of calling the representative into account, the formal agreement can be ended. Although the initial act of handing over authority to the representative is indispensable, if it leads to the represented being regarded as passive 'recipients' of the representative acts and commitments, an essential part of representation is missed. Subjects must also have control over the representative and not solely the other way around (Pitkin 1972: 232).

The 'mandate'– issued by the represented and binding them, limited in scope and/or time, initiated and/or terminated in a characteristic way – is the formal component of political representation. It implies a set of rules and techniques that organises the input and the output of the process of representation – i.e. the election of representatives and information about the preferences of the represented – that are closely linked with legitimacy and efficiency (Hirst 1990; Judge 1999; Sartori 1987). Although representation is much more than structures, regulations, and elections, they are an indispensable part of it.

A second approach to representation focuses on the representatives, on who they are and what they stand for (Pitkin 1969; Griffiths 1960; Birch 1971, 1993; Braud 1985). Descriptive representation stresses the accurate composition of the parliament. Taken together, the representatives mirror the people they represent. Who they are and what they look like is what counts. The representatives provide information about the (perceived) desires, views or interests of the constituents. Therefore, the resembling composition also assures that the representatives *would* act the way the represented would. In this view, direct democracy is the ideal (Brennan and Hamlin 1999).

A specific kind of representation through 'standing for' is symbolic representation (Phillips 1969; Griffiths 1960; Birch 1971, 1993; Braud 1985). A king or a flag represents a nation because of symbolic qualities. Not the resemblance, but the fact that people acknowledge the symbolic quality of an object or a person is what constitutes representation.

Gendering formal and descriptive representation – Historically, women and men were not considered to have the same capacities to give and receive the authority to represent (Pateman 1988; Paxton 2008). Generally, women were granted the right to vote and to be a candidate later than men. This excluded them for a long time from formal and descriptive participation. Although it was claimed that a woman participated through her father's and subsequently her husband's votes (Sapiro 1981), and an exclusively male parliament represented them symbolically (Mansbridge 1999; Phillips 1995), the absence of the right to vote implied that representatives were not directly accountable to women. Today, women in most countries are fully enfranchised. Nonetheless, in most states women are still underrepresented on a formal and descriptive level; e.g. on candidate lists and in assemblies. To counter the lack of representativeness of the political institutions, parity laws and sex quotas have been applied in progressively more countries to break through barriers hindering women's formal and descriptive participation (*see* Chapter Nine by Norris and Krook in this volume; Dahlerup 2006; Krook 2004; Meier 2002; Squires 1996). Proponents of descriptive representation point to the importance of role models, to justice and democratic values – there exists no democratic argument to justify male overrepresentation in political decision making structures – and to the legitimacy of institutions, especially in the case when substantive representation fails (Phillips 1995; Williams 1998). The traditional argument against is that it might entail representatives of mediocre quality (Birch 1993; Norton 1993).

What and who is represented (and by whom)?

Representation as 'acting for' – Formal, symbolic, and descriptive representation do not deal with a crucial aspect of representation, notably 'what is going on during representation' (Pitkin 1969: 9). That is the domain of representation as 'acting for'. Substantive representation is about what representatives do: 'acting in the interest of the represented, in a manner responsive to them' (Pitkin 1972: 209). This conception of representation places the subject and the relationship between the representative and the represented in the center of attention. What is to be represented? How is the principal represented? Who decides on what is in the interest of the represented: the representative or the represented? Depending on the answers to these questions, the representative sees his/her role as a trustee (independent from the represented) or as a delegate (with no independency). The representative's position with regard to the represented should not be considered static, absolute, and polarised (Pitkin 1969; Judge 1999; Eulau and Wahlke 1978; Sobolewski 1968). A representative can behave as a trustee or a delegate and also as a 'politico' expressing both orientations, either simultaneously or serially (Elau *et al.* 1978: 119). A representative's behaviour is determined by 'meta-political' considerations concerning, for instance, the nature of the issues and the capacities of both the representatives and the represented: representatives will act as trustees when they are considered to be superior in wisdom and experience to the represented and political problems are supposed to have a clear and objective solution that can be defined through a rational investigation; representatives will act as delegates when representatives and the represented are considered to have equal capacities and when political issues are more linked with personal preferences, thereby making objective, rational deliberation inapt (Pitkin 1969: 19–21). Moreover, the representative's acts and activities are based primarily on the judgment of the party and not on her/his own opinions or on those of the electorate (Pitkin 1972: 215; Judge 1999; Sobolewski 1968). The 'constituency' of the representative is plural and consists of concentric circles: the nation or the territory, the political party, and functional groups (Fenno 1978).

Recently, the debate regarding 'what is represented?' and more specifically the trustee position is taken one step further by scholars such as Mansbridge[3] (1998, 2003) and Saward (2006), who consider 'creative' acts to be fundamental aspects of representation. 'Anticipatory representation' (Mansbridge 1998, 2003) is motivated by winning future voters and is based on what the representative thinks the voter of the next election will prefer. In my view, this implies that, to a certain extent, the interests of the represented are a creation by which the representative hopes to please the future voter, who will in turn approve the representative's actions by reelecting her/him. The creative aspect of representation is more explicitly dealt with in Saward's work on political representation. He rejects the assumption often present in the delegate-trustee debate that interests exist

3. Jane Mansbridge (1998, 2003) distinguishes four 'faces of representation'. 'Representation by promising' implies that the representative will act for the represented according to what he/she promised during the election. Voters vote for the candidate because of what he/she promises and plans to do. In the case of 'introspective' or 'gyroscopic representation', on the contrary, voters vote for a candidate because they expect the candidate to act in a certain way according to internal principles and convictions. 'Surrogate representation' occurs when representation takes place notwithstanding the fact that there exists no formal tie between the representative and the represented (for instance, because they are situated in different constituencies). 'Anticipatory representation' is motivated by winning the future voters and is thus based on what the representative thinks the voter in the next election prefers. In this case, voting behaviour is based on retrospection.

prior to their representation; that they are 'out there' and can be brought into the representational process. During representation the representative creates the represented, as well as him/herself and the audience, via 'representative claims': 'The "interests" of a constituency have to be "read in" more than "read off"; it is an active, creative process, not the passive process of receiving clear signals from below' (Saward 2006: 310). Pushed to its limits, this implies that the represented exists by virtue of the representative, who subsequently seems to become the principal and the represented agent.

Gendering substantive representation – Gendering substantive representation refers to representation of women's interests and gendering the general interest. A crucial evolution in feminist political theory in the 1980s and 1990s concerns the demarcation of 'women's interests' (*see* Campbell *et al.'s* Chapter Eleven in this volume). In the early 1980s scholars like Virginia Sapiro, Irene Diamond and Nancy Hartsock tried to define women's interests (Sapiro 1981; Diamond and Hartsock 1981). According to Sapiro, political women's interests are a consequence of the different social positions that women occupy. More precisely, it is the 'private distribution of labor' – i.e. the tasks of giving birth to and care for children – that makes women take up different socioeconomic positions than men and that gives them distinct interests (as a group) that are politically 'representable'. According to Diamond and Hartsock, on the contrary, women's common interests are not the consequence of the division of tasks inside the household but of the gendered division of productive labor (Diamond and Hartsock 1981: 194–196). They prefer the more enclosing terms *wants* and *needs* above the utilitarian vocabulary coinciding with the promotion of interests. They thereby refer to female values, behaviour, and psyche that have been determined through two studies on the socialisation of women in that period (Rich 1976; Chodorow 1978). The scholars of group representation of the 1990s, on the contrary, keep their distance from an essentialist image of the woman (Phillips 1995, 1998; Young 1997). 'That which has to be represented' (women's interests)[4] results from the diversified life experience of different groups of women. Women's interests then, are *a priori* undefined, context related, and subject to evolution.

What is at stake in the case of gendered representation is not only the inclusion of women's interests, but also the gendering of the general interest (Lovenduski 2005: 19; Stokes 2005: 20; *see also* Mazur and McBride in this volume). In opposition to Phillips, Iris Marion Young suggests that the link between being a woman and representing women is not about interests and needs, but about social perspectives, in particular the way in which people interpret things and events from within their structural social situation (Young 1997, 2000). Social groups are structured around differences such as gender, race, nationality, and religion,

4. Phillips uses the terms 'interests' and 'needs' together. According to Phillips, interests and needs both come forth out of the life experience of women, and together they are what needs to be represented (Phillips 1995: 73). This chapter applies the same enclosing definition of women's interests.

but she stresses that these groups cannot be defined through common interests or through similar opinions. Therefore, women cannot be represented as a group based on such shared interests and opinions. Substantive representation of a social group means representing the social perspective of that group deriving from its structural position in society. It is crucial in a democratic dialogue because in that way it will count for all citizens, provide information about the diversity of social perspectives, and lead to more justice.

A second important evolution in the feminist political theory concerns the way in which the relationship between descriptive and substantive representation is perceived. The 'critical mass theory' – more precisely the way Drude Dahlerup's statements about the importance of numbers of women were interpreted (Dahlerup 1988; Childs and Krook 2005) – supposed a strong relationship between being female and acting for women: women *will* make a difference if they have the numerical strength (*see* Dahlerup's account in this volume, Chapter Seven). The 'politics of presence theory' (Phillips 1995, 1998), on the contrary, does not refer to numbers of women. Furthermore, it contends that the link between women MPs and the political representation of women is 'half-fastened': the *possibility* that women are represented increases when women are present.[5] According to Phillips, the link between descriptive and substantive representation is based on women's life experiences. It is this structural position in society that causes a specific background of experiences and knowledge (Tamerius 1995). Because of their biology and their roles in society, women have personal experiences that are different from men as well as a gendered perspective on situations and experiences that are objectively the same. Furthermore, shared experiences and perspectives foster group identification, which in turn fosters sharing experiences. The latter is also due to socialisation and to working in groups and contexts that exclude the other sex.

This shared gendered life experience not only provides 'resources' in terms of consciousness and expertise for the substantive representation of women, but also impacts upon their assessment of priority of and engagement for representing women (Tamerius 1995; Phillips 1995). Furthermore, the presence of women also enables a 'politics of transformation' (Phillips 1995, 1998). Interests and needs are not external data entered in political decision making; they take shape during political decision making. Only in the most optimal circumstances, in particular when a group is systematically present in the process of working out alternatives, is it capable of formulating new subjects and challenging dominant conventions. Young (1994, 2000) also contends that making the social perspective of women present can only be achieved by persons who share the experience that goes with a structural position in society, as the people in this position are sensible to certain subjects, questions or events. Paraphrasing Mansbridge and Saward: female representatives have specific resources of knowledge and expertise to create the

5. A similar argumentation can be found with Anna Jónasdóttir (1988), Melissa Williams (1998), and Jane Mansbridge (1999).

female representative and her interests, and to claim to represent them. These resources can be tapped into when representatives behave as trustees and rely on their own insights and internal principles; what Mansbridge terms 'gyroscopic' representation.

Necessity and interdependency of the dimensions

None of the dimensions described above – formal participation, descriptive or substantive representation – are essential to representation. A representative can be imposed on me, but still represents me if she takes my interests to heart. I can acknowledge a person to be my formal representative, even if he neither looks like me, nor acts for me, or even if he harms my interests. However, since the essence of representation is the making present of the absent, the represented has to be made present by the representative in at least one way, be it formally, descriptively, symbolically, *or* substantively. In other words, at least one of these dimensions needs to be present in order to claim that representation takes place. Given the variety of instances in which representation takes place, representation is not an ideal type.

Theoretically, the formal, descriptive/symbolic and substantive dimensions of representation are also not interdependent. One dimension can occur without the presence of the other dimensions. For example, an MP who does not look like me and was not elected by me can substantively represent me (for instance, in the case of 'surrogate representation'). However, empirical research shows a strong relationship between these dimensions. Formal participation (e.g. as candidates and electorate) often is a prerequisite for descriptive (e.g. female legislators) and substantive representation (e.g. through inclusion of women's issues in the party programme). Furthermore, feminist scholars point to the existence of a necessity and causal relationship between descriptive and substantive representation (addressed in the latter part of this chapter).

There exist quantitative and qualitative degrees of descriptive and substantive representativeness (in terms of sex and gender) according to: the number of representatives who stand or act for the represented or the number of moments when substantive representation takes place; the quality of descriptive and substantive representatives (measured for instance by degree of resemblance, status, power, financial resources, or degree of activity); and the quality of substantive representation (measured for instance by range, inclusiveness, degree of congruency with the will of the represented). An example of a position between descriptive representation and nonrepresentation in terms of sex and gender is what Carroll (1984) terms 'closet feminists': female politicians who refuse to identify with the women's movement. An example of a position closer to the positive side of the continuum can be found in what Dovi (2002, 2007) labels 'preferable descriptive representatives' that have 'strong mutual relations with the dispossessed groups of historically disadvantaged groups' (Dovi 2002: 729). An in-between position on the substantive representation–nonrepresentation continuum in terms of sex and gender could be discerned by the extent to which expertise and knowledge was investigated in the representation of women, whereby a 'lower' degree of substantive representation implies a low level of expertise and knowledge, for instance in the case of voting for women (Tamerius 1995). Degrees of substantive representation could also be defined by looking at the range of the women's interests represented: a 'higher' degree of substantive representation of women is reached when a more diverse group of women is represented (Trimble 1993, 1997, 2000; Celis 2006).

Empirical research on gendering representation

Empirical research investigating the gendered dimensions of representation deals with the formal and descriptive participation of women and/or their substantive representation. As mentioned before, the necessity order and causal relationship between these aspects is above all an empirical question. It has been a key question in empirical research regarding political representation of women since the 1970s and still is today, be it that its theoretical underpinnings evolved and its focus was broadened to include institutions.

Empirical research regarding gendered aspects of formal and descriptive representation focuses on describing the evolution towards full enfranchisement, on mapping the numerical force women and men constitute in politics (e.g. Karam 1998), and on explaining the status quo. As Lovenduski's work has demonstrated, recruitment, selection, and election of candidates cause descriptive under representation of women in politics, parliaments, and governments worldwide (*see* Chapter Eight by Kenny in this volume; Leyenaar 1997).

Descriptive representation is not only about the presence and the number of women, but also about whether the representatives *would* act the way women would act themselves. This concern is dealt with in empirical research that investigates the attitudes of female representatives regarding the representation of women's interests and their views on general matters. The most frequently analysed attitudes in this respect are: the recognition of the existence of women's interests (e.g. Skjeie 1998); sensitivity to a responsibility to devote attention to them (e.g. Whip 1991); to lend priority to them (e.g. Thomas and Welch 2001); and the degree of congruence between the points of view of women MPs on the one hand and the female citizens (e.g. Mateo-Díaz 2005) and women's movement (e.g. Reingold 2000) on the other. According to a number of recent studies, women MPs as a group have a greater potential to represent women (e.g. Whip 1991); these conclusions, however, were not always applicable to all women MPs (e.g. Mateo-Díaz 2005) or for every attitudinal dimension (e.g. Reingold 2000). It is clear that these attitudes are situated in a grey zone between descriptive and substantive representation since they are an important prerequisite for 'acting for' women, a category that I nevertheless reserve for 'acts' as distinguished from 'thoughts'.

Empirical research about the gendered aspect of substantive representation has traditionally evolved around the question: 'Do women represent women'?

This link between descriptive and substantive representation of women has been empirically tested since the 1970s. Empirical research on gendered substantive representation mainly focuses on parliaments and on legislative activity: initiating, accompanying and voting of legislation in favour of women (e.g. Reingold 2000; Swers 2002a; Wolbrecht 2002), and participation in parliamentary debates in favour of women (e.g. Cramer Walsh 2002; Trimble 2000). Some studies confirm the existence of a link between the fact that the representative is a woman and voting for women (e.g. Swers 2002a, 2002b, 2002c), speaking in favour of women (e.g. Cramer Walsh 2002) and working on legislation in favour of women (e.g. O'Regan 2000; Carroll 2001). Other studies discard the existence of such a connection (e.g. Tremblay 1998). These studies also contend that a multitude of political, parliamentary, social and individual situations hamper the wish to represent women in practice, or interfere with its contents. Party affiliation seems to be the most influential factor (e.g. Purdy 1991; Reingold 2000).

Whether or not a 'critical mass' of women MPs influence women's substantive representation has been a main question in empirical research on the necessity and causal relationship between descriptive and substantive representation of women (*See* Chapter Seven; Childs and Krook 2006; Mackay 2004). The expectation that women are likely to 'make a difference' once they constitute a 'critical mass' (Kanter 1977, Dahlerup 1988) is a key feature in this research (Childs and Krook 2005; Lovenduski and Norris 2003). Although the theses of Drude Dahlerup were often misinterpreted and although there exists but little proof for the critical mass effect on substantive representation (Grey 2002; Trimble 1997), it is a powerful argument for claiming more female representatives (Childs and Krook 2005).

The descriptive 'presence of women' can be conceived in an individual way, as most scholars do, but also in structural terms. In the field of substantive representation, the recent 'institutionalist turn' implies investigating the role played by women's policy agencies and the women's movement (*see* Chapter Six Mazur and McBride in this volume; 2008). Here also, the main question is whether or not and in what way the presence of these institutions (descriptive level) foster the substantive representation of women.

The research regarding descriptive and substantive representation has long been predominantly Anglo-American and mainly focused on the U.S. and Western Europe. However, questions regarding the participation of women in the formal and descriptive dimensions of representation and as to whether descriptive representation (in the form of individuals or institutions) enhances substantive representation, is relevant and possible in each political system in which descriptive representation occurs. They are taken into account in recent research on democratisation processes in Russia, East Central Europe, Latin America and South Africa (Waylen 2007; Nechemias 1994; Matland and Montgomery 2005) and on the enlargement of the EU to include east central European nations (Galligan *et al.* 2007). Also Latin America is obvious research territory, given the widespread use of gender quotas and the installation of women's policy agencies (Htun and Jones 2002; Heath *et al.* 2005; Franceschet 2005; Stoffel 2008; Zetterberg 2008).

In the major part of the research relating to the active parliamentary representation of women by female MPs as well as the role women's policy agencies play in the substantive representation of women, a thematic selection of women's interests was made in advance, and subsequently used to measure activity in favour of women. The large or limited thematic selection carried out by various empirical researches generally takes two forms. First, the thematic selection often contains subjects concerning the traditional roles of women and/or subjects with a clear feminist accent. A second thematic operationalisation that one finds in many researches consists of selecting a number of current themes of the women's movement. To illustrate this, I concentrate on the operationalisation of women's issues in research regarding the parliamentary representation of women. Nevertheless, the discussion and conclusion also apply, for instance, to state feminism research by RNGS, also partially featuring a thematic approach to substantive representation (e.g. abortion, prostitution, job training, and political representation) (Mazur and McBride Chapter Six in this book).

Traditional and feminist women's interests – In their research about the impact of female representatives on the representation of women, Dodson and Carroll included women's rights bills that on the one hand, relate directly to women or that have a feminist undertone and laws concerning women's traditional arenas of interest, and on the other hand, that relate to the role of women as 'dispensers of care' inside the family as well as in society, and to themes such as health care and education (Dodson and Carroll 1995). In more recent research, one also often finds an operationalisation of women's interests in a similar 'double' way (e.g. Reingold 2000; Cramer Walsh 2002; O'Regan 2000; Carroll 2001; Meyer 2003; Taylor-Robinson and Heath 2003). Christine Wolbrecht, for instance, investigated women's rights' legislation concerning job possibilities, salary equality, women's health, abortion rights and education, to assess whether female representatives in the *House of Representatives* from 1953 to 1992 were responsible for the growth and the diversification of women's rights (Wolbrecht 2002). Wolbrecht concluded that women MPs proposed more of these laws and were most active in proposing new subjects and new policy solutions.

The thematic demarcation of women's interests in empirical research raises some problems. First, although the content of women's interests has not been without discussion since the 1980s, the selection of women's interests is rarely accounted for. In addition, a reflection on the possible consequences of the inclusion and exclusion of issues on the research results is mostly absent. Second, when including 'traditional' women's interests, they are sometimes interpreted so widely that the link with women's interests is almost lost. It is hardly sustainable to consider every theme related to children and family (Cramer Walsh 2002; Carroll 2001) as a women's interest. These themes can, of course, given the traditional role of women, contain a gender dimension, but that does not *per se* apply to every theme regarding children or family.

The main problem with the illustrated thematic delimitation of what one considers in the research as women's interest is that it tends to 'freeze' or essentialise women and their interests and to deny diversity among women. It also hinders the research question to travel to different political contexts and time periods. Furthermore, a thematic demarcation does not keep pace with the previously described evolution on the theoretical level that actually distances itself from an essentialist female identity. Therefore, it does not seem to be an interesting trail for future empirical research that wants to connect with the more recent theory about female representatives and the representation of women.

Interests of the women's movement – A second thematic operationalisation consists in selecting a number of current themes of the women's movement. In some cases, researchers select one or more current feminist themes; in other cases, they start from an overview of programme or attention points of a specific women's network or organisation. As opposed to thematic operationalisation as described above, researchers avoid the subjective manipulation of the selection – and thus also in a certain way the definition – of women's interests (e.g. Dolan 1997; Swers 2002a, 2002b, 2002c). In this case, the selection is left to an external actor: the women's movement or a women's network. Burrell, for instance, based her research on the themes of the chart of the National Women's Political Caucus: equal representation in the *National Commission for Neighborhoods,* tax reduction for childcare facilities, flexible hours for federal civil servants, family planning, federal abortion subsidies, rise of minimum salaries, and gay rights (Burrell 1994). Based on the voting behaviour of these subjects, Burrell showed that in the period from 1987 to 1999 women supported these laws more than men.

The generalisation of the programme of the women's movement, even though it avoids a subjective selection by the researcher and even though it leads to a very large palette of involved women's interests is, however, facing three limits. Firstly, as a method of operationalising women's interests and as substantive representation of women, it supposes the existence of a women's movement that is able to formulate claims. This might not be the case in non democratic states, and thus this operationalisation might hinder travelling to other political contexts. A second objection is that the total population of women is not backing the demands of the women's movement (Sawer 2000). In other words, the representation of feminist interests cannot be identified without problems with the representation of women's interests. Thirdly, the feminist programme taken into consideration is mostly reduced to its leftist–progressive variety (an exception being Swers 2002a, 2002b, 2002c; regarding the variety in the women's movements *see* Mazur and McBride in this volume). The diversity of points of view and visions of the feminist movement is mostly neither recognised nor translated into the research. Karen Offen distinguishes two threads in (European) feminism, in particular a relational and an individual current (Offen 2000: 21–22). The relational feminist current strives to a gendered but equal organisation of social relations between sexes and stresses complementarities, equality as 'equal value', and the partnership between men and women as the foundation for society. The individualist feminist current, on the other hand, gives the individual and the equality between individuals a central place. The strong focus on the latter in the empirical research tradition causes the researched themes to be only a partial reflection of the demands of the women's movement and therefore an even worse reflection of the interests of all female citizens. And again, the latter and the first point of critique make clear that this form of operationalisation might not be suited for travelling to other cultural and temporal contexts.

An open and formal operationalisation of women's interests – The empirical research tradition does not travel well. Furthermore, there exists a discrepancy with the recent theories formed about 'women representing women' that give a lot of space to diversity and evolution within women's interests, and wish to avoid the essentialisation of women. Taking into account the diverse and changing character of women's interests and its theoretical *a priori* 'undefinability' is what empirical research will best achieve if it does not determine the content of women's interests in advance. The concrete outline of women's interests therefore also has to be a subject for study. In other words, the research on the relationship between descriptive and substantive representation is only a second research step following the study of the content of substantive representation of women as such. Next to the advantage of a better connection with the theory, this operationalisation could also be a master key enabling the research on the substantive representation of women to travel across cultural and temporal contexts and become apt for cross cultural and historical comparisons.

Theoretically, this can be done in two ways. The first way would be to trace exhaustively what women themselves consider as their interests and to check afterwards what the relationship is between the representation of these interests and the sex of the representatives. This option immediately creates many new problems; among others, its size, the methodology to be used to map women's interests, and – again – the changing character of women's interests. A second way to operationalise the research that enables one to take the theoretically *a priori* undefinable character of women's interests into account consists in using a formal definition of substantive representation of women that does not make claims regarding the content. A formal delimitation of 'what has to be represented' dismisses the researcher of the task to carry out an 'essentialisating' selection. Such an operationalisation or research step can be found in research by Reingold (1992); Trimble (1993, 1997, 2000); Childs (2001, 2004); Bratton (2002); Wängnerud (2000); and Celis (2006).

Reingold used a very large operationalisation of women's interests in her research, notably that which politicians themselves pointed out as being women's interests (Reingold 1992). Trimble based her research on the Hansard Index, a written copy of the debates in the Canadian parliament, accessible through keywords (Trimble 1993, 1997, 2000). Each time an MP referred to women, their lives or their political needs, this was encoded under the keyword 'women'. She could thus also draw conclusions concerning the activities of men and women MPs regarding gendering the apparently gender-neutral legislation. This seems very relevant, given the current theories that indeed point out the possibility that women can have, concerning any subject whatsoever, a potentially different experience and thus a specific interest or perspective. Furthermore, the approach made comparisons between men and women MPs possible, which is also indispensable to make statements concerning the specific contribution of women MPs to the substantive representation of women.

Not delimitating women's interests in advance and, on the contrary, leaving it to the representatives, one also finds research that describes the perception of the contribution of female representatives to the representation of women. Sarah Childs (2001, 2004) did in-depth interviews with 34 of the 65 'new intake' women of the Labour MPs in the first three months after the 1997 election. Half of the interviewed Labour women stated that their presence allowed the expression of women's interests concerning themes such as violence on women, childcare, education, equal chances and employment.

Lena Wängnerud (2000) and Kathleen Bratton (2002) also apply a formal definition of (the representation of) women's interests. However, they have a different view on the operationalisation used by Trimble, Reingold and Childs because they fix the object of the representation of women's interests. Bratton defines women's interest legislation as 'bills that may decrease gender discrimination or alleviate the effects of such discrimination and those that are intended to improve the socioeconomic status of women' (Bratton 2002: 123). According to Wängnerud's definition, women's interests have to contain three elements: 1) the recognition of women as a social category; 2) the recognition of a power unbalance between men and women; and 3) the wish to implement a policy that increases the autonomy of female citizens. Although discrimination and autonomy are broad concepts, they connect with a rather equality oriented, individualistic vision of 'what is in the interest of women'. A similar approach thus again contains the danger that the diversity among women will not be taken into account.

In my own research on the representation of women in the Belgian Parliament, I used a formal operationalisation that strongly follows the one used by Trimble and Reingold (Celis 2006). I operationalised 'representing women('s interests)' as follows: *to denounce a situation that is disadvantageous for women, to formulate a proposal to improve the situation of women or to claim a right for women with the same goal.* I mapped such interventions between 1900 and 1979, during the most central political debates in the Belgian Parliament: the budget debates in the Lower House. Through this formal definition, I obtained a view on what the MPs themselves considered as women's interests, which contained a wide variety of women's interests as well as perspectives on what was in the interest of women. Subsequently, I compared the parliamentary represented women's interests with the series of demands of various women's movements. This operationalisation allowed me, firstly, to obtain an indication of whether and to what extent the parliamentary representation of women connected to what 'women themselves' wished and, secondly, to detect a specific contribution of women MPs – notably, they broadened the dominant vision of what was 'in the interest of women' and realised a higher congruence between the parliamentary substantive representation of women and the way 'women themselves' perceived their interests. Although the formal approach also has a number of disadvantages – mainly capturing only explicit claims that were considered appropriate in the specific context – its main advantage entails in not giving an essentialist content to the substantive representation of women and respects the theoretical assumption that women's interests are *a priori* undefined, context related, and subject to evolution.

Conclusion

Gendering representation is a feminist research praxis that describes, analyses, and explains the gendered dimensions of political representation. Its central question regards the inclusion and exclusion of women and gender in various dimensions of representation; i.e. formal participation, descriptive and substantive representation. The aim of gendering representation lies also in enhancing the inclusiveness of the concept of political presentation and its praxis in terms of sex and gender. A key contribution to the latter ambition is the theory which links descriptive and substantive representation: descriptive representativeness possibly furthers substantive representativeness. Whether that is actually the case is an empirical question. Empirical research is challenged though by theoretical evolutions in respect of the diverse character of women's interests and gendered perspectives. A formal operationalisation of substantive representation meets these demands. Besides the advantage of synchronising empirical research and recent theories about representation, applying a formal operationalisation will make the research question more apt for travelling to other cultural and temporal arenas, and application in a wide range of political and cultural contexts. Longitudinal and international comparative research can, in turn, broaden our knowledge about the content, actors, sites and contexts of substantive representation across time and space (Celis *et al.* 2008).

References

Alcoff, L. (1991) 'The problem of speaking for others', *Cultural Critique* Winter 1991–92: 5–32.

Beetham, D. (1992) 'Liberal democracy and the limits of democratisation', *Political Studies* 40 (5): 40–53.

Birch, A. (1993) 'Political Representation', in Birch, A. (ed.) *The Concepts and Theories of Modern Democracy*, London-New York: Routledge, pp. 69–79.

— (1971) *Representation: Key concepts in political science*, London: Pall Mall Press.

Bratton, K. (2002) 'The effect of legislative diversity on agenda setting: evidence from six state legislatures', *American Politics Research* 30 (2): 115–142.

— (2005) 'Critical mass theory revisited: the behavior and success of token women in state legislatures', *Politics and Gender* 1: 97–125.

Braud, P. (1985) 'Théories de la représentation. Introduction', in F. d'Arcy (ed.) *La représentation*, Paris: Economica, pp. 33–37.

Brennan, B. and Hamlin, A. (1999) 'On political representation', *British Journal of Political Science*, 29: 109–127.

Bryson, V. (2003) *Feminist Political Theory: An introduction*, Houndmills-NewYork: Palgrave Macmillan.

Burrell, B. C. (1994) *A Woman's Place is in the House: Campaigning for Congress in the feminist era*, Ann Arbor: University of Michigan Press.

Carroll, S. (1984) 'Women candidates and support for feminist concerns: the closet feminist syndrome', *Western Political Quarterly* 37 (2): 307–323.

— (2001) 'Representing Women: Women state legislators as agents of policy-related change', in S. Carroll (ed.) *The Impact of Women in Public Office*, Bloomington, Indianapolis: Indiana University Press, pp. 3–21.

Caul, M. (1999) 'Women's representation in parliament: the role of political parties', Party Politics 5 (1): 79–98.

Celis, K. (2006) 'Substantive representation of women: the representation of women's interests and the impact of descriptive representation in the Belgian parliament (1900–1979)', *Journal of Women, Politics and Policy* 28 (2).

Celis, K., Childs, S., Kantola, J. and Krook, M. L. (2008) 'Rethinking women's substantive representation', *Representation*, 44 (2): 99–110.

Childs, S. (2001) 'In their own words: New Labour women and the substantive representation of women', *British Journal of Politics and International Relations* 3 (2): 173–190.

— (2004) *New Labour's Women MPs,* London-New York: Routledge.

Childs, S. and Krook, M. L. (2006) 'Gender and politics: the state of the art', *Politics* 26 (1): 18–28.

— (2005) 'The Substantive Representation of Women: Rethinking the critical mass debate', Paper presented at the 2005 APSA Annual Meeting, Washington.

Chodorow, N. (1978) *The Reproduction of Mothering: Psycho-analysis and the sociology of gender*, Berkeley: University of California Press.

Cramer Walsh, K. (2002) 'Female Legislators and the Women's Rights Agenda', in C. S. Rosenthal (ed.) *Women Transforming Congress*, Oklahoma: University of Oklahoma Press: Norman, pp. 370–396.

Dahlerup, D. (1988) 'From a small to a large minority: women in Scandinavian politics', *Scandinavian Political Studies* 11 (4): 275–298.

— (ed.) (2006) *Women, Quotas and Politics*, London-New York: Routledge.

Diamond, I. and Hartsock, N. (1981) 'Beyond interests in politics: a comment on Virginia Sapiro's "When are interests interesting? The problem of political representation of women"', *The American Political Science Review* 75 (3): 717–721.

Dodson, D. and Carroll, S. (1995) *Voices, Views, Votes: The impact of women in the 103rd Congress. The impact of women in public office*, New Jersey: Rutgers.

Dolan, J. (1997) 'Support for women's interests in the 103th congress: the distinct impact of congressional women', *Women and Politics* 18 (4): 81–94.

Dovi, S. (2002) 'Preferable descriptive representatives: will just any woman, black, or Latino do?', *The American Political Science Review* 96 (4): 729–743.

— (2007) *The Good Representative*, Oxford: Blackwell Publishing.

Eulau, H. (1967) 'Changing Views of Representation', in I. de Sola Pool (ed.) *Contemporary Political Science: Toward empirical theory*, New York: McGraw-Hill Book Company, pp. 53–85.

Eulau, H. *et al.* (1978) 'The role of the representative: some empirical observations on the theory of Edmund Burke', in H. Eulau and J. Wahlke (eds) *The Politics of Representation: Continuities in theory and research*, Beverly Hills: Sage, pp. 111–126.

Eulau, H. and Wahlke, J. (eds) *The Politics of Representation: Continuities in theory and research*, Beverly Hills: Sage.

Farrell, D. (2006) 'Inclusiveness of Electoral Systems', paper presented at the seminar Inclusive Politics, Radboud University, Nijmegen, May 29 2006.

Fenno, R. E. (1978) *Home Style: House members in their districts*, Boston: Little Brown.

Franceschet, S. (2005) *Women and Politics in Chile*, London: Lynne Rienner.

Franceschet, S. and Krook, M. L. (2005) 'State Feminism and Gender Quotas in the "North" and "South": Comparative lessons from Western Europe and Latin America', Paper presented at the International Studies Association Annual Meetings, March 22–25, 2005, San Diego, CA.

Fraser, N. (1989) 'Struggle over needs: outline of a socialist-feminist critical theory of late capitalist political culture', in N. Fraser (ed.) *Unruly Practices: Power, discourse and gender in contemporary social theory*, Cambridge: Cambridge University Press.

Galligan, Y., Clavero, S. and Calloni, M. (2007) *Gender Politics and Democracy in Post-Communist Europe*, Leverkusen: Barbara Budrich Publishers.

Gilligan, C. (1982) *In a Different Voice: Psychological theory and women's development*, Cambridge, Mass.: Harvard University Press.

Goertz, G. and Mazur, A. (2008) (eds) *Politics, Gender, and Concepts: Theory and methodology*, Cambridge: Cambridge University Press.

Grey, S. (2002) 'Does size matter? Critical mass and New Zealand's women MP's', *Parliamentary Affairs* 55 (1): 19–29.

Griffiths, A. Phillips (1960) 'How can one person represent another?', Aristotelian Society supplementary volume 34: 187–208.

Guinier, L. (1994) *The Tyranny of the Majority: Fundamental fairness in representative democracy*, New York: Free Press.

Heath, R. M., Schwindt-Bayer, L. A. and Taylor-Robinson, M. M. (2005) 'Women on the sidelines: women's representation on committees in Latin American legislatures', *American Journal of Political Science* 49 (2): 420–436.

Hirst, P. (1990) *Representative Democracy and its Limits*, Cambridge: Polity Press.

Htun, M. and Jones, M. (2002) 'Engendering the right to participate in decision-making: electoral quotas and women's leadership in Latin America', in N. Craske and M. Molyneux (eds) *Gender, the Politics of Rights and Democracy in Latin America*, Basingstoke: Palgrave, pp. 432–456.

Jónasdóttir, A. G. (1988) 'On the Concept of Interests: Women's interests and the limitation of interest theory', in K. B. Jones and A. G. Jónasdóttir (eds) *The Political Interests of Gender*, London: Sage Publications.

Judge, D. (1999) *Representation: Theory and practice in Britain*, London-New York: Routledge.

Kanter, R. M. (1977) 'Some effects of proportions on group life: skewed sex ratios and responses to token women', *American Journal of Sociology* 82(5): 965–991.

Karam, A. (ed.) (1998) *Women in Parliament: Beyond numbers*, Stockholm: IDEA.

Krook, M. (2004) 'Gender quotas as a global phenomenon: actors and strategies in quota adoption', *European Political Science* 3 (3): 59–65.

Leyenaar, M. (1997) *How to Create a Gender Balance in Political Decision Making: A guide to implementing policies for increasing the participation of women in political decision making*, Luxembourg: European Commission.

Leyenaar, M., Niemoller, K., Laver, M. and Galligan, Y. (1999) *Electoral Systems in Europe: A gender impact assessment*, Brussels: European Commission.

Lijphart, A. (1984) *Democracies: Patterns of majoritarian and consensus governments in twenty one countries*, New Haven: Yale University Press.

Lister, R. (1997) *Citizenship: Feminist perspectives*, London: Macmillan.

Lovenduski, J. (2005) *Feminizing Politics*, Cambridge: Polity Press.

Lovenduski J. and Norris, P. (2003) 'Westminster women: the politics of presence', *Political Studies* 51(1): 84–102.

Lovenduski, J. *et al.* (eds) (2005) *State Feminism and Political Representation*, Cambridge: Cambridge University Press.

McBride Stetson, D. (ed.) (2001) *Abortion Politics, Women's Movements, and the Democratic State: A comparative study of state feminism*, Oxford: Oxford University Press.

Mackay, F. (2004) 'Gender and political representation in the UK: the state of the discipline', *Journal of Politics and International Relations* 6(1): 99–120.

McLean, I. (1991) 'Forms of representation and systems of voting', in D. Held (ed.) *Political Theory Today*, Cambridge: Polity Press, pp. 172–196.

— (1996) *The Concise Oxford Dictionary of Politics*, Oxford: Oxford University Press.

Mansbridge, J. (1998) 'The Many Faces of Representation', *Working Papers*, Harvard: John F. Kennedy School of Government, Harvard University.

— (1999) 'Should blacks represent blacks and women represent women? A contingent "yes"', *The Journal of Politics* 61 (3): 628–657.

— (2003) 'Rethinking representation', *American Political Science Review* 97 (4).

Marin, L. (2001) *On Representation*, Stanford: Stanford University Press.

Mateo-Díaz, M. M. (2005) *Representing Women? Female legislators in West European parliaments*, Oxford: Oxford University Press.

Matland, R. (1995) 'How the election system structure has helped women close the representation gap', in L. L. Karvonen and P. Selle (eds) *Women in Nordic Politics: Closing the gap*, Brookfield: Dartmouth.

Matland, R. and Montgomery, K. (2005) *Women's Access to Political Power in Post-Communist Europe*, Oxford: Oxford University Press.

Mazur, A. (ed.) (2001) *State Feminism, Women's Movements, and Job Training: Making democracies work in the global economy*, London-New York: Routledge.

Mazur, A. and McBride Stetson, D. (eds) (1995) *Comparative State Feminism*, Thousand Oaks: Sage.

— (2008) 'State Feminism' in G. Goertz and A. Mazur (eds) *Politics, Gender, and Concepts: Theory and methodology*, Cambridge: Cambridge University Press, pp. 244–69.

Meier, P. (2002) *Guaranteeing Representation: Democratic logic or deficit? A qualitative comparative analysis of techniques enhancing representativeness and the argumentation on their behalf in a plural society*, Unpublished doctoral thesis, Vrije Universiteit Brussel.

Meyer, B. (2003) 'Much ado about nothing? Political representation policies and the influence of women parliamentarians in Germany', *Review of Policy Research* 20 (3): 401–421.

Nechemias, C. (1994) 'Democratization and women's access to legislative seats: the Soviet case, 1989–1991', *Women and Politics* 14 (3): 1–18.

Norton, P. (1993) *Does Parliament Matter?* London: Harvester Wheatsheaf.

Offen, K. (2000) *European Feminisms 1700–1950: A political history*, Stanford, California: Stanford University Press.

O'Regan, V. (2000) *Gender Matters: Female policymakers' influence in industrialized nations*, Westport-London: Praeger.

Outshoorn, J. (ed.) (2004) *The Politics of Prostitution: Women's movements, democratic states and the globalisation of sex commerce*, Cambridge: Cambridge University Press.

Paolino, P. (1995) 'Group-salient issues and group representation: support for women candidates in the 1992 Senate elections', *American Journal of Political Science* 39 (May): 294–313.

Parks, R. (1982) 'Interests and the politics of choice', *Political Theory* 10 (4): 547–565.

Pateman, C. (1988) *The Sexual Contract*, Cambridge: Polity.

Paxton, P. (2008) 'Gendering democracy' in G. Goertz and A. Mazur (eds) *Politics, Gender, and Concepts: Theory and methodology*, Cambridge: Cambridge University Press.

Pennock, R. (1968) 'Political representation: an overview', in R. Pennock and J. W. Chapman (eds) *Representation: Nomos X*, New York: Atherton Press, pp. 3–27.

Phillips, A. (1995) *The Politics of Presence*, Oxford: Clarendon Press.

— (1998) 'Democracy and representation: Or, why should it matter who our representatives are?' in A. Phillips (ed.) *Feminism and Politics*, New York: Oxford University Press, pp. 224–240.

Pitkin, H. F. (1969) *Representation*, New York: Atherton Press.

— (1972) *The Concept of Representation*, Berkeley and Los Angeles: University of California Press.

Purdy, E. R. (1991) *The Representation of Women and Women's Issues: Differences in voting patterns of male and female members of the House of Representatives*, Ann Arbor: University of Michigan Press.

Reingold, B. (1992) 'Concepts of representation among female and male state legislators', *Legislative Studies Quarterly* 17 (4): 509–537.

— (2000) *Representing Women: Sex, gender and legislative behavior in Arizona and California*, Chapel Hill, NC: University of North Carolina Press.

Rich, A. (1976) *Of Women Born: Motherhood as experience and institution*, New York: Bantam Books.

Sapiro, V. (1981) 'When are interests interesting? The problem of political representation of women', *The American Political Science Review* 75 (3): 701–716.

Sartori, G. (1987) *The Theory of Democracy Revisited*, Chatham, NJ: Chatham House Publishers.

Saward, M. (2006) 'The representative claim', *Contemporary Political Theory* 5 (3): 297–318.

Sawer, M. (2000) 'Parliamentary representation of women: from discourses of justice to strategies of accountability', *International Political Science Review* 21 (4): 361–380.

Skjeie, H. (1998) 'Credo on difference – women in parliament in Norway' in A. Karam (ed.) *Women in Parliament: Beyond numbers*, Stockholm: International Institute for Democracy and Electoral Assistance, pp. 183–189.

Sobolewski, M. 1968. 'Electors and representatives: a contribution to the theory of representation', in R. Pennock and J. Chapman (eds) *Representation: Nomos X. Yearbook of the American Society for Political and Legal Philosophy*, New York: Atherton Press, pp. 95–107.

Squires, J. (1996) 'Quotas for women: fair representation?', *Parliamentary Affairs* 49 (1): 71–88.

— (1999) *Gender in Political Theory*, Malden, USA: Blackwell Publishers Inc.

Squires, J. and Wickham-Jones, M. (2004) 'New Labour, gender mainstreaming, and the women and Equality Unit', *British Journal of Politics and International Relations* 6 (1): 81–98.

Stoffel, S. (2008) 'Does state feminism contribute to state retrenchment in the field of women's rights? The case of Chile since the return of democracy', *Representation*, 44 (2) 141–154.

Stokes, W. (2005) *Women in Contemporary Politics*, Cambridge: Polity.

Sunstein, C. (1991) 'Preferences and politics', *Philosophy and Public Affairs* 20(11).

Swers, M. L. (2002a) *The Difference Women Make: The policy impact of women in congress*, Chicago – London: University of Chicago Press.

— (2002b) 'Research on women in legislatures: what have we learned, where are we going', *Women and Politics* 23 (1/2): 167–185.

— (2002c) 'Transforming the agenda: analyzing gender differences in women's issue bill sponsorship', in C. Simon Rosenthal (ed.) *Women Transforming Congress, Congressional Studies Series 4*, Oklahoma: University of Oklahoma Press: Norman, pp. 260–283.

Tamerius, K. (1995) 'Sex, Gender, and Leadership in the Representation of Women', in G. Duerst-Lahti and R. M. Kelly (eds) *Gender Power and Leadership, and Governance*, Ann Arbor: University of Michigan Press, pp. 93–112.

Taylor-Robinson, M. M. and Heath, R. M. (2003) 'Do women legislators have different policy priorities than their male colleagues? A critical case test', *Women & Politics* 24 (4): 77–100.

Thomas, S. and Welch, S. (2001) 'The Impact of Women in State Legislatures: Numerical and organizational strength', in S. Carroll (ed.) *The Impact of Women in Public Office*,. Bloomington, Ind.: Indiana University Press, pp. 166–181.

Thomassen, J. 1994. 'Empirical research into political representation: failing democracy or failing models?' in M. Kent Jennings and T. E. Mann (eds) *Elections at Home and Abroad: Essays in honor of Warren E. Miller*, Anne Arbor: University of Michigan Press, pp. 237–264.

Tremblay, M. (1998) 'Do female MPs substantively represent women? A study of legislative behavior in Canada's 35th parliament', *Canadian Journal of Political Science* 31 (3): 435–465.

Trimble, L. (1993) 'A few good women: female legislators in Alberta, 1972–1991', in C. Cavanaugh and R. Warne (eds) *Standing on New Ground: Women in Alberta*, Edmonton: University of Alberta Press, pp. 87–118.

— (1997) 'Feminist policies in the Alberta legislature, 1972–1994', in J. Arscott and L. Trimble (eds) *In the Presence of Women: Representation and Canadian governments,* Toronto: Harcourt Brace, pp. 128–154.

— (2000) 'Who's represented? Gender and diversity in the Alberta legislature', in M. Tremblay and C. Andrew (eds) *Women and Political Representation in Canada, Women's Studies Series 2*, Ottawa: University of Ottawa Press, pp. 257–289.

Wängnerud, L. (2000) 'Testing the politics of presence: women's representation in the Swedish riksdag', *Scandinavian Political Studies* 23 (1): 67–91.

Waylen, G. (2007) *Engendering Transitions: Women's mobilization, institutions and gender outcomes*, Oxford: Oxford University Press.

Weldon, L. S. (2002) 'Beyond bodies: institutional sources of representation for women in democratic policymaking', *The Journal of Politics* 64 (4): 1153–1174.

Whip, R. (1991) 'Representing women: Australian female parliamentarians on the horns of a dilemma', *Women and Politics* 11 (3): 1–22.

Williams, M. (1998) *Voice, Trust, and Memory: The failings of liberal representation,* Princeton, New Jersey: Princeton University Press.

Wolbrecht, C. (2002) 'Female Legislators and the Women's Rights Agenda', in C. Simon Rosenthal (ed.) *Women Transforming Congress*, Oklahoma: University of Oklahoma Press: Norman, pp. 170–194

Young, I. M. (1997) 'Deferring group representation', in I. Shapiro and W. Kymlicka (eds) *Ethnicity and Group Rights*, Nomos 39, Yearbook of the American Society for Political and Legal Philosophy, New York: New York University Press, pp. 349–376.

Zetterberg, P. (2008) 'The Downside of Gender Quotas? Institutional Constraints on Women in Mexican State Legislatures', *Parliamentary Affairs*, 61 (3): 442–460.

Chapter Four

Feminising Political Parties

Sarah Childs and Rainbow Murray

Introduction

It is 20 years since Pippa Norris and Joni Lovenduski published their edited book *Gender and Party Politics* (Lovenduski and Norris 1993). Despite its age, it remains a 'go-to' book for comparative analysis of gender and parties. Crucially it revealed that traditional analyses, which largely fail even today to address issues of sex and gender in anything but a simplistic fashion, can only ever be limited. Across its eleven chapters *Gender and Party Politics* documents the demands of women, and the response of parties for both the inclusion of women and the consideration of women's interests in politics (Lovenduski 1993). Contending that liberal democracies offer women the 'means to claim equality of representation by utilising the political opportunities offered by the party systems' (Lovenduski 1993: 3), each chapter shows how different party systems responded in 'varying degrees' to the demands made by women. It captures how 'gender has affected party policies and how the imperatives of party politics influences the patterns of women's representation' (Lovenduski 1993: 3). The book highlights women's demands for greater inclusion within parties, via member recruitment drives, and as key post holders, via internal party quotas, as well as demands for a re-gendering of party policy, not least in respect of gender equality policies (Lovenduski 1993: 3).

In 1993 Lovenduski noted that while gender had become an explicit issue for many political parties, the 'extent' and 'manner' of party accommodation varied. Reforms were most successful in Scandinavia; leftist parties were more accommodating than rightist ones, although parties across the political spectrum were beginning to seek greater numbers of women representatives; and for the most part 'women kept to the rules of the game', seeking changes within rather than across parties. Moreover, while there was some policy convergence to attract the female voter, particular party policies for women largely reflected parties' own ideologies (Lovenduski 1993: 6). The importance of political context is emphasised too (Kittilson 2005; Lovenduski and Norris 1993): party competition, party modernisation, system level constitutional change and altered party-state relations (Norris and Lovenduski 1995), interacting with the 'vital' activity of women themselves (Lovenduski 1993: 7, 14), affected outcomes. As Lovenduski makes clear, women's demands for feminisation – in respect of both the inclusion of women and the inclusion of women's interests – are likely to be contested, and hence women making these demands must 'pay attention to the ideology and organisation of their party' (Norris and Lovenduski 1995: 13).

Such questions continue to frame contemporary analysis of gender and party politics. Indeed, Lovenduski's tripartite framework for categorising parties' equality strategies – equality rhetoric, promotion and guarantees – is pre-figured in *Gender and Party Politics* (Lovenduski 1993: 7–8). And in her chapter with Pippa Norris on the UK, data detailing the numbers and roles of women within the main UK political parties, whilst remaining critical, has simply not been reproduced since, despite strenuous effort (Childs and Webb 2012).[1] Norris and Lovenduski further note the different organisational trajectories of women in the UK's two main parties and the different demands they had been making in the 1970s-1990s; and the different electoral imperatives of Labour and the Conservatives – not least in terms of timing – with Labour in need of the 'woman voter' in the 1980s (Norris and Lovenduski 1995: 57–9). These inter-party differences are still ongoing.

There has been, regretfully, no second edition or comparative text published on political parties since. In part, this reflects the subsequent and extensive attention that gender and politics scholarship has given to political recruitment/women's descriptive representation (Childs and Lovenduski 2013; Norris 1997) and to studies of women's substantive representation (*see* Chapters Three, Eight and Nine of this volume). But it also reflects the exacting nature of providing in-depth accounts of political parties in a comparative setting (not least in terms of researchers' time, access, and breadth of knowledge), as well as the still limited number of scholars of gender and politics who simply cannot study – in the absence of more bodies to undertake empirical research – all the questions the sub-discipline has sought to address in the intervening twenty years.[2] In the UK, extensive analysis of the Labour Party (Childs 2008; Perrigo 1995; Perrigo 1996; Russell 2000) has more recently been supplemented by book length gendered analysis of both other main parties, the Liberal Democrats (Evans 2011) and the Conservative Party (Childs and Webb 2012). In such studies, parties' organisation, ideology, personnel and activities are mapped and analysed from gendered perspectives, and in so doing they question much of the accepted wisdom of parties scholarship. To these case studies, large N global analysis can be added (Kittilson 2013; Kittilson 2005). These are rightly premised upon the claim that only with comparison are scholars able to show 'how party rules and processes' mediate women's participation and representation in political parties (Kittilson 2013).

Early research sought to document the presence and role of women within parties and to identify the determinants and dynamics of their inclusion, albeit mostly in respect of how this related to women's parliamentary recruitment and representation. Given women's continued unequal presence within political parties and within legislatures this research focus remains as important as ever.

---

1. The data was not centrally held.
2. That said, there have been country case and party case study analyses. English language literature includes Murray 2010; Williarty 2010; Young 2000 on Canada and the US.

Yet today as a community of scholars we often lack comprehensive and systematic empirical data about women's participation both as ordinary party members, as party activists and as actors in the higher echelons of political parties; we know much more about women in parliaments. Further, studies should explore the kinds of women who participate politically, identifying patterns of engagement that likely reflect differences of class, race, age, sexuality, disability, and motherhood, amongst others. Similarly, the role of women qua women within parties invites greater investigation: we know that historically parties often have had women's organisations that mobilised women for the party – ladies' auxiliaries (Young 2000). But some studies have suggested (during the 1980/90s in the UK Labour party and the 2000s in the Conservative party, for example) that these became organisations more explicitly for women (Childs 2008), whilst recently, as discussed further below, such organisations seeking group representation may well have fallen out of fashion (Cross and Young 2004; Williarty 2010; Kittilson 2013).

Studies investigating the formulation and content of party policy, both explicitly gendered and apparently non-gendered, are necessary too in order to better inform understandings of women's substantive representation and its links with women's presence in parties and not just with women elected representatives (Childs and Webb 2012; Kittilson 2013; Phillips 1995). Links between women in political parties and women's group/movement activism also warrant further research. Our interest here may be about linkages of participation between these political actors. Are the same women active in both, for example? Is there movement between the two sites of political participation, over time and space? Do women come together to work collectively across parties and civil society associations? In other words, what are the nature of representational relationships between women active in civil society groups and women active in parties?

Finally, recent research by feminist institutionalists, informed by developments in both gender theory and institutionalism, investigates political parties as explicitly gendered institutions (Lovenduski 1998; Lovenduski 2005). The recognition that sex and gender are different concepts points to a research agenda which investigates 'what else is happening when the numbers of women are changing within particular institutions' (Lovenduski 1998: 338). The focus here is on how masculinities and femininities interact in organisations, institutions and processes (Lovenduski 1998: 339). Although mostly applied to parliaments thus far, political parties should be regarded as gendered institutions and so examined: constituted both by formal rules and regulations but also via informal norms and practices which 'have differential effects for men and women' (Lovenduski 1998). Feminist institutional research exposes 'the incompleteness of accounts that leave out the relational dynamics of gender' (Lovenduski 1998: 352). Such accounts are crucially able to capture change over time (Kittilson 2013). Indeed, feminist and/or women's intervention inside and outside of parties constitutes one means of engendering a feminisation of our political parties and political institutions (Lovenduski 2005; Childs and Webb 2012).

A recently developed research agenda for gender and politics research on political parties identifies five foci (Childs 2008; Childs and Webb 2012): (1) the level of women's participation in party structures, including, but importantly not limited to, the parliamentary party, with such enquiries exploring whether parties employ specific mechanisms in both party structures and the parliamentary party to guarantee women's descriptive representation; (2) whether women's participation is substantive across the party's various structures and activities or symbolic and limited to certain forms or places; (3) the nature of the role, remit and ideology of any women's organisations and, in particular, whether these are integrated formally into the wider party structure and policy making bodies, and to whom they are accountable, both upwards and downwards; (4) whether a party regards women as a corporate entity capable of being represented (both descriptively and substantively) and if so, whether the party is susceptible to feminist arguments for this. This might include whether the party makes gender based and/ or feminist claims rather than non-gendered, neutral or anti-feminist claims; and finally (5) the extent to which party policies are gendered and/ or feminist.

In addition to these particular concerns, contemporary gender and parties scholarship also addresses issues of party laws and party regulation. When political parties are considered public utilities, they can and should be (more) fully regulated and, given that existing party regulations are underpinned by normative assumptions about the nature of democracy, a case can be made to regulate political parties informed by feminist principles (Childs 2013). Party funding – monetary and non-monetary or in-kind – has been a hitherto under-tapped resource to both incentivise and penalise parties that fail to sufficiently feminise (Childs 2013; Norris and Krook 2011). This research also considers new party types, with the emergence of the 'corporatist catch all-party' which mobilises rather than dis-empowers its membership whilst acknowledging group interests via internal organisation and policy-making processes (Williarty 2010). Debate over the nature and future of party women's organisations includes competing accounts of whether the era of the women's organisation as Quasi Women's Policy Agency is over (Kittilson 2013; Cross and Young 2005). Finally, the role of party ideology in shaping parties' organisational response to feminisation is the focus of an expanding research agenda (Celis and Childs 2012; Kittilson 2006; Opello 2006).

In the remainder of this chapter we elaborate on two contemporary concerns: intra-party democracy and feminised party change. Both speak to scholarship about parties. The former offers a feminist reading and a definitional challenge to an increasingly important concept and empirical area of research which has hitherto failed to consider gendered perspectives and the issue of women's participation and representation in political parties. The latter illuminates the process of change within parties as they adapt to internal and external pressures to feminise.

A feminist reading of intra-party democracy[3]

The extant intra-party democracy (IPD), and gender and politics literatures have rarely engaged explicitly with each other's concerns. Where it does consider gender, the IPD literature mostly focuses on parliamentary candidate selection and internal party representation. Here, demands for sex quotas are usually found to conflict with greater internal party democracy.[4] The imposition by a party of an obligation to select a female candidate is seen as an infraction of the autonomy of members to select their preferred candidate. When gender and party scholars address issues of internal party organisation and structure, relations and power, they have rarely drawn on the conceptual frameworks of IPD. However, subjecting traditional IPD research to a gendered reading and undertaking an IPD-sensitive reading of the gender and politics literature reveals that both share overlapping concerns. The IPD literature, moreover, has much to offer women political party members and activists as well as scholars of gender and politics, even if the latter may very well turn out to be critical of some of its concepts. In particular, a feminist account of IPD challenges extant considerations about what constitutes IPD, the effect of processes of IPD to date and, in turn, the health of our political parties and wider democracy. In so doing, gender and politics scholarship has the potential to make the test/markers of IPD more fulsome and demanding.

That political parties in many western democracies have sought to enhance the democratic basis of their internal structures and processes is widely agreed upon in the parties literature, even as the consequences of these changes are more contested (Cross and Katz 2013; Katz and Mair 2010; Young and Cross 2002). IPD is broadly agreed to involve:

1. The direct election of party leaders (Scarrow 1999b; Young and Cross 2002);
2. Individual referenda (ratifying and/or consultative) on policy (Katz and Mair 2010; Scarrow 1999a; Young and Cross 2002), with the attendant downgrading of party conferences and committees from substantive policy-making bodies to leadership showcases (Heffernan 2007; Pettit 2006, 2011);
3. Vertical (unmediated) political communication, from the centre/leadership downwards, for example via email and electronic polling (Katz and Mair 2010), rather than horizontal communication between areas, regions, and constituencies (Seyd, in Cross and Young 2002; Heffernan 2007);

---

3. This section draws on Childs in Cross and Katz (2013).

4. In respect of candidate selection – the acid test of IPD for Gallagher and Marsh (cited in Bille 2001: 364; *see also* Mikulska and Scarrow 2011) – sex is explicitly identified as a candidate characteristic that parties seek, but it also plays out in arguments that suggest women's descriptive representation conflicts with greater IPD, and in the apparent tension between internal democracy at the party level (the greater inclusiveness of members in the processes of candidate selection) and representativeness at the system level (*see* Chapter by Childs in Cross and Katz 2013 for a more extensive discussion of this; *see also* Rahat and Katz 2008).

4. A refusal to differentiate members by group identity and a rejection of hierarchical membership (Young and Cross 2002);
5. Decentralised and democratised candidate selection, with a greater role to individual party members (Bille 2001; Blyth and Katz 2005; Rahat and Hazan 2001) through broad-based ballots (Katz 2001), albeit in ways that pre-empt local associations (Young and Cross 2002) and local party activists (Katz 2001; Katz and Mair 2002). Candidate selection may very well take the form of primary elections (Baldez 2007; Mair 2010).

Whether these characteristics result in an actual redistribution of power within parties remains a moot point and, of course, is an empirical question. Yet for gender and politics scholars, additional criteria of IPD must surely come into play. We might ask: can a political party be judged internally democratic if women continue to be under-represented at all levels of the party, including at the top, even when recent gains in women's participation are noted? Can they be so judged if women are included but not integrated, that is, lacking substantive power? In answering the question, 'in respect of whom must women have power?' a single shift in women's power relative to their male peers, who historically would have held more power, could only ever be limited. Rather, women need to gain power relative to the historically and overwhelmingly male leadership for it really to 'count' as a plus on the IPD balance sheet. A fully engendered conception of IPD has, then, to imply more than the mainstream conception of IPD: not only must women gain power but they must also gain power relative to where power lies, too. In other words, there is little value for IPD in women gaining greater presence in political parties, if this occurs precisely at the point where power becomes more narrowly concentrated at the top of political parties.

Then there is the question of what kinds of power women members must have relative to the party leadership – as individuals or as a group? This relates to questions of whether claims for women's representation (descriptive and substantive) are about women as a group, or women as individuals. Take Lisa Young and Bill Cross' (2002) representational party. Here women are included in separate women's organisations and there are formalised means for group representation. Contrast this with the more internally democratic plebiscitary party. Here women are included as individual members, rather than as representatives of women, and women lack mechanisms or structures that represent women as a group, descriptively and/or substantively. This latter party form accordingly looks rather inhospitable to 'feminist' and/ or 'gender conscious' women's group mobilisation and organisation within parties. If just over one third of 142 parties in 24 post-industrial countries had some form of women's organisation (Kittilson 2011a), gender and party scholars arguably need to know more than the fact of their existence (Lovenduski and Norris 1993; Young 2000). We might also want to question as unnecessary and unhelpful the construction of women's group representation in opposition to individual representation (Kittilson 2011a: 6 makes the same point).

In reflecting on the implications for a feminist definition of IPD, three tentative claims can be made. First, the greater presence of women amongst parties' parliamentary representation does represent a shift of power from men to women. A political party has become more democratic when women number more highly amongst elected representatives. This is because a hitherto excluded group (women) is now more included in its parliamentary representation. Women's greater parliamentary presence also has the potential to effect the distribution of power amongst the party leadership more broadly, as women leaders gain power that traditionally was the preserve of men – again a marker of greater IPD. Furthermore, if these women seek to act for women in their party – as a collective entity – and particularly if they do so in conjunction with a party's women's organisations, their presence may enhance IPD further through acting as a pressure group on the party leadership, likely affecting policy concerns, and potentially policy-making processes too.

Women party members – at all levels – seeking to act for women additionally influence wider discussions of policy making and IPD. IPD debates suggest that parties have moved away from bottom-up policy making towards top-down leadership efforts – something that would be considered the antithesis of IPD. Yet in drawing this conclusion, the sex of the now over-powerful leadership now matters more than ever. As women make their way up the party's ranks, culminating in senior party, legislative and executive presence, some of the leadership's power to make policy will be transferred to women leaders (feminist criticisms of gendered institutions notwithstanding (Lovenduski 2005)). While this might be regarded as a negative according to mainstream IPD, as power remains within the party leadership, it might be considered more positive for advocates of a re-gendered party politics. This is because whilst individual party members, both male and female, may only be able to accept policy over which they have little say, the policies themselves may be more feminised than hitherto, as a result of the role that senior party and elected women play in policy development. Indeed, where women within a party have mobilised for the substantive representation of women, they can be considered to have acted as a pressure group (Sainsbury, in Lovenduski and Norris 1993: 289) or 'faction' (Boucek 2009). As such, party women might more generally be able to improve party performance, policy making, and IPD as they signal to party leaders 'which policies are acceptable'. Whether this meets the requirement of the double shift – from men to women, and between the party leadership and party members – remains a critical empirical question. And of course such a conclusion also begs the question of to whom, and in what ways, senior party women and women-elected representatives are accountable.

Secondly, although the use of sex quotas in delivering women's greater parliamentary representation and internally within parties is often perceived as an anti-democratic effort according to IPD literature, this conclusion can and should be contested. Not only is this just one reading of the adoption of sex quotas, it also fails to recognise the intersection of party and system level democracy. A strong case can be made that women's parliamentary representation may require a limit on (traditionally understood) IPD for the good of system level democracy. Without so acting, parties will be anti-democratic in the sense of excluding or descriptively under-representing half the population in their parliamentary representation.

Thirdly, and most relevant to this chapter, traditional IPD reforms, other than those relating to candidate selection, look likely to enhance the power of women in political parties, either directly or indirectly. Susan Scarrow (1999b: 353) maintains that neither the adoption of parliamentary sex quotas, nor explicit calls to recruit more women by political parties, has significantly altered the composition of the wider party memberships. This apparent continued state of affairs surely invites new research, theoretical and conceptual. In everyday terms, why is it that women's participation in electoral politics remains limited? Is this for the same reasons as noted in the early gender and politics research? Is women's continued under-representation problematic and if so why, and are these the same reasons as before? And what might be done about this? At the same time, we should acknowledge that across Western Europe the presence of women in parties' more senior positions has improved over time. On party national executive committees women's presence has risen from 15 per cent in 1975 to approximately 30 per cent (Kittilson 2006: 42), in part a reflection of the adoption by parties of internal sex quotas. Again, such improvements invite reconsideration, not least to identify processes of successful reform. But what of this particular development for notions of IPD? Even without a large increase in women party members overall, IPD reforms which shift power to other hitherto less activist members will likely involve an important shift to women – previously less or un-active women party members – and therefore have the potential to empower women relative to men. Moreover, this contention that women party members might have acquired more power might hold even if party members' influence overall is reduced relative to the party leadership. This is because even the limited participation of larger numbers of women members might be an improvement on the previously existing state of affairs, that is, the dominance of ordinary women members by more activist male members. Nor does it stop these newly empowered women members from seeking greater IPD as they gain more power, even if it is only relative. And they may well have relations, either formal or informal, with women in the party's leadership.

The necessity and benefit of subjecting traditional conceptions of IPD to a feminist reading should be apparent to gender and politics scholars. IPD is an increasingly central area of enquiry amongst party scholars (Cross and Katz 2013), critically reflecting on observed changes (symbolic and substantive) within parties on the ground. However, without including gender within its terms of reference, this scholarship will misrepresent what is going on as parties reform their structures, internal processes and, in turn, experience redistribution of power. From a feminist perspective, parties that exclude women, or only include them minimally or symbolically, suffer from a significant democratic deficiency; those that have larger numbers of women populating their party can be considered more democratic; those in which power has been redistributed to women and men, and relative to the party leadership can be considered the most internally democratic. And yet it is not quite so simple as this. What counts as IPD according to most party scholars sits in tension, if not opposition, with many of the kinds of measures advocated by many gender and politics scholars as necessary for women's equal descriptive and substantive representation– most notably sex quotas for parliamentary representation, but also sex quotas for internal party positions, and mechanisms for group representation. To suggest that these are counter to IPD fails to acknowledge the feminist claim that democracy is premised upon political equality that must also include between women and men. In sum, a feminist reading of IPD illuminates not only gaps in IPD's conceptual framework but also challenges some of those concepts for being blind to unequal gender relations.

Parties and party change: Lessons from the french case[5]

The French gender parity law offers a particularly interesting opportunity to study the effects of compulsory feminisation on political parties, as Lovenduski highlights in her more recent *Feminizing Politics* (Lovenduski 2005). Parity legislation, passed in 2000 in France, compels all political parties to field an equal number of male and female candidates to most elections. In elections using proportional representation (including local, European and some constituencies of the Senatorial elections), party lists are rejected automatically unless they comply with the parity legislation. For legislative elections, conducted under single member plurality, parties lose part of their state funding if they fail to field sufficient women candidates.[6] As a result, parties of all sizes and ideologies have found themselves obliged to transform a number of their practices, including their candidate recruitment practices, their internal organisation and their electoral strategies (Murray 2010). These processes have proven significantly more challenging for some parties than for others.

One of the most important issues raised by the parity legislation was the apparent difficulty in reforming candidate selection. Aside from the need for more female candidates was the pressing issue of how to adapt existing candidate selection procedures to the requirement for feminisation. Within party lists, placement on lists became an issue of ever-greater importance, with men disproportionately monopolising the positions at the top of the list. This was both to ensure their own re-election and to secure favourable positions for themselves within local executives, as the candidate at the top of the winning list will normally become the mayor or the president of the county or regional council. For Senatorial elections, this process was rather more prescriptive, as the legislation required strict zipping – in other words, women needed to be placed in strict alternation with men on

5. This section draws on Murray (2010).
6. Parties receive funding in two portions; the first relates to how many votes they receive, and the second to how many seats they win. Parties who do not respect parity lose a fraction of the first portion of funding, making the legislation more restrictive for smaller parties who do not win seats (and who therefore do not affect the composition of parliament). From 2000–2012, parties lost 1 per cent of their funding for every percentage point that their proportion of women candidates fell below 50 per cent. For example, a party fielding 40 per cent women lost 10 per cent of their funding. In 2012, this was increased to 1.5 per cent for each percentage point.

party lists. For those parties with two or more male incumbents, the necessity of placing a woman second on the party list equated to the forcing out of office of the lower placed male incumbent. To avoid this scenario, a number of male incumbents defected to other parties in order to head their lists, thus compromising the prospects of the women candidates on the lists of both the male incumbent's original and their subsequently adopted parties. Some candidates also forged their own 'dissident' lists. Where the defecting male candidates were successful in securing their own re-election, they sometimes rejoined the original party fold after the election, but this practice inevitably had an impact on the partisan balance of power after the election, and made it much harder for political parties to control their candidate lists and to manage their parliamentary party groupings after the elections.

For parliamentary elections, the risk of dissident candidates has also been a threat, with some candidates standing against the official party nominee in a defiant refusal to cede their seat to a woman candidate. The most notable example of this was in 2012, when former Socialist presidential candidate Ségolène Royal was parachuted into a safe parliamentary seat, only to lose to the male Socialist who had originally intended to defend the seat, refused to step aside and fought as a 'dissident socialist'.

It is not only the incumbents themselves who can create headaches for party officials attempting to enforce gender parity. It is common practice in France for members of parliament (deputies) also to hold local office concurrently, resulting in powerful politicians with strong local political fiefdoms. These deputies often command a loyal support base within the local party, and their supporters may be highly resistant to any attempts by the party to introduce an alternative candidate. The local deputy may also be well placed to groom his or her (usually his) successor, with a colleague from local politics often primed to replace the deputy upon retirement. The consequence is that male incumbents are very difficult to remove, and retiring male incumbents often have a male successor lined up. This leads to a collective action problem, whereby each constituency selects a male candidate, hoping that another constituency somewhere else will select a woman in order to fulfil the requirement of gender parity across the full set of constituencies. Resolving this problem requires national co-ordination, and sometimes imposition,[7] in order to ensure that a sufficient number of constituencies choose a female candidate (Murray 2010). Different parties have tried to resolve this conundrum in different ways. The Communists have sought to negotiate with party members while recognising the primacy of party members, whereas the Socialists have reserved certain seats for women in order to oblige members in some constituencies to select a woman candidate (these tend to be seats without a male incumbent seeking re-election). The Greens have been pro-active in parachuting women into seats in order to meet the requirement of gender parity. The UMP has been much more cautious and more reluctant to interfere with local selection procedures.

7. *See* for UK comparison: Childs 2004.

The French case is therefore a classic example of the tension created by gender quotas between internal democracy within parties, and a centrally-driven demand to feminise (Lovenduski 1993: 13–14, and as observed in the previous section of this chapter). In the era of electoral-professional parties (Panebianco 1988), the role of party members is much diminished, and influence over candidate selection is one of the few perks of party membership that remain. However, if party members resist feminisation by prioritising well-networked and influential men within the constituency, it can be very difficult for parties to meet the requirement of gender parity. The ability of the national party to impose women candidates is therefore a necessary (although not sufficient[8]) condition of achieving gender parity, yet this comes at the expense of autonomy and influence for local members (Hazan and Rahat 2010).

The need to ensure a gender balance of candidates becomes even more complex for political parties when placed alongside the other balancing acts required in the candidate selection process. In particular, French parties are faced with two other, often competing, demands. First, many parties form electoral alliances with other parties prior to the elections, whereby they agree not to stand against an electoral partner in certain constituencies. The sacrifice of these constituencies to another party is traded off against the enhanced prospect of victory in those seats where they do field candidates, due to the lack of competition from their electoral partner. However, deciding which constituencies to sacrifice, and what to do with the candidates who would otherwise have defended those constituencies, can lead to delicate decisions. This combines with the second complication, which is the need to appease different factions within each party. Many parties in France are riven with internal divisions, exacerbated by the presidentialisation of politics, resulting in different groups within each party who are loyal to different potential leaders within the party. The French party system contains many small parties whose origins lie in an offshoot from a bigger party; the opportunity for each party's leader to gain profile in the presidential elections makes the option of exit from a major party more appealing than in some other party systems. To prevent such divisions from destroying the party, each leader must therefore try to balance out the different factions, ensuring that none becomes too powerful and that none becomes so disillusioned as to have grounds to split away and form a separate party. The Socialists have been accused of using gender parity as an excuse to reconfigure the balance of power between factions in unfair ways, by targeting male candidates within a particular faction for replacement with female candidates from a different faction. Preserving internal party unity, which is essential for the survival of the leadership and also for the electoral credibility of the party, requires that no one faction be singled out in this way for unfair treatment. As a result, maintaining a fair balance between competing groupings within the party may take precedence over ensuring an equitable gender balance.

The ability of parties to adapt to gender quotas is also influenced by the parties' ideology (Lovenduski 2005: 63). Work by Miki Caul Kittilson (1999, 2001, 2006)

8. Party leaders must have not only the power but also the will to impose women candidates.

has highlighted the greater willingness of parties of the left to feminise. Attitudes towards gender quotas and feminisation are intertwined with several related aspects of a party's ideology. In order to support gender quotas, parties need to consider gender imbalances to be problematic, which is not always the case, such as in the New Centre (formerly UDF) party. If the current sex balance is considered acceptable or even desirable, any attempt to change it may be resisted, with women candidates considered less suitable than the men that they would replace (*see* Chapter Ten of this volume for discussions of quota discourses (Dahlerup 2006)). Parties also need to consider gender quotas to be an acceptable remedy to the problem of women's under-representation. Parties who shun other forms of top-down intervention and who favour a laissez-faire approach to governance will be unlikely to welcome the use of compulsion to enforce gender equality. Such parties, to the extent that they are willing to support feminisation, might prefer to do so through 'equality promotion' but not 'equality guarantees' measures such as offering more training to women candidates. Such measures may help to address supply-side problems but, as Lovenduski (2005: 91) highlights, they are ineffective in addressing the more serious problems of demand. Finally, even a party that supports the goals and the means of quotas will still need sufficient commitment to override competing priorities within the party such as those highlighted above.

Nonetheless, parties who oppose gender parity in principle might yet be persuaded to support it in practice if other imperatives motivate them to do so (Murray 2010). Parties eager to modernise their public image may use quotas as an instrumental (some might suggest cynical) measure designed to appeal to women voters and to project a sympathetic and inclusive image for the party. Alternatively, the penalties applied for failing to implement a quota may prove sufficiently persuasive, especially in the case of parties without alternative resources who therefore cannot afford to lose financial subsidies or to risk having their party lists rejected. Parties also operate under the classic electoral imperative of needing to provide a united front on policy issues. For parties of both the left and the right in France, the question of gender quotas has presented some internal division. On the left, widespread support for quotas has been tempered by philosophical objections to quotas that are perceived as demeaning and divisive. On the right, widespread opposition to quotas has met with resistance from Right-wing feminists and from party leaders anxious not to cede political ground on an electorally popular issue (Murray, Krook and Opello 2012; Opello 2006). In both cases, the firm stance taken by the party leadership in favour of parity has forced the rest of the party to toe the official line – highlighting the role played by leadership political will. Over time, as gender parity has become a more established aspect of French political culture, ideological resistance has gradually given way to resigned acceptance (Murray 2012a; Sénac-Slawinski 2008).

The concept of parity has even begun to influence other aspects of politics in unprecedented ways. For example, Nicolas Sarkozy's Right-wing government introduced gender quotas for the boards of large companies in 2011, reflecting a dramatic ideological shift in a party better known for being pro-business, anti-interventionist and non-feminist. The combined influences of political expediency, international and cultural pressures and the need to appeal to diverse electorates, together have taken primacy over certain parties' more traditional ideological instincts. In a similar way, the far-right Front National party has been among the best performers in terms of implementing the parity law, despite being one of the few parties openly to oppose the law. The Front National initially complied in order to evade the penalties, but has also benefited electorally from a feminisation of its candidates and its leadership (in the form of Marine le Pen, who succeeded her father as party leader in 2011). Women candidates have helped to soften the extremist image of the party, and have reduced the dramatic gender gap in the party's electorate, which is no longer two-thirds male (Mayer 2013; Murray 2012b). The FN is one of several French parties to have been headed by a woman, even though men retain the vast majority of positions of power in the major parties.

Women's contribution to French parties goes far beyond their role as candidates, voters and even leaders. Women's sections within parties have been influential in feminising the policy agenda and pushing for internal party reform. Several French parties now have internal gender quotas for their party's decision-making organs, as a result of pressure from party women. In *Gender and Party Politics*, Amy Mazur and Andrew Appleton outline some of the foundational work undertaken by women within French parties, and this work has been complemented by Opello (2006). Women's sections have long been more vocal and effective on the left, with Opello highlighting the relatively weak mobilisation by women within parties of the right. However, the French mainstream right has long featured a number of outspoken feminist women, several of whom have served as women's ministers, chairs of the parliamentary committee on gender equality or directors of the Parity Observatory, an official body tied to the office of the Prime Minister. Since the introduction of the parity law, cross-party collaboration on gender issues has been accompanied by a stark partisan divide in terms of women's representation, with Left-wing parties getting ever closer to gender parity while the proportion of women deputies in the Right-wing UMP party continues to stagnate at barely 13per cent. Following a very disappointing outcome for women in the 2012 election, including several instances where strong women candidates were forced to give way to prominent men who were parachuted into their constituencies as the official candidate,[9] a new women's section formed within the UMP. Spearheaded by Rachida Dati, the former Justice Minister, 'A Droite Toutes'[10] now comprises more than 100 elected women. Their stated goals include 'to make French political parties evolve, even if it means constraining them further, in order that they be

9. Rachida Dati herself was ousted by the former prime minister, François Fillon, so that he could move from a rural to a Paris constituency. His goal was to establish himself in Paris in order to seek to become the next mayor of Paris, a powerful and prominent position from which to launch his future presidential campaign. Dati's colleague, Brigitte Kuster, was also forced to stand down against a male former minister, despite being the mayor (and thus, in the traditions of French politics, the natural candidate) of the Paris constituency in question.

10. This is a play on words, with A Droite meaning 'on the right' and 'toutes' being the feminine form for all (ie all women).

models of good practice, that they scrupulously apply the existing laws, and that they become more representative of our society' (www.adroitetoutes.fr; authors' translation). They also demand greater parity and gender equality throughout French politics and society.

The repeated incidences of powerful men within parties forcing women to step aside in order to pursue their own ambitions are an indication that power and status within the party in France still take primacy over equality. This has been reflected in other acts of resistance against feminisation by men keen to preserve their own power and political fiefdoms. Although the overall trend has been one towards greater equality, there have been several instances of backlash, protectionism and subversion of the spirit of parity. Gender quotas have been incorporated tactically into wider power games within French parties and French politics. Many of the key positions within local politics that help to reinforce local power bases and act as launch-pads for national politics, such as local mayors and presidents of county and regional councils, have remained male-dominated, despite the feminisation of local and regional councils. Several electoral reforms enacted since the original introduction of parity have actually served to reinforce male control of these domains, thus subverting the spirit of parity. For example, the minimum district magnitude required for senatorial elections to be conducted under proportional representation was increased from 3 to 4, thus leading to a higher proportion of seats being elected under a majoritarian system that was exempt from the parity legislation. In Senate seats governed by PR, and hence by parity, the proportion of women has increased significantly, whereas in majoritarian districts there has been very little progress. Similarly, the Sarkozy government pushed through reforms to local politics even though the reforms were widely denounced, including by women within the UMP, as being detrimental to parity. (The reforms have since been scrapped under François Hollande's government.) These reforms were a subtle way, concealed under the guise of broader electoral reform, of ensuring that male elites within the party were able to maintain their power bases. These important local positions act as springboards into national politics, strengthen the local implantation of deputies, and offer a buffer from which to bounce back in the event of electoral defeat at the national level. The preservation of these roles for men within a context of widespread feminisation is indicative of the biggest flaw with gender parity: while women have gained access to less powerful positions in large numbers, men have used their positions of power within parties and elected politics to ensure that the most important offices have largely resisted parity. The pragmatism that inspired parties to sign up for gender parity despite ideological resistance to quotas is reflected in the ongoing covert attempts to resist and subvert parity. While ideological resistance has declined and women's mobilisation has increased, the classic problem remains: the self-interest of those in power will motivate them to preserve their dominant status wherever possible.

Conclusion

That political parties were, and should remain, central to gender and politics scholarship reflects the central role political parties play in democratic politics: as sites of participation and representation. As the party politics literature tells us, parties are the link between the represented and those who govern them. Accordingly, women's participation in and representation via parties, as well as gendered critique of parties, should be a key concern for democrats and must be a key concern for feminists (Childs 2008; Kittilson 2012; Murray 2010). Women's participation in political parties is, as Miki Caul Kittilson (2012) so nicely phrases it, best understood as a process of 'democratic inclusion, albeit contested, slow, [and] uneven'. Norris and Lovenduski's *Gender and Party Politics* marked a significant feminist intervention in comparative parties and gender and politics scholarship; its influence has been extensive on the latter, although less so, unfortunately, on the former. Some twenty years ago, *Gender and Party Politics* spotlighted the failure of non-gendered accounts to recognise political institutions, including parties, as gendered. They also failed to recognise the party changes associated with the demands that women were making as they entered political parties, and that parties' responses to demands for women's inclusion garnered different responses across parties and countries. In so doing, apparently neat typologies and accounts of party organisation, type and change missed the complexity of gendered party politics. In the intervening years there has been much gendered analysis undertaken, although there is still much to do: writing in her 2005 book, *Feminizing Politics*, Lovenduski is explicit:

> Finally I aim once again to draw attention of political scientists to the importance of gender to the study of politics. I hope this intervention will not only inform and extend discussion of the methods that best achieve equality of women's representation and provides resources for its advocates, but also add to the pressure to incorporate gender into the mainstream of political science (Lovenduski 2005: 10 emphasis added).

Significant advances in the field of gendered party politics have been made in the twenty years since the seminal contribution of Norris and Lovenduski (1993). However, it is clear that this is an area that remains under-researched and that requires greater integration into the wider study of political parties. If parties are the main agents of democracy, and women comprise more than 50 per cent of the global population, it stands to reason that no study of democracy can be complete without acknowledging the gendered nature of parties as institutions. The trend in recent years towards the gradual feminisation of politics – accelerated in places through the use of sex quotas – has presented unique challenges to the internal organisation of parties. Understanding how parties have adapted to (and sometimes resisted) these changes must be central to future research agendas on party organisation.[11]

11. Although earlier work by Lovenduski and Norris in this area garnered more attention from

References

Appleton, A. and Mazur, A. (1993) 'Transformation or Modernization: The rhetoric and reality of gender and party politics in France', in J. Lovenduski and P. Norris (eds) *Gender and Party Politics*, London: Sage, pp. 86–112.

Baldez, L. (2007) 'Political parties: old concepts and new challenges', *Latin American Politics and Society* 49 (3): 69–96.

Bille, L. (2001) 'Democratizing a democratic procedure', *Party Politics* 7 (3): 363–80.

Blyth, M. and Katz, R. (2005) 'From catch all politics to cartelization', *West European Politics* 28 (1): 34–61.

Boucek, F. (2009) 'Rethinking factionalism', *Party Politics*, 15 (4): 455–85.

Celis, K. and Childs, S. (2012) 'The substantive representation of women: what to do with Conservative claims?' Political Studies, 60 (1).

Childs, S. (2004) *New Labour's Women MPs: Women representing women*, London: Routledge.

— (2008) *Women and British Party Politics: Descriptive, substantive and symbolic representation*, London: Routledge.

— (forthcoming) 'In the absence of electoral sex quotas: regulating political parties for women's representation', *Representation.*

Childs, S. and Lovenduski, J. (2013) 'Political Representation', in G. Waylen, K. Celis, J. Kantola and L. Weldon (eds) *The Oxford Handbook of Gender and Politics*, Oxford: Oxford University Press, pp. 489–514.

Childs, S. and Webb, P. (2012) *Sex, Gender and the Conservative Party*, London: Palgrave Macmillan.

Cross, W. and Katz, R. (2013) *The Challenges of Intra-Party Democracy*, New York: Oxford University Press.

Cross, W. and Young, L. (2002) 'The rise of the plecbiscitary democracy in Canadian political parties', *Party Politics* 8 (6): 673–699.

— (2004) 'The contours of political party membership in Canada', *Party Politics* 10 (4): 823–43.

Dahlerup, D. (2006) 'What are the effects of electoral gender quotas?', Fukuoka, Japan: International Political Science Association.

Evans, E. (2011) *Gender and the Liberal Democrats: Representing Women?* Manchester: Manchester University Press.

Hazan, R. and Rahat, G. (2010) *Democracy Within Parties: Candidate selection methods and their political consequences*, Oxford: Oxford University Press.

Heffernan, R. (2007) 'Tony Blair as Labour party leader' in A. Seldon (ed.) *Blair's Britain*, Cambridge: Cambridge University Press, Ch. 8.

Katz, R. (2001) 'The problems of candidate selection and models of party democracy', *Party Politics* 7 (3): 277–96.

gender and politics scholars than from most parties scholars, the legacy of Lovenduski's research continues to grow and will be felt across the discipline for many more decades to come.

Katz, R. and Mair, P. (2002) 'The ascendancy of the party in public office', in R. Gunther, J. R. Montero and J. J. Linz (eds) *Political Parties: Old concepts and new challenges*, Oxford Oxford University Press, Ch. 5.

— (2010) 'The cartel party thesis: a restatement', *Perspectives on Politics* 7 (4): 753–66.

Kittilson, M. C. (1999) 'Women's representation in parliament: the role of political parties, *Party Politics* 5(1): 79–98

— (2005) 'In support of gender quotas', *Politics and Gender* 1 (4): 638–45.

— (2006) Challenging Parties, *Changing Parliaments*, Columbus: Ohio State University Press.

— (2013) 'Party politics' in *The Oxford Handbook of Gender and Politics*, G. Waylen, K. Celis, J. Kantola and L. Weldon (eds) Oxford: Oxford University Press, pp. 536–53.

Lovenduski, J. (1993) 'Introduction: The dynamics of gender and party', in in J. Lovenduski and P. Norris (eds) *Gender and Party Politics*, London: Sage, pp. 1–15.

— (1998) 'Gendering research in political science', *Annual Review of Political Science* 1: 333–56.

— (2005) *Feminizing Politics*, Cambridge: Polity Press.

Lovenduski, J. and Norris, P. (eds) (1993) *Gender and Party Politics*, London: Sage.

Mair, P. (2010) 'The Parliamentary Peloton', *London Review of Books* 32 (4): 31–33.

Mayer, N. (2013) 'From Jean-Marie to Marine Le Pen: electoral change on the far right', *Parliamentary Affairs* 66 (1): 160–78.

Murray, R. (2010) *Parties, Gender Quotas and Candidate Selection in France*, Basingstoke: Palgrave.

— (2012a) 'Parity in France: a dual-track solution to women's under representation', *West European Politics* 35 (2): 343–61.

— (2012b) 'Progress but still no présidente: women and the 2012 French presidential elections', *French Politics, Culture and Society* 30 (3):45–60.

Murray, R., Krook, M. and Opello, K. (2012) 'Why are gender quotas adopted? Party pragmatism and parity in France', *Political Research Quarterly* 65 (3): 529–43.

Norris, P. (ed.) (1997) Passages to Power, Cambridge: Cambridge University Press.

Norris, P. and Krook, M. L. (2011) 'Gender Equality in Elected Office' (OSCE: draft report).

Norris, P. and Lovenduski, J. (1995) *Political Recruitment*, Cambridge: Cambridge University Press.

Opello, K. (2006) *Gender Quotas, Parity Reform, and Political Parties in France*, Lanham, MD: Lexington Books.

Panebianco, A. (1988) *Political Parties: Organization and power*, Cambridge: Cambridge University Press.

Perrigo, S. (1995) 'Gender struggles in the British Labour Party from 1979–1995', *Party Politics* 1 (3): 407–17.

— (1996) 'Women and change in the Labour party 1979–1995', in J. Lovenduski and P. Norris (ed.) *Women in Politics*, Oxford: Oxford University Press, pp. 118–31.

Pettit, R. (2006) 'Rebellion by the seaside: how single member plurality has affected membership dissent at the Labour Party conference', Representation 42 (4): 289–301.

— (2011) 'Exploring variations in intra-party democracy: a comparative study of the British Labour Party and the Danish centre left', *British Journal of Politics and International Relations* 14 (4): 630–50.

Phillips, A. (1995) The Politics of Presence, Oxford: Oxford University Press.

Rahat, G. and Hazan, R. (2001) 'Candidate selection methods', Party Politics 7.

Rahat, G. and Katz, R. (2008) 'Democracy and Parties: On the Uneasy relationship between Participation, Competition and Representation', *Party Politics* 14 (6): 663–83).

Russell, M. (2000) 'Women's Representation in UK Politics', London: Constitution Unit.

Sainsbury, D. (1993) 'The Politics of Increased Women's Representation: The Swedish case', in J. Lovenduski and P. Norris (ed.) *Gender and Party Politics*, London: Sage, pp 263–90.

Scarrow. S. (1999a) 'Democracy within –and without – parties', *Party Politics* 5 (3): 275–82.

— (1999b) 'Parties and the Expansion of Direct Democracy', *Party Politics* 5 (3): 341–62.

Sénac-Slawinski, R. (2008) 'Justifying parity in France after the passage of the so-called parity laws and the electoral application of them', *French Politics* 6 (3): 234–56.

Williarty, S. (2010) *The CDU and the Politics of Gender in Germany: Bringing women to the party*, Cambridge: Cambridge University Press.

Young, L. (2000) *Feminists and Party Politics*, Ann Arbor: University of Michigan Press.

Young, L. and Cross, W. (2002) 'The rise of plebiscitary democracy in Canadian political parties', *Party Politics* 8 (6): 673–99.

Vignette – *Gender and Party Politics*: The 'Feminisation' of the Conservative Party

Theresa May MP

> Theresa May is a British Conservative Politician. She was first elected to the House of Commons in May 1997. She held a number of senior posts when the Conservative Party was in opposition, including Chairman [*sic*] of the party, Shadow Secretary of State for Transport, Shadow Leader of the House of Commons and Shadow Secretary of State for Work and Pensions. She has been Home Secretary since the coalition government was elected in 2010 and between May 2010 and September 2012 she was also Minister for Women and Equalities. Theresa May has been at the forefront of the campaign to modernise the Conservative Party and she has played a critical role in bringing gender equality onto the mainstream political agenda in Britain. As such she has had direct experience of attempts to make gender visible within a major political party and she is well situated to reflect on how gender affects party politics.

The year that I was first elected to the House of Commons, 1997, was a significant one for women in politics. The number of female MPs increased dramatically to a level that was at the time a historic high. This was predominately due to the massive increase in the number of female Labour MPs at the 1997 general election – out of the 120 women elected that year, just thirteen were Conservatives. This was partly a consequence of the heavy defeat suffered by the Conservative Party as a whole at that election. However, this fact could not distract from the serious under-representation of women on the Conservative benches both prior to and after 1997, and the need for us to address this problem.

Of course, it was quite clear that the Labour Party's success in electing more women to Parliament had been a result of their use of all-women shortlists, imposed by the party on its constituency selections. Although this tactic naturally succeeded in increasing the proportion of women selected, it struck many of us in the Conservative Party as not being a long-term solution as it failed to address the real reasons as to why women were not getting selected, and why women were not even seeking to get selected in the first place. So the challenge for the Conservative Party was therefore: how could we encourage more women to get involved in politics, and encourage more local constituency associations to select women as candidates, without resorting to the top-down imposition of all-women shortlists?

There were two key aspects that we identified: firstly, reforming our selection procedures in order to ensure a level playing field for women; and secondly, making sure that women had the mentoring and networking opportunities that seemed to be so easily available to men.

From 2001 onwards, including during the period that I was Party Chairman, we made a number of reforms to our selection procedures in order to open up the system to women and ethnic minorities. For example, we replaced the 'Parliamentary Selection Board' – which was said to have been based on Sandhurst's army officer training procedure – with a new assessment process better suited to the modern demands of transparency and fairness; and I introduced selection primaries in some seats. Along with Andrew Lansley, I called for the introduction of a priority list of candidates in order to increase the supply of good-quality candidates from all backgrounds. Following the 2005 election, this 'A list' was introduced with a clear requirement that 50 per cent should be women. As part of further changes later, we also ensured that the shortlists drawn up by local associations – from which the final candidate would be selected – were 50 per cent women. One of the more interesting additional reforms that we piloted shortly before the last election was the use of all-postal ballot primaries, where members of the public could select the Conservative candidate whether or not they were party members. This innovative mechanism was used in two constituencies and it is interesting to note that a woman was selected in both.

In addition to these procedural changes, I was clear that we needed to encourage more women to stand as candidates and to have opportunities to meet other women involved in politics. In 2005, I co-founded *women2win*, which has led the campaign within the party to encourage more women to come forward, including through hosting events across the country and providing support to women seeking to be selected as candidates.

As a result of these steps, we have made strong progress in increasing the number of Conservative women in Parliament. Today, we have more female MPs than we have ever had before, and Conservatives make up 35 per cent of women in the House of Commons compared to 10 per cent in 1997. Indeed, both the total number and proportion of women MPs has continued to rise since 1997.

This development has not been simply for show. Because women now have a stronger voice within the Conservative Party, it is Conservatives in government who have been leading the debate on issues such as shared parental leave, violence against women, and the vital role of women in tackling international poverty.

We have achieved this progress because individual constituency associations have decided to select women on merit, not because women have been forced upon them. However, there remains a long way to go, both for the Conservative Party and for British politics as a whole. Women today still make up less than 25 per cent of the House of Commons. So far from resting on the progress we have made, we must re-double our efforts in the years ahead in order to make our Parliament more representative of the British people.

The Rt Hon Theresa May MP

Chapter Five

Gender and Political Institutions

Fiona Mackay with Faith Armitage and Rosa Malley

> Feminists use institutionalist approaches to answer questions about power inequalities in public life. When feminists adopt institutionalist research strategies that include gender, they seek to illuminate and change the status of women.
>
> (Lovenduski 2011: vii)

Introduction

Institutions – the formal and informal 'rules of the game' – shape political life and political outcomes. Feminist political scientists, applying a gendered lens, expose the ways in which political institutions are also gendered, and the processes by which particular gendered patterns of power are replicated or challenged. A new approach – feminist institutionalism – has evolved around these twin insights and what they might mean for analysis and action about gendered inequalities in politics.[1]

The goal has been to explore the potential for, and limits of, a synthesis of neo-institutionalism (NI) and feminist political science (FPS) in order to develop new tools and analytical frameworks to help us to answer some of the big questions and real world puzzles about gendered power inequalities in public and political life. For example, in what ways are formal institutions (like parliaments, political parties, governments and constitutions) and informal institutions (such as norms and conventions) understood to be gendered? How do political institutions affect the daily lives of women and men? Why do outcomes from political institutions (including political representation and policy outcomes) have such profound gendered consequences for different groups of women and men? What are the processes and mechanisms that account for the considerable resilience of many

1. Feminist Institutionalism builds on the pioneering work of Joni Lovenduski and others. The Feminism and Institutionalism International Network (FIIN) was established in 2006. It is a collaborative project to develop a feminist institutionalism approach which synthesises insights from institutionalist theory and institutionally-focussed feminist political science. *See* www.femfiin.com.

political institutions to change, even in the face of, for example, new ideas about gender relations? And, finally, for feminists concerned as they are with the normative project of transformational change: what is the potential for institutional innovation, reform and change in pursuit of gender equality and gender justice; and what are the gendered barriers and limits to such change?

In this chapter, we chart ways of understanding political institutions as gendered, particularly the development of a feminist institutionalism. We provide a brief overview of current developments and new directions. In particular we discuss two areas that are emerging as central concerns of enquiry to researchers: institutional change (and stability); and the identification of informal institutions, their interaction with formal institutions, and their effects. In the latter part of the chapter, we provide two illustrative case studies.[2] First, Faith Armitage observes that studying the Speakership of the House of Commons offered an opportunity to examine an institution with a particular gendered history, and to consider how efforts both to 'modernise' and to 'feminise' parliament affected the Speakership and its attendant informal masculine norms and rituals. Rosa Malley's comparative study of cultures in the UK and Scottish parliaments reveals similarities and differences in the gendered rules and norms of the two institutions. Moreover, as an observer in both, she – as a young female researcher – experienced Westminster to be 'daunting' whereas she found Holyrood much more informal and more inclusive of women.

Political institutions, institutionalism and gender[3]

The potential 'for scholarly affinity' between institutionally-focused feminist political science and institutionalists was highlighted more than a decade ago by Joni Lovenduski (1998). But efforts at systematic engagement and synthesis are more recent.[4] As Lovenduski notes,

> Feminist political scientists want to discover and explain gender effects in political life, a project that inevitably leads them to focus on how political institutions are formed and sustained and how gender is embedded in them (Lovenduski 2011: viii).

Taking the lead from neo institutionalist analysis, institutions are theorised as formal and informal structures, rules, routines and norms that are embedded in the organisation of political life. They comprise the rules-in-form (the official rules) and the rules-in-use (how things are done around here) that exist above, below, between and within political organisations (Lowndes 2010). While institutions are seen to be powerful constraints on actors, their behaviour, and their preferences,

2. These were undertaken by early career researchers and mentees of Joni Lovenduski: Drs. Faith Armitage and Rosa Malley.
3. The main body of the chapter draws upon more substantial reviews in Kenny and Mackay 2009; Krook and Mackay 2011; Mackay 2011; Mackay, Kenny and Chappell 2010.
4. *See* references and review in Krook and Mackay 2011.

they are also viewed as products of human agency, constructed through processes of negotiation, conflict and contestation.

Institutions arise through accident, evolution and by conscious design. However, even if institutions are created for a specific function or to promote particular desired values, the outcomes are variable and uncertain. Institutionalist scholars, particularly historical institutionalists, stress the difficulties and unintended consequences of institutional design and the inability to control the embedded and contested process of institutionalisation as institutions evolve over the 'long haul' (*see* especially Goodin 1996). Once institutions are created, they are seen to be difficult to change. Indeed, as Mahoney and Thelen note: 'the idea of persistence of some kind is virtually built into the very definition of an institution' (Mahoney and Thelen 2010: 4). Institutions are path dependent – in other words shaped by past choices and legacies as well as ongoing interactions – oft times contradictory with other institutions.

Although the variants of new institutionalism (of which there are at least four: rational choice, historical, sociological and discursive) differ in their explanations of institutional creation, structure and agency, and power (Mahoney and Thelen 2010), there is considerable common ground. Whether feminist political scientists ally themselves to one or another of the variants (Lovenduski 2011: x-xi; *see also* Mackay and Waylen 2009), or combine elements (Krook and Mackay 2011), it is argued that NI offer new tools and frameworks that enable feminists to better capture multiple dynamics of continuity and change through concepts like informal institutions, critical junctures, path dependency, feedback mechanisms, and institutional conversion, layering, drift and erosion. Feminist research, in turn, brings a specific lens that can help NI scholars to theorise the gendered nature of formal institutions, the operation and importance of informal institutions, make visible the relations of power within and across institutions, and identify the sources and variable outcomes of attempted institutional change. In identifying changing gender relations as a potential cause of institutional change, feminism also 'increases the capacity of 'new' institutionalists to model causality'(Lovenduski 2011: xi).[5]

Increased interest in institutional-level analysis by FPS has gone hand-in-hand with the development of more complex understandings of gender. In so doing research has moved on from 'documenting sex imbalance and sexism' at individual level to an analysis of the underlying structures which underpin 'institutionalised advantages and disadvantages' (Duerst-Lahti and Kelly 1995: 44; *see also* Lovenduski 1998). This interest was driven, in part, by the need to move beyond description in order to situate political actors in their specific political institutions and wider contexts (Childs 2004); and to explain the persistence of inequality and range of exclusionary practices that operate within political institutions.

Feminist scholars have argued that gender provides a central structuring dynamic of political and public institutions and important mechanisms by which

5. Feminists also have serious critique of NI, not least for its neglect of gender. *See* recent surveys in Kenny 2007, Krook and Mackay 2011, Mackay, Kenny and Chappell 2010. However, the purpose of this chapter is to focus on the benefit of synthesis for FPS.

particular arrangements are naturalised and institutionalised, or resisted and discarded. Patterns of behaviour are shaped by cultural codes of masculinity and femininity and by institutional norms and values. Although both feminine and masculine codes are present in political institutions, the masculine ideal is dominant and underpins institutional structures and practices: shaping 'ways of valuing things, ways of behaving and ways of being' (Duerst-Lahti and Kelly 1995: 20). According to Lovenduski, masculinist ideologies are 'central to the workings of public institutions and therefore to political life, conventionally defined' (Lovenduski 1998: 340). Dominant masculinities are thus presented as common-sense, as the human standards for norms, conventions and practices.

Not only are gender relations seen to be 'institutional', they are also theorised as 'institutionalised'; in other words, embedded and naturalised within political institutions as gender regimes complete with 'rules, procedures, discourses and practices'; regimes in which 'many men are comfortable and most women are not' (Lovenduski 2005: 147). Such regimes not only constrain and shape the social interaction of institutional actors but also impact upon the operation and effect of institutions (Acker 1992; Connell 2002; Kenney 1996). And as Kenny notes these are contests with concrete outcomes for women as the actors who are frequently disadvantaged in power plays over institutional design processes, institutional implementation, and contests around the accumulation of institutional resources (Kenny 2007: 91). Furthermore, these patterns of power intersect with other social divisions such as those based on race/ethnicity, class, sexuality and so on. Gender relations and gender rules (including norms) – and their institutionalised forms in institutional 'gender regimes' (Connell 2002) – are thus part of the wider legacies and ongoing dynamics with which reform efforts must contend (Mackay, Kenny and Chappell 2010).

Current developments and new directions

In this section we discuss some recent and current work which has developed under the broad rubric of FI. We focus on FI perspectives on institutional continuity and change (in other words, how institutions stay the same and how change happens); and, secondly, on the growing realisation of the importance of informal rules and norms and their interplay with formal institutions (in other words, the way institutions are lived on a daily basis).

FI perspectives on institutional continuity and change

Institutional continuity and change, and the contingent, and often unanticipated, consequences of institutional reform and redesign are of interest to feminist political scientists. It is accepted that better explanations of change are needed; explanations that refine understandings of how change is generated via exogenous and endogenous processes, and how these processes interconnect. This is emerging as an area where FI has engaged fruitfully with recent developments in NI, particularly the dynamic conceptions of institutional change pioneered by historical institutionalists Kathleen Thelen and her collaborators.

Institutionalist models of change that draw a sharp analytical distinction between institutional creation (often viewed as resulting from external shock and dramatic rupture) and institutional reproduction (through endogenous processes of path dependency and institutional lock-in), whilst still widely used, are coming under increasing challenge. Newer and more dynamic models have been developed that emphasise 'bounded innovation' and characterise the boundaries between institutional reproduction and institutional creation or institutional change as blurred. Employing a loose notion of path dependency, it is argued that periods of institutional reproduction overlap with moments of institutional creation in partial and often unpredictable ways, and with unanticipated outcomes. As such, institutional actors experience a combination of 'lock in' and 'innovation', where already existing institutional structures to some extent 'lock' actors onto certain paths.

However, this does not preclude action by institutional actors and still leaves scope for innovation. These intuitions give rise to understandings of institutions as not only or always acting as a constraint but also as providing strategic resources (*see*, for example, Thelen 2003, 2004). Models such as these emphasise the importance of ongoing political contestation and the daily 'enactment' of institutions as key drivers of institutional change (Mahoney and Thelen 2010; Streek and Thelen 2005). Apparently small shifts in institutional power dynamics such as changing political alliances, and the cumulative effects of seemingly inconsequential decisions may add up to significant developments over time. These include the creation of new institutional forms through the change mechanisms such as layering (where new institutional elements are added to older elements, eventually supplanting them), conversion (where old institutional arrangements are co-opted and reinterpreted for new purposes), displacement (the wholesale removal of old institutional elements and their replacement with new) and drift (where old institutional arrangements are actively neglected and/or coopted) (Mahoney and Thelen 2010; Streek and Thelen 2005).

These new frameworks need to be rethought via a gender lens but are seen to hold great promise for fruitful adaptation and synthesis (Waylen 2011). They accord with the 'messiness' and empirical complexity of real world scenarios. As such, they may enable greater understanding of the variable and partial success of new feminist institutions created to challenge existing gender norms and gendered power asymmetries such as the introduction of gender candidate quotas (Freidenvall and Krook 2011; Krook 2009; Lovenduski 2005; Murray 2010; Squires 2007, and chapters six and seven of this volume) gender mainstreaming (Rai 2002; Squires 2007), the establishment of and subsequent fates of women's policy agencies (Outshoorn and Kantola 2007; Squires 2007), and the integration of gender concerns in the design of new formal institutions in the judicial, constitutional and parliamentary arenas (Chappell 2011; Kenny 2011; Mackay 2009; Waylen 2011). Whilst the approach may prove most fruitful for analysing feminist institution building, it also holds promise for understanding continuity and change in older and more resilient institutions.[6]

6. Our thanks to the anonymous reviewer for making this distinction.

That is not to underplay the power of path shaping continuities and the ongoing importance of legacies, including gendered legacies. These nuanced models still retain the insight that decisions made early in the life of an institution have particular significance because of the openness or 'permissiveness' of the opening stages in a sequence. Once chosen, paths are shaped and reinforced by factors such as large set up costs, strong learning and co-ordination effects, and normative processes. Thinking about democratic transitions and their gendered effects, Waylen (2011) asks to what extent outcomes emerge as a result of path dependent processes set in train at the point of transition, and to what extent they are a result of on-going contestation and more gradual institutional change?

Hana Hašková and Steven Saxonberg (2011) provide a compelling account of how path dependency can be understood as both powerful drag and incremental change. Instead of a radical break with the past, they argue that post-communist family and child care policies in the Czech Republic and Slovakia are more influenced by decisions made during the communist period (and indeed the pre communist 'bourgois' regime) than decisions made in the post communist era. Critical junctures were not exogenous shocks like regime change, but instead apparently mundane decisions and events that shaped, and continue to shape, future policies and gender relations, and also attitudes toward gender roles in a feedback effect. Institutional development is characterised here as a more incremental process whereby a sequence of decisions is made, each highly conditioned by the previous decision: not a clear trajectory but instead a series of small adjustments. As such, they argue against an overly deterministic notion of path dependency but rather change understood as sequenced problem solving, in which cognitive and normative resources upon which decision makers draw upon, including gendered norms, are influenced by previous decisions.

FI scholars have used such theoretical tools to gain insight into how far feminist reformers have been able to take advantage of 'permissive' stages in the life of new institutions to advance gender equality (Chappell 2011; Kenny 2011, 2013; Mackay 2009; Waylen 2011). Louise Chappell examines the extent to which, in the early days of its operation, the International Criminal Court has been able to realise its reformist potential to better protect women's human rights in times of war and conflict. The creation of a new international institution such as the ICC offers 'a rare opportunity to monitor the development of an institution from its genesis, an opportunity that can potentially yield important insights about the evolution of formal institutions' (2011: 163). However studies of restructuring processes and new institutions suggest both the extent to which new institutions are shaped by past legacies and ongoing interactions with other institutions, and the importance of ongoing contestation. In this respect, the concept of 'nested newness' (Mackay 2009) alerts us to the ways in which '"old" gender practices, norms, and expectations often underpin new institutions in ways which can blunt their reformist potential' (Chappell 2011: 166).

According to Vickers (2011) there are (at least) two institutional types: an individual institution in which gender regimes are discursively-constructed and changed by internal gender/power struggles; and interlocking networks of political institutions, which are 'culturally masculinised' such as central institutions including parliamentary legislatures fused with executives, judicial and prison systems. These are harder to change, and apparently changed by different processes. When complex institutional networks are restructured, some aspects of path dependence may be dislodged opening up new paths, especially if structural change is supported by ideational and discursive shifts. This analysis points to the importance of the coincidence of structural and ideational or discursive shifts. Ideas and discourses are thus a potential source of institutional change and a way of re-gendering politics for example through legislated gender quotas that legitimate both women's presence and their actions (Franceschet 2011; Freidenvall and Krook 2011).

Formal and informal rules – Gender and the 'hidden life' of institutions[7]

Informal institutions and their interplay with formal institutions are crucial if we want to understand wider processes of continuity and change and explain how similar formal rules result in variable outcomes. A notable feature of FI – in common with institutionalists from across the different schools – is the equal theoretical, empirical, and methodological status accorded to both kinds of institutions. North's ubiquitous definition of institutions as 'the rules of the game' (1990: 3) goes on to emphasise that such rules comprise of both formal and informal dimensions.

Informal norms and institutions as defined by Gretchen Helmke and Steven Levitsky (2004: 727) are 'socially shared rules, usually unwritten, that are created, communicated, and enforced outside of officially sanctioned channels', and that mediate the impact of formal rules. Informal institutions studied by comparative politics scholars have included patronage and other broader cultural practices; however little attention has been paid to the informal institutions of gender or to the gendering effects of other informal institutions. The central insight of FI is that both formal and informal institutions are gendered. FI argues that analysis is needed to explain how formal and informal institutions interact – in complementary or contradictory ways – to shape political outcomes. Institutional configurations and their effects may be gender neutral or gender-biased; these are empirical questions to be explored through detailed research (Kenny 2013, Chappell and Waylen 2013).

For example, Susan Franceschet (2011) develops an institutionalist and gendered comparative analysis of the interaction of formal and informal institutions, which structure the legislative process in ways that influence the actions of female legislators, and either facilitate or obstruct favourable policy outcomes for women. Her work on Argentina and Chile exposes the formal and informal institutions that structure the legislative environment and influence legislator behaviour and policy outcomes, ranging from formal electoral rules to

7. Section title is taken from Chappell and Waylen 2013.

informal norms such as combative or consensual political styles. These interactions impact upon all politicians, male and female, and on outcomes. However, they also have gendered effects in that they impact differently upon women and men, because they are embedded within wider gendered structures and gender norms. Particular configurations of institutions may encourage or discourage the articulation of perspectives that advance women's rights or the development of women's policy. There may also be gendered costs and benefits for particular behaviour. For example, women legislators who break informal conventions may pay a higher price than men because they contravene gendered norms as well as general legislative conventions.

Focussing on the dividends that accrue as a result of political masculinities, rather than the penalty paid by political femininities, Elin Bjarnegård turns the spotlight on the gendered operation and impact on political recruitment of the informal institution of clientelism amongst male political elites. Powerful informal norms of clientelism persist in many parliamentary democracies despite formal rules of equal opportunities. Using theories of masculinities to capture these informal gendered rules and practices, and the 'homosocial capital' upon which they are based, she provides a powerful explanation of how male dominance is reproduced through gendered mechanisms (Bjarnegård 2013).

Institutional reform and innovation

The understanding that institutions consist of formal rules and informal norms and, second, that institutions are complex systems that may work in permissive or obstructive ways are particularly pertinent when examining processes of institutional reform and innovation, as Box 5.1 illustrates. Informal rules and norms can serve a number of purposes: they may emerge to complement and reinforce formal institutions; or they may 'plug the gaps' when formal institutional solutions are not available; conversely, they may provide alternative norms and practices in situations where formal rule changes are unlikely or unwelcome. In an effort to explain why informal institutions exist, some analysts suggest that informal rules emerge when formal institutions are incomplete; when actors prefer, but cannot achieve, a formal institutional solution; or when actors are pursuing goals that are not publicly acceptable, either because they are unlikely to stand the test of public scrutiny or will attract international condemnation (Helmke and Levitsky 2004; *see also* Leach and Lowndes 2007). Although both kinds of institutions comprise rules of appropriate behaviour (March and Olsen 1984) they may arise and be subject to amendment by means of distinct processes. They may work in concert to intensify or work against each other to dilute particular political outcomes.

Box 5.1: The Speakership, Gender and Parliamentary Change – Faith Armitage

The Office of the Speaker is deeply stamped with a masculine character. To date, there have been 158 incumbents of the Office and all but one has been male. Its masculine character has traditionally been conveyed most obviously through a distinctive official outfit – consisting of a full-bottomed wig, morning coat, ruffled white shirt, knee breeches, tights and buckled shoes – worn by successive Speakers until very recently. Throughout the centuries, all Members of the Commons have had to observe a formal dress code. But whereas the dress code for 'ordinary' MPs has kept pace with the times, the evolution of the Speaker's outfit came to a halt in the 18th century.

However, in 1992, Betty Boothroyd, the first woman elected Speaker, chose not to wear the full-bottomed wig and exchanged the knee breeches for a skirt. According to her, this was not an autonomous decision, but rather required assent from 'the usual channels' of the House. The wig has not reappeared on the scene since then. In fact, the current incumbent, John Bercow, dispensed with the rest of the antique court dress, and wears an academic-style black gown over a lounge suit. Explaining his decision, Bercow said:

> [I]f we're to recover respect for Parliament, that will be achieved [...] by the comprehensiveness and radicalism of our reforms to the House, both in terms of cleaning up Parliament and strengthening our scrutiny of the executive and advancing to centre stage the role of the backbencher. We will not recover respect for politics or Parliament by dressing up in fancy uniforms and being pompous (interview, 24 November 2009).

Norms of dress for MPs at Westminster are still gendered as they are in British society at large but the Speaker's uniform gradually has been brought more into line with what 'ordinary' MPs in the chamber are wearing, and the changes mean that the Speakership today projects a less obviously masculine image than it did in the days of powdered wigs and buckled shoes. As a result, it is perhaps less of a stretch, nowadays, for female MPs to imagine themselves in the role. Perhaps the Speakership represents less of an 'ill-fitting suit' for women (Puwar 2004) simply because of the modernisation of something seemingly as trivial as an outfit.

Speakership elections suggest another way in which the institution is gendered, and how this might be changing in response to wider cultural and institutional changes within the House. Up until around the 1970s, Speakership elections tended to be conducted as backroom 'gentlemen's agreements' because of an accretion of unwritten norms and understandings about the Speakership which were shared by successive parliamentary elites (*see* Armitage 2012). For example, it was accepted that the Government of the day had the right to choose the Speaker-elect, after consultation with leaders of the Opposition. The Government understood that it should choose a man who was popular on all sides of the House, an able backbencher, but someone with little or no ministerial experience, if it wanted to get its chosen Speaker through on the nod. The odd woman may have been in the room, by virtue of her position of influence in the party, but their numbers in the House in general were still low, and until 1992, no woman was ever put forward by her party as a candidate. Indeed, it is worth noting that when she won the election in 1992, Boothroyd was only the 27th woman ever to be elected to the House of Commons.

Actual contests for the Speakership were rare in the twentieth century because of these norms and understandings. When they have occurred – as they did with increasing frequency toward the end of the century due to gradual changes in the culture of the Commons and the prevailing mindset and career patterns of MPs (Armitage 2012) – they have elicited displays and accounts of heroic masculinity. In the following illustrative extracts from Hansard, men invoke military or athletic experiences and achievements as a qualification for the Speakership:

> I remember when we first met. It was at the beginning of the war, and we were both at the Staff College at Camberley. You were there as a second lieutenant. Within a very short time you became a brigadier on the staff of the Second Army in the invasion of Europe (the 'Father of the House' congratulating John Selwyn Lloyd, Speaker-elect, HC Deb 12 January 1971 vol 809 c31).

> You were a gunner, I flew aeroplanes, and my hon. Friend was in tanks. There is no more demanding environment than to be in a tank and to learn to get on with all sorts of conditions and people (an MP nominating an alternative to the frontrunner, speaking to the Father of the House, HC Deb 23 October 2000 vol 355 c61).

Many more such examples could be found. Such speeches contribute an additional note to the dominant public and parliamentary discourse about the House of Commons as a masculine place – a 'bear pit' or a boys' public school. Specifically, they project an image of the Speakership as an office requiring 'manly' men. Such speeches are not necessarily intentionally exclusive of women, however, even as the proportion of women in the Commons increased, some men still judged it necessary or advantageous to showcase their 'heroic masculinity' – as this speech extract from the 2009 Speakership election suggests:

> As someone who in his younger days – much younger days – played rugby against the South African Springboks, I am used to coping with the roughest of confrontations and able to insist on fairness being done

> in the toughest of circumstances (a candidate giving his address to the Commons, HC Deb 22 June 2009, c. 626).

This 2009 Speakership election was a watershed for the Commons, as it marked the first time the election was conducted by secret ballot – unheard of in the Commons, where all other votes up until that time were public. The new election procedures had been approved by the Commons in 2001, and were precipitated by the mini-scandal of the 2000 Speakership election. There were 12 candidates, it lasted more than seven hours and some felt the traditional procedures were unfair and did not allow the most popular candidate to emerge. The 2009 Speakership election took place in the midst of the major scandal of the MPs' expenses crisis, which precipitated other important parliamentary reforms long championed by those concerned to strengthen parliament and reduce the Executive's dominance in the Commons. These included the creation of a backbench business committee, secret elections for select committee chairs, and secret elections for Deputy Speakers. Under the new rules for electing Deputy Speakers, it was stipulated that there must always be at least one man and one woman in the four-person Speaker + Deputy Speakers 'team'.

Diverse cases such as recruitment reforms in post-devolution Scotland (Kenny 2013; *see also* Kenny 2011); gender quota reforms in Sweden and France (Freidenvall and Krook 2011; Murray 2010); and the creation of the new International Criminal Court (Chappell 2011) all provide ample evidence of the way in which 'old rules' embodied in gender norms and legacies may work to frustrate or dilute new institutions promoting gender equality.

Researching these dynamics can uncover informal mechanisms of resistance including, 'forgetting' new rules and espoused norms (Mackay 2009) and 'remembering' old rules and norms (Leach and Lowndes 2007). These mechanisms can result in the reassertion of traditional gender relations and norms; strategies of partial or non-compliance, the reluctance of key actors fully to utilise new powers and rules that promote gender equality and gender justice. For example, judicial interpretations in new international institutions such as the International Criminal Court at times uphold 'gender norms that treat women's rights as less significant than other rights', despite extensive formal 'women-friendly' provisions (Chappell 2011); and the emergence of informalisation through various practices such as informally sanctioned rule-breaking, lack of rule enforcement and adoption of alternative conventions in Scotland, which undermine the gender reforms which accompanied devolution (Kenny 2011, 2013).

These mechanisms are not confined to new or young institutions and operate in different ways in different systems. Despite formal equal access in parliamentary democracies, informal practices of exclusion persist (Bjarnegård 2013). Federal systems provide ample opportunity for informal rules to mediate the impact of formal rules about divisions of powers and responsibilities. For example, Jill

Vickers argues that Courts often allow national governments in federal systems to 'stretch' jurisdictions over issues relating to the economy and security (Vickers 2010). Despite formal constitutions protecting the rights of women, states may relinquish authority to sub-state levels – or even non-state 'acknowledged authorities' – on matters of 'personal law' and 'family policy'. In so doing, formal provisions that are gender-neutral or gender-equal can, through the informal conventions by which they are interpreted and enacted, produce –or reinforce norms and biases of gender inequality.

'Gaps' and 'soft spots' exist between rules and their interpretation, enactment and enforcement. These are analytical spaces within which institutions are contested in ongoing processes (Mahoney and Thelen 2010: 18). Informal rules play out in different scenarios during periods of reform and transition. On the one hand, they may reinforce change when there is good fit and tight coupling between the old informal and the new formal. On the other hand, they may serve as a primary site of resistance 'existing in parallel – or even in direct contradiction – to formal rules' (Leach and Lowndes 2007: 186). Informal rules can thus serve to modify newness (rules, structure and roles) and reincorporate old ways and old paths 'leaving power relationships intact' (Leach and Lowndes 2007: 186). Banaszak and Weldon argue that 'attending also to informal institutions increases our analytic leverage, providing systematic explanations of the causal mechanisms by which informal institutions shape gender inequality' (Banaszak and Weldon 2011: 267).

Whilst the weight of empirical evidence points towards old, informal rules as a key mechanism of resistance to gendered change, it is nonetheless possible to theorise instances in which institutions may be regendered (in a positive direction) through developments in, or the mobilisation of, progressive informal rules and norms modifying more negative formal rules; or progressive formal rules impacting upon traditional informal rules (Beyeler and Annesley 2011). Opportunities to alter existing institutions are presented when formal and informal institutions are in tension or outright conflict. Positive examples include the introduction of gender quotas – formal rules about political candidature and political leadership – which may result in subsequent changes in informal norms and rules and increase gender equality (Krook 2009).

Answering the questions raised by gendered institutions requires a multi-method approach. It has been a long and slow process but FPS researchers have increasingly borrowed tools and concepts from sociology, organisational studies, social psychology and linguistics as well as from institutional analysis (Lovenduski 1998; Mackay 2004). Work is progressing, but there are considerable challenges to successfully 'capturing' gender as it operates in institutions through informal rules, norms and practices and their interplay with formal rules and laws, and attending to the incremental change that happens as a result of ongoing contestation 'under the radar'. As in other parts of political science (*see* Gains 2011; Rhodes *et al.* 2007), FPS researchers are beginning to turn to ethnographic techniques to uncover the hidden and gendered lives of political institutions. Rosa Malley's research (*see* Box 5.2) uses observation and 'shadowing' to explore and compare parliamentary cultures and how they are 'lived' on a daily basis by female and male politicians.

Box 5.2: Feeling at Home: Inclusion at Westminster and the Scottish Parliament – Rosa Malley[8]

It is my first shadowing placement at Westminster and I am to meet the MP's researcher at Central Lobby. Arriving at the main visitors' entrance outside the Palace, a stern looking policeman asks me why I am here. Unsure how much information he requires, I start to explain that I am 'shadowing' a Member of Parliament (MP) and have arranged to meet their researcher. He interrupts me upon hearing the name of the MP and points me to security. Photo taken, bags checked and person frisked, I follow instructions towards Westminster Hall. Inside is incredibly large and somewhat gloomy, and I am very aware of the echo of my feet and small wheelie-bag reverberating as I walk through the Hall. I lift my bag to minimise the noise and carry on. Walking along St Stephen's Hall on my way to Central Lobby, I pass large paintings depicting battle scenes. I am asked, once again, at the entrance to Central Lobby what I am here for. I say the MP's name and am directed to a parliamentary official, wearing a ceremonial dark evening suit decorated with a large brass medallion, on the main desk. After explaining who I am meeting, I sit on a green leather bench. My feet do not touch the ground, and looking up to the grandly decorated curved roof, I feel very small, and suddenly nervous about the day ahead.[9]

> I have just arrived for my first shadowing placement at the Scottish Parliament and am waiting in the large reception area to be met by someone on behalf of the Member of the Scottish Parliament (MSP) I am shadowing. To my surprise, the MSP comes down to meet me herself rather than sending an assistant. Her friendliness and informality strike me immediately as we exchange initial greetings. This develops as she carefully explains the activities during the time I will be spending with her. Today is mainly taken up by a committee and we go directly there. Small incidents throughout the day develop my sense of ease and perception of informality in the Scottish Parliament. For instance, the MSP I am shadowing is concerned I will get a cup of tea in the break of the committee I am observing. During the break, two MSPs separately, and spontaneously, chat to me and ask about my research. I am further struck by the contrasting atmosphere from Westminster when watching the casual interaction between MSPs and other staff such as security guards and interns. Later, the MSP I am shadowing casually invites me to join her and a fellow MSP for dinner that evening.[10]

8. This vignette draws substantially on Malley 2012
9. Fieldnotes, Westminster, 4 March 2009.
10. Fieldnotes, Scottish Parliament, 23 March 2010.

These field notes, written while conducting participant observation at Westminster (March–May 2009) and the Scottish Parliament (March–May 2010), are illustrative of differences in the two institutions' parliamentary cultures. Whereas I experienced Westminster as daunting, the informality of the Scottish Parliament was striking from the outset. The Scottish media and an academic consensus are broadly dismissive of the 'new politics' aspirations of plural, participative and consensual politics espoused during the campaign for devolution. They point to dominance of the executive, to partisan politics and to the weekly wrangle between the party leaders to support the assertion that the Scottish Parliament looks more similar to Westminster than its founders intended (*see*, for example, Cairney 2011).

While true, these accounts fail to acknowledge substantial differences between these two institutions in how they are experienced by representatives in an everyday sense. Looking at behaviour in the debating chambers of these parliaments, it is evident that that the Scottish Parliament is more inclusive than Westminster for women and other historically under-represented groups. My research draws on over sixty interviews and participant observation through 'shadowing placements' with politicians. Participant observation – a relatively underused method in political science – provides a way of seeing how everyday institutional conventions, rituals and behaviours contain gendered norms of behaviour.

Westminster: 'Two swords apart'

Debating in the chamber has been cited as evidence of a traditionally masculine gender regime at Westminster (Lovenduski 2005). The chamber is the most public arena where women have to 'manage' their femininity (Puwar 2004). Previous studies demonstrate that many women perceive debate as macho and are less likely to participate aggressively (Childs 2004; Shaw 2000; Sones, Moran, and Lovenduski 2005). This is supported by my data. The aggressive, and dominant, style of interaction in the chamber is perceived by a majority of MPs as masculine and is thought to reflect the Oxbridge Union style of debating. For instance, a Labour woman MP is unequivocally critical of the 'bear pit' atmosphere of the chamber: 'I find it quite difficult really. It's Prime Minister's Questions today and that'll be like a bear pit and that's a very difficult time to get your views across because it's so intense, and hectic, and so antagonistic.'[11]

A Conservative woman MP, who is not initially disposed to a gendered critique of Parliament, reflects that behaviour in the Chamber may be part of the 'subtle discrimination here in Parliament – the way it works tends to play to male traits more than female traits: 'There are more risks, because if your voice becomes shrill, you will immediately become ridiculed'.[12]

---

11. Interview 21, 3 February 2010.
12. Interview 20, 4 March 2010.

A Labour MP supports this observation in arguing that some of the qualities necessary for the more adversarial occasions are more difficult for women to perform:

> On the big occasions, what works is a macho, tub-thumping, loud voice – boom-boom-boom, the classical rhetorical devices and all of that. And although not all men are comfortable with that and some women are, by and large, most of my women colleagues, like me, hate it.[13]

Scottish parliament: A consensual chamber?

There is broad agreement that behaviour in the chamber of the Scottish Parliament is more similar to Westminster's yah-boo politics than the consensual politics envisaged by its founders. Nonetheless, and unlike Westminster, debate in the Scottish Parliament is not perceived, on such a scale, as exclusionary in terms of gender or class. For example, a Labour woman MSP spontaneously identifies the debating style as evidence of the effective mobilisation of feminist demands in the Scottish Constitutional Convention. She argues feminists were not prepared to abide by debating rules they associated with elite schools: 'I think there was a lot of women like myself, who were involved politically for a long time and we certainly weren't coming here to follow rules of debate that had been decided in private schools in deepest England somewhere'.[14] She addresses the aggressive style of debate, joking ('we have been known to heckle'), but does not describe it as exclusionary and defends it on the grounds of political differences.

Two women MSPs (who it should be noted have never been MPs and so are merely speculating on Westminster debate), argue that although robust, debate in the Scottish Parliament compares favourably with that of Westminster. A Labour woman argues that the Scottish Parliament chamber is less daunting ('It's very relaxed. It's a much easier place to get up and speak in'[15]) and an SNP woman argues that although raucous, behaviour in the Scottish Parliament chamber is less macho: 'It can get rowdy sometimes which is sometimes really good, sometimes not really good if all the rowdiness is directed at you. But it's not got the same, sort of, testosterone type aggressive, boorish type of debating that goes on.'[16]

The founding ideal of consensual behaviour in the chamber of the Scottish Parliament was part of the more general aspiration to make the Scottish Parliament a more inclusive parliament than Westminster, where cut-and-thrust politics was perceived as particularly alienating to women. Its failure to manifest itself as intended might therefore be viewed as a broader

13. Interview 29, 6 January, 2010.
14. Interview 61, 18 May 2010
15. Interview 72, 26 May 2010.
16. Interview 53, 13 May 2010.

failure to create a more inclusive parliament. However, these findings suggest that adversarialism, perceived as exclusionary in Westminster, does not have the same effects for MSPs. Though aggressive, and therefore more associated with masculinity according to socially constructed gender roles, ritualistic behaviour in the Scottish Parliament is not observed or reported as exclusionary.

This indicates that the origins of political rituals matter. The norms of behaviour that have developed in the Scottish Parliament reflect a broad plurality of Members involved in the construction of the institution. In Westminster, rituals have developed over the long course of its institutional history. There are different (and competing) narratives as to why they exist. The rituals are perceived by a significant group of MPs to reflect the historical dominance of upper-class white men. The Scottish Parliament rituals are known or at least traceable. Women were involved in the development of ritualised norms of behaviour in the chamber and hence may feel a sense of ownership over them.

Behaviour in the debating chambers of Westminster and the Scottish Parliament highlights the similarities and differences between these two institutions. Adversarial exchange and partisan posturing illustrate the extent to which party politics dominates in both. However, despite the similarities, debate in the Scottish Parliament is not experienced as exclusionary to nearly the same extent as Westminster. Holyrood's parliamentary culture looks to be more inclusive of women and other historically under-represented groups. This is a substantial difference between these two institutions that is under-estimated in mainstream studies of these parliaments. Moreover, it suggests that the presence of women representatives has been crucial for creating a parliamentary culture that is more inclusionary.

Conclusions

There is no single feminist institutionalist approach but central features and concerns are shared: they are pluralistic in approach; pay attention to both formal and informal institutional environments; see institutional change (and stability) as driven by gendered processes from within and without, and consider actors as having agency, albeit bounded by various constraints. Already a canon of work is developing but much work lies ahead. Nonetheless, the synthesis of institutionally focused feminist scholarship and NI into a feminist institutionalism has considerable potential to improve our understanding and analyses of the nature, function and impact of political institutions.

We need to consider what is the aim of FI in terms of scope and focus. An overly narrow focus, for example, solely on women representatives or policy initiatives around gender equality can limit analysis of the broader question of how and with what effect state and political institutions are gendered (Waylen 2011). Part of the strategy must be to engage with 'mainstream' scholarship and, as Joni Lovenduski has argued: 'Pay attention to questions in the rest of political science, use it ruthlessly and attack where necessary (or irresistible.)' (2009: 2). This suggests the need for a dual focus on both feminist guided change (gender equity reforms) and on the gendering of wider political processes.

Research strategies are needed which examine both the formal and informal rules within a particular institutional domain; their interaction with practices and discourses; and the interaction effects of other institutions in the dense institutional environment within which they are nested. Combined methods will enable us to capture and analyse institutional dynamics, gender power, and the causes and consequences of gendered inequalities in political life. For example, understanding the gendered nature of institutions allows reformers to understand why seemingly neutral rules can result in outcomes that profoundly disadvantage women; exposing informal gender rules and norms at play in institutional arenas alerts us to ways in which such informal institutions may operate to undermine and dilute reforms intended to improve gender equality. As such, the study of gender and institutions provides Words – useful knowledge, ideas and analysis – to inform Deeds: the action and new strategies that may lead to transformation and change.

References

Acker, J. (1992) 'From sex roles to gendered institutions', *Contemporary Sociology* 21 (5): 565–569.

Annesley, C. and Gains, F. (2010) 'The core executive: gender power and change, *Political Studies* 58 (5): 909–929.

Armitage, F. (2012) 'From elite control to democratic competition: procedural reform and cultural change in UK House of Commons Speakership elections', *British Politics* 7 (2): 135–162.

Banaszak, L. A. and Weldon, L. (2011) 'Informal institutions, protest and change in gendered federal systems', *Politics and Gender* 7 (2): 262–274.

Beyeler, M. and Annesley, C. (2011) 'Gendering the institutional reform of the welfare state' in M. Krook and F. Mackay (eds) *Gender, Politics and Institutions*, Basingstoke: Palgrave Macmillan, pp. 79–94.

Bjarnegård, E. (2013) *Gender, Informal Institutions, and Political Recruitment*, Basingstoke: Palgrave Macmillan.

Cairney, P. (2011) *The Scottish Political System since Devolution: From new politics to the new Scottish Government*, Exeter: Imprint Academic.

Chappell, L. (2006) 'Comparing political institutions: revealing the gendered "logic of appropriateness"', *Politics and Gender* 2 (2): 223–235.

— (2011) 'Nested newness and institutional innovation: expanding gender justice in the international criminal court', in M. Krook and F. Mackay (eds) *Gender, Politics and Institutions*, Basingstoke: Palgrave Macmillan, pp. 163–180.

Chappell, L. and Waylen, G. (2013) 'Gender and the hidden life of institutions', *Public Administration* 91 (3): 599–615.

Childs, S. (2004) New Labour's Women MPs: Women representing women, London: Routledge.

Connell, R. (2002) *Gender*, Cambridge Polity Press.

Duerst-Lahti, G. and Kelly, R. M. (1995) *Gender Power, Leadership and Governance*, Ann Arbor, MI: University of Michigan Press.

Franceschet, S. (2011) 'Gendered institutions and women's substantive representation: female legislators in Argentina and Chile', in M. Krook and F. Mackay (eds) *Gender, Politics and Institutions*, Basingstoke, pp. 58–78.

Freidenvall, L. and Krook, M. (2011) 'Discursive strategies for institutional reform: gender quotas in Sweden and France' in M. Krook and F. Mackay (eds) *Gender, Politics and Institutions*, Basingstoke, pp. 42–57.

Gains, F. (2011) 'Elite ethnography: potential, pitfalls and prospects for getting 'up close and personal', *Public Administration* 89 (1): 156–166.

Goodin, R. (1996) 'Institutions and their Design' in R. Goodin (ed.) *The Theory of Institutional Design*, Cambridge: Cambridge University Press, pp. 1–53.

Hašková, H. and Saxonberg, S. (2011) 'The institutional roots of post-communist family policy: comparing Czech and Slovak Republics', in M. Krook and F. Mackay (eds) *Gender, Politics and Institutions*, Basingstoke: Palgrave Macmillan, pp. 112–128.

Helmke, G. and Levitsky, S. (2004) 'Informal institutions and comparative politics: a research agenda', *Perspectives on Politics* 2 (4): 725–740.

Kenney, S. (1996) 'New research on gendered political institutions', *Political Research Quarterly* 49 (2): 445–446.

Kenny, M. (2007) 'Gender, institutions and power: a critical review', Politics 27 (2): 91–100.

— (2011) 'Gender and institutions of political recruitment: candidate selection in post-devolution Scotland', in M. Krook and F. Mackay (eds) *Gender, Politics and Institutions*, Basingstoke: Palgrave Macmillan, pp.21–41.

— (2013) *Gender and Political Recruitment: Theorizing institutional change*, Basingstoke: Palgrave Macmillan.

Krook, M. (2009) Quotas for Women in Politics, New York: Oxford University Press.

Krook, M. and Mackay, F. (2011) *Gender, Politics and Institutions: Towards a feminist institutionalism*, Basinstoke: Palgrave Macmillan.

Leach, S. and Lowndes, V. (2007) 'Of roles and rules: analysing the changing relationship between political leaders and chief executives in local government', *Public Policy and Administration* 22 (2): 183–200.

Lovenduski, J. (1998) 'Gendering research in political science', Annual Review of Political Science 1 (333–56).

— (2005) *Feminizing Politics*, Cambridge: Polity Press.

— (2009) 'Thoughts on Feminist Institutionalism so Far, Notes from Roundtable: Feminism and Institutionalism: promising synthesis or another case of "master's tools"?' Presented at the European Conference on Politics and Gender, Queens University Belfast.

— (2011) 'Forward', in M. Krook and F. Mackay (eds) *Gender, Politics and Institutions*, Basingstoke: Palgrave Macmillan.

Lowndes, V. (2010) 'The Institutional Approach' in D. Marsh and G. Stoker (eds) *Theories and Methods in Political Science*, Houndmills, Basingstoke: Palgrave Macmillan, pp.60–79.

Mackay, F. (2004) 'Gender and political representation in the UK: the state of the 'discipline', *British Journal of Politics and International Relations* 6 (1): 99–120.

— (2009) 'Institutionalising "New Politics" in Post Devolution Scotland: "Nested Newness" and the Gendered Limits of Change', Presented at the Political Studies Association Annual Conference, Manchester.

— (2011) 'Conclusion: Towards a feminist institutionalism?' in M. L.Krook and F. Mackay (eds) *Gender, Politics and Institutions: Towards a feminist institutionalism*, Basingstoke: Palgrave Macmillan, pp. 181–196.

Mackay, F. and Kenny, M. (2009) 'Already doin' it for ourselves?: Skeptical notes on feminism and institutionalism', *Politics and Gender* 5 (2): 271–280.

Mackay, F., Kenny, M. and Chappell, L. (2010) 'New institutionalism through a gender lens: towards a feminist institutionalism', *International Political Science Review* 31 (5): 1–16.

Mackay, F. and Waylen, G. (2009) 'Critical perspectives on feminist institutionalism', *Politics and Gender* 5 (2): 237–280.

Mahoney, J. and Thelen, K. (2010) 'How historical institutionalists explain change', in J. Mahoney and K. Thelen (eds) *Explaining Institutional Change: Ambiguity, Agency, and Power*, pp. x-xx.

Malley, R. (2012) 'Feeling at home: inclusion at Westminster and in the Scottish Parliament', *Political Quarterly* 83 (4): 714–717.

March, J. and Olsen, J. (1984) 'The new institutionalism: organizational factors in political life', *American Political Science Review* 78 (2): 734–749.

Murray, R. (2010) *Parties, Gender Quotas and Candidate Selection in France*, Basingstoke: Palgrave Macmillan.

North, D. (1990) *Institutions, Institutional Change and Economic Performance*, Cambridge: Cambridge University Press.

Outshoorn, J. and Kantola, J. (eds) (2007) *Changing State Feminism*, Basingstoke: Palgrave Macmillan.

Puwar, N. (2004) *Space Invaders: Race, gender and bodies out of place*, London: Berg Publishers.

Rai, S. (ed.) (2002) *Mainstreaming Gender: Democratizing the state?*, Manchester: Manchester University Press.

Rhodes, R.A.W., t'Hart, P. and Noordegraaf, M. (eds) (2007) *Observing Government Elites: Up close and personal*, Basingstoke: Palgrave Macmillan.

Shaw, S. (2000) 'Language, gender and floor apportionment in political debates', *Discourse and Society* 11 (3): 401–418.

Sones, B., Moran, M. and Lovenduski, J. (2005) *Women in Parliament: The new suffragettes*, London: Politicos.

Squires, J. (2007) *The New Politics of Gender Equality*, Houndmills, Basingstoke: Palgrave Macmillan.

Streek, W. and Thelen, K. (eds) (2005) *Beyond Continuity: Institutional change in advanced political economies*, Oxford: Oxford University Press.

Thelen, K. (2003) 'How institutions evolve', in J. Mahoney and D. Rueschemeyer (eds) *Comparative Historical Analysis in the Social Sciences*, Cambridge: Cambridge University Press.

— (2004) *How Institutions Evolve: The political economy of skills in Germnay, Britain, the United States and Japan*, Cambridge: Cambridge University Press.

Vickers, J. (2010) 'A two-way street: federalism and women's politics in Canada and the United States', *Publius* 40 (3): 412–435.

— (2011) 'Gendering federalism: institutions of decentralization and power-sharing', in M. Krook and F. Mackay (eds) *Gender, Politics and Institutions*, Basingstoke: Palgrave Macmillan, pp. 129–146.

Waylen, G. (2011) 'Gendered institutionalist analysis: understanding democratic transitions' in M. Krook and F. Mackay (eds) *Gender, Politics and Institutions*, Basingstoke, : Palgrave Macmillan, pp. 147–162.

Vignette – Gender and Political institutions: 'Twinning' – the Scottish Experience

Alice Brown CBE

> Professor Alice Brown CBE is an academic, feminist campaigner and longstanding contributor to Scottish public life. Alongside her impressive academic career at the University of Edinburgh, she has served on a wide range of public bodies, including the Equal Opportunities Commission in Scotland. She was the first Scottish Public Services Ombudsman (2002–2009) and she was a member of the Consultative Steering Group that drew up the procedures for the Scottish Parliament. Professor Brown used academic evidence to support the case for ensuring the fair representation of women in the new Scottish Parliament, helping to design mechanisms to promote women's representation and was a founder of the women's organisation 'Engender'. As such, she typifies the interaction between feminist deeds and words that is the focus of this book and has a deep knowledge of how political institutions are gendered.

As an academic, I believe that it is not only important to strive for excellence in research and teaching but to consider how best to engage with, contribute to and have an impact on public debate and policy. There could be no better example of how it was possible to engage, contribute and impact than that of the events that led up to the establishment of the Scottish Parliament in 1999. For me, it was a unique opportunity to play a part in ensuring that the new House was not dominated by male politicians. It was an experience that I will never forget.

The campaign for a Scottish Parliament covered many years but it reached a peak during the Thatcher governments in the 1980s and 1990s. The Scottish Constitutional Convention involved a wide range of political parties and representatives from Scottish civic society in preparing plans for a Scottish Parliament – a new institution with a new electoral system and different ways of working. Part of the vision of a new democracy in Scotland was the aspiration that women should play an active and equal role in the future governance of Scotland.

The Scottish Trades Union Congress' (STUC) Women's Committee, and activists like Ronnie McDonald and Yvonne Strachan, were instrumental in articulating the need for a new parliament that had equal representation of women as well as men. Indeed it was this group of women who first made the case for '50:50' and began the campaign to realise this ambition. They argued that to guarantee gender balance in the new Scottish Parliament, each constituency should elect two members, one man and one woman from lists of male and female candidates.

The challenge was, however, not only to persuade the different political parties to adopt positive action measures in their selection of candidates but how to achieve gender balance in a new, more proportional, electoral system. The Additional Member System would return 56 Members of the Scottish Parliament (MSPs) elected through first-past-the-post in parliamentary constituencies and a balance of 73 MSPs elected via regional lists (a total of 129 MSPs). The picture was complicated too by the fact that, at the time, the Labour Party's domination of Scottish politics meant that they were likely to achieve the majority of their seats in constituencies while the other parties would have to rely on obtaining the majority of their seats through the regional lists.

This is where the role of academics like myself came in. Drawing on experience of practice in other countries, notably Sweden, Norway and Finland, and on academic research and knowledge of electoral systems and positive action measures, it was possible to demonstrate how gender balance could be achieved by the different parties in a way that was compatible with the electoral system and its likely different impact on individual political parties. While there are different techniques that can be used in relation to regional lists – placing women candidates near the top of the list and/or 'zipping' by alternating female and male candidates – it was necessary to consider how the constituency seats could be managed. Further, learning lessons from challenges to the Labour Party's policy of 'All Women' shortlists in 1997, we sought ways of overcoming potential legal barriers of designating seats for women only.

It was then that the idea of 'twinning' was proposed. Under this proposal, we suggested that constituencies could be twinned or paired in order that an equal number of men and women candidates could stand for election. I recall one evening in particular when myself, and a number of the women involved, spread out a large map of Scotland on a table so that we could give some thought to which constituencies could best be twinned with one another.

The 'twinning' scheme provided a practical solution and way of achieving gender balance. Under the scheme, the woman with the highest number of votes would be selected as the Labour candidate for one of the twinned seas, at the same time as the man with the highest number of votes would be selected for the other. The next stage was to convince leading politicians in the Labour Party that it both should and could be done – not necessarily an easy task. However, the twinning initiative was indeed adopted by the Labour Party (in Scotland, the mechanism was used to select Labour candidates for all constituencies with the exception of four Highlands and Islands constituencies) and certainly produced the desired results with 28 women and 28 men elected from the Labour Party, i.e. the 50:50 result that many women had campaigned for, but through a different route to that originally proposed.

Unfortunately the other political parties who did not adopt positive action measures were not as successful in terms of gender balance. Nevertheless, a total of 48 women MSPs were elected (37 per cent) to Scotland's first parliament since 1707. The number of women elected in just one day exceeded the total who had been elected to represent Scottish constituencies at general elections to the House of Commons over the previous 81 years, that is since 1918 when women were first eligible to stand for election to parliament. This was a remarkable and historic achievement.

On the day of the opening of the Scottish Parliament, the sun was shining and it was a public holiday. There was great excitement and buzz in Edinburgh. I had the privilege to be invited to the opening ceremony but nothing could have prepared me for the moment when the procession of MSPs and others who had marched up the High Street to the sound of pipe bands reached the parliament building. The doors burst open and in came the first cohort of MSPs. Suddenly the result of all the work and campaigning was evident as a sea of colour entered the chamber and the first women to be elected to the Scottish Parliament proudly took their seats. I have to confess to sharing that pride in the knowledge that the advocacy and expertise of women had had an impact – it had helped realise the vision of a more gendered balanced parliament.

Chapter Six

Women, Gender Politics and the State: The Words and Deeds of RNGS

Amy G. Mazur and Dorothy E. McBride

The long campaign to gender the state, that is, to make gender differences explicitly part of the state's processes and policies in Western democracies, took a new turn when states formally incorporated the idea of women/gender by charging structures explicitly with the task of promoting the status of women and achieving gender equality.[1] Whether such structures, called women's policy agencies and gender equality mechanisms, have had any effect on state power structures or policies was the question that inspired the work of the Research Network on Gender, Politics and the State (RNGS).[2] Over seventeen years of collaboration, researchers in the network completed rigorous comparative studies exploring the effectiveness of over seventy gender equality mechanisms in thirteen Western postindustrial democracies. Of special interest was their ability to respond to demands of women's movement activists over the last thirty years of the 20th century. A final outcome of this research was a new politics and theory of state feminism elaborated in the capstone book, *The Politics of State Feminism: Innovation in Comparative Research* (McBride and Mazur 2010).

This chapter looks at the contributions of RNGS research to scholarship and practices in the campaign to gender the state in Western democracies; first is a focus on how the new politics of state feminism has changed conventional approaches to thinking about and studying women and the state. The chapter goes on to link these research outcomes – the 'words' of RNGS—RNGS 'deeds'. It reviews how RNGS findings and methods have informed policy discussions and decisions about women's rights and gender equality in the political arena by looking at nine instances in four venues: policy recommendations to governmental organisations; research funded by women's policy agencies; expert reports to international organisations; dissemination to and networking with policy practitioners and activists.

1. This occurred in Western democracies beginning in the 1970s with a few exceptions (U.S. 1920; France 1965; Canada 1954).
2. Everything you ever wanted to know about RNGS can be found on the RNGS website: http://libarts.wsu.edu/pppa/rngs/html.

RNGS words: The new politics of state feminism

This first section presents a survey of the implications of the new politics and theory of state feminism for understanding the complexity embodied in the study of women's movements, women's policy agencies, and gendering the state. The findings described here are possible due to RNGS' rigorous scientific approach to qualitative and quantitative comparative conceptualisation, data collection, and analysis. Many of the research results were unexpected or contrary to conventional assumptions. Thus, in addition to summarising research results, this section serves as an inventory of the latest contributions to the field. We cover five topics: ideas about women, gender politics and the state and how to study the topic; how women's movements speak for women; women's movements' success with the state; variation, comparison and explanation of findings; and representation of women through state feminism (Lovenduski and Guadagnini 2010).[3]

Ideas about women, gender politics and the state and how to study the topic

What is the state? Any effort to answer that question is likely to encounter a variety of views, from seeing states as monolithic patriarchal entities acting almost as individuals to seeing only blurred distinctions between states, governments and groups. Thirty years of studying women's movement activism has convinced many, including RNGS, that the idea of the monolithic state is not only unhelpful, but blinds those who assume it to be that way to what is really going on. RNGS found that the state comprises a variety of arenas for political action and debate, which validates work such as that by Pringle and Watson (1992). In this context, the state is permeable to advocates for change not always or inevitably but possibly and observably. Thus, advocates for women and gender equality women's movement actors can get access to the inside workings of the state.

Not only is the state open to pressure by activists from outside, it is likely that agencies inside the state will act as advocates for movement goals in policy debates as they did in 66 per cent of the cases in the RNGS research. When gender equality mechanisms are able to influence the terms of debates in policy subsystems such as on abortion reform or job training and to insert gendered ideas derived from women's movements, the result weakens the male gender-based 'logic of appropriateness' that policy actors have assumed.[4] In other words,

3. This is a direct link to the contributions of Joni Lovenduski to the RNGS capstone analysis. We see through Joni Lovenduski's life's work and RNGS' policy activities a roadmap for building bridges between science and politics where gender expertise grounded in the scientific method and rigorously designed studies serves as the path to the development of effective authoritative policies and structures that promote gender equality and women's rights. Ultimately, we believe, these endeavours can make democracies more democratic and improve lives of women and men.

4. This notion was first elaborated in early non feminist work on new institutionalism. Chappell (2006) and others, including Joni Lovenduski, have identified the gender bias of institutions in terms of a gender-biased 'logic of appropriateness'.

women's policy agencies forming temporary alliances with women's movement actors and presenting their views can, for one policy moment, gender the state to represent women's interests. Multiply such moments by many agencies, debates and countries, and we can see how new institutionalism can become feminist institutionalism.[5]

Thus, feminist criticism that the state is by definition resistant to gendering and the inclusion of women must be set aside as an assumption for research. Rather, whether or not the state will change to incorporate feminised ideas and advocates for women must become a question for empirical research. RNGS shows that states have accepted a changed gendering. Therefore, it's possible...let's find out when, where and why.

How women's movements speak for women

Although individual women are fully capable of speaking for themselves and making their wishes known, it is women's movements that express many of the ideas and goals of women in societies. Despite decades of research on social movements, reliable knowledge about the impact of movements on states and state structures remains limited. We have found that one of the problems with studying the ways that women's movements speak to the state on behalf of women has been weak conceptualisation of movements – both social movements and women's movements (McBride and Mazur 2008).

To conduct the RNGS study as well as future research on movements and the state we discovered that two assumptions are key. First, is the analytical separation of movement discourse from those actors that are part of movements. Movement discourse is the range of ideas and desires developed by women as they think about their place as women in society. The discourse is the essential core of any movement and separates it from other phenomena in a political society. At the same time, since the discourse is likely to be as varied as the women who produce it, it is impossible to study more than a tiny part of the production of discourse empirically. Women's movement actors, however, are those entities, formal and informal groups, that – articulate movement discourse in the public sphere. Actors and their statements are eminently observable.

The second key assumption is to remove the element of protest as an essential dimension of the definition of social movements and women's movements. Most social movement research relies on nominal definitions that require contentious activism against the state as a defining element of any social movement. However, especially when looking at women's movements, such a requirement prevents inquiry into a range of interactions with state actors and in policy arenas. It is important to make discovering the ways movements approach states a question for empirical research. This opens the way to see penetration by women's movement actors of state institutions and activities as well as protest against them.

---

5. An important focus of Joni Lovenduski's oeuvre.

The speech (oral and written) of women's movement actors in public settings as well as policy actors in women's policy agencies takes the form of frames.[6] Such frames in public debate are composed of the diagnosis of an issue, in other words, the problem that needs attention by policy makers, and a prescription for fixing the problem – a policy goal. Framing is the language of the politics of state feminism. Connections between women's movement actors and women's policy agencies and other state actors are made through explicitly gendered frames that show agreement or conflict in public debate and policy formation. When policy debates are gendered, it is more likely that movement actors will be included in the policy arenas. At the end of policy debates, if policies have content that is compatible with the frames that movement actors articulated, it is evidence of a positive state response to the movement. When women's policy agencies present frames that agree with those of movement actors and are effective in convincing policy actors to adopt the same frames and include movement actors in the process, we have evidence of state feminism.

Finally, we recognise that women's movement discourse may or may not be feminist discourse, that is, it may or may not challenge subordination, target gender hierarchies, or explicitly promote gender equity. For example, movement actors may seek votes for women because they see women as mothers and want their special perspective represented, or they may seek votes for women to overcome inequality and challenge men for power. It is important to differentiate between feminist and non-feminist frames in studying actions and outcomes pertaining to women's movement actors and agencies.

Women's movement actors may be successful in working with women's policy agencies in gendering policy debates to include attention to how policies affect women. In the RNGS project we called this outcome Movement State Feminism. Only in those instances where feminist frames find similar success is there the potential for movement actors and their agency allies to challenge the fundamental traditional gender logic of power. Given this potential, RNGS calls this outcome Transformative State Feminism.

Women's movement success with the state: State feminism

RNGS research findings show that women's movements have been successful in getting positive responses from states' policymaking apparatus. Such responses may be found in policy content or in incorporating movement actors into policy arenas, or both, the latter called Dual Response. Only 17 per cent of the cases found movement actors completely left out. The reasons for variations in rates and degrees of success are complex, context specific, and conditional. At the same time, the chances for success are significantly improved when women's policy agencies step up and advocate movement frames. In some debates on some issues, agencies make the difference between success and failure for women's movements

6. The RNGS project used the term micro-frame to distinguish the statements of movement actors and women's policy agencies from more general issue frames.

when other favourable conditions for movements are not present, in other words, they play an essential 'back-up' role.

The most effective agencies are Insiders.[7] It is the alliance between movement actors and insider agencies achieving state Dual Responses that is the core of movement state feminism. With such positive state responses comes cultural change within the state arenas because women's interests and participation have become part of the business of government. Such successes are due to the activities of movement actors and agencies in sensitising policy actors to the gendered aspects of policy problems, but these changes are often not permanent. There is an ongoing need for state feminism – effective alliances between agencies and movement actors in policy debates – to retain the gendering of policy frames and approaches over time.

Gendering the state in a transformative way is much rarer than movement state feminism. RNGS found a small incidence of cases (only 18 per cent) of movements and agencies both gendering policy debates with feminist frames that challenge gender hierarchies and promote gender equity and gaining feminist state responses. This is not due to a lack of feminist demands from movement actors; the rate of such frames increased over the decades of the study. Similarly, it was not due to women's policy agencies failing to put these ideas forward. Rather we found that agency feminist allies face a great many barriers in bringing feminist perspectives into the dominant state culture.

These limits on agency effectiveness do not deny the importance of women's policy agencies in understanding the unfolding relationships between women, women's movements and state actors. There has never been any doubt that what states do is a subject that enhances efforts to understand the effectiveness of social movement activism. RNGS research shows that institutional allies *inside* states are also an important part of understanding that effectiveness and should be a component of social movement theory. These allies have a place in the development of movement strategies as well as explaining and assessing movement success *vis-à-vis* the state.

Variation, comparison and explanation

The previous section summarised what we know generally about state feminism in Western postindustrial democracies. Now we review the analysis of the data as RNGS looked for patterns to compare and explanations for variations. The successes of women's movement actors across the thirteen countries in the study tended to increase over the last decades of the 20th century. At the same time, the activities of women's policy agencies on their behalf have not followed a longitudinal trajectory. There are various ideas about what might explain the pattern of successes and alliances.

---

7. Insiders are agencies that advocate movement actors' frames in a debate and are successful in gendering the frames used by policy actors.

- resource mobilisation theory suggests actors tend to be more successful with the state when they go after issues that are a high priority, are cohesive in their demands, and have more followers.
- political opportunity structure theory considers that the policy environment makes the difference between success and failure, such things as open access to policy arenas, weak counter movements, and compatible policy ideas.
- government (executive and parliament) formed by Left-wing parties close to movement organisations and ideas are more amenable to movement overtures.

After extensive mixed methods analysis,[8] we found that these conventional theories for explaining movement outcomes do not hold up. The puzzles and patterns of state feminism do not lend themselves to grand overarching solutions. Rather, explanation requires two components: (1) exploration of a variety of combinations of characteristics and contexts; and (2) a mixed methods approach to uncover their complexity. Putting RNGS qualitative and quantitative analyses together over time, policy sector, and country, we can offer some explanations for movement success that do hold up:

- the priority of an issue to women's movement actors as a whole;
- the degree of openness to outside actors in policy subsystems;
- the compatibility of frames of women's movement actors with those of policy actors; and
- alliances between movement actors, Left-wing parties and Left wing members of parliament (not necessarily the governing majority).

The complexity of state feminism is especially challenging when comparing and explaining the effectiveness of women's policy agencies (Insiders) in helping movement actors gain positive state responses. Many scholars suggest that structures, powers, administrative resources, and leadership make agencies more or less effective partners for movement activists. While such factors may be important in specific cases, our conclusion is that which characteristics are most helpful depends on the policy arenas where debates occur. Thus, there is no master design for creating an insider women's policy agency. These findings cast doubts about the expected link between institutional capacity and effectiveness as well.

This last observation points to one of the most important RNGS findings in the study of movement success and state feminism: the influence of policy sector. Rather than regional groupings or country patterns, the fate of advocates for women

---

8. In the capstone analysis, we used descriptive statistics, statistical analysis, qualitative comparative analysis and causal mechanism case studies.

addressing the state and its agencies more likely depends on the policy sector where the claim is made. Policy sectors refer to specific areas of government action based on large functional areas of government action, for example, environment, agriculture and health. Constellations of state and non-state actors or stakeholders form a policy subsystem to debate proposals and affect the direction of policy in that specific area. In the RNGS study, researchers gathered data about policy sectors where particular policy debates played out, such as, abortion reform, job training, or prostitution policy. Time after time, we found that patterns of state feminism movement success, the presence of insider agencies, and explanations for their success varied according to the policy sector, even though debates about those issues may have taken place at different times and in different countries.

Representation of women through state feminism

The RNGS data on women's movements, policy debates, women's policy agencies and state responses enticed Joni Lovenduski, working with Marila Guadagnini, to unpack state feminism politics and theory to see how they informed ideas about the political representation of women (Lovenduski and Guadagnini 2010). Using RNGS data to test propositions from feminist representation theory, they challenge previous research and help broaden state feminism theory and its applications. This work closely follows the questions, outlined in Chapter Three, that feminist scholars ask about substantive representation. Here we summarise this analysis.

Looking at the 'how' of representation in terms of efforts to gender policy debates Lovenduski and Guadagnini confirm that women's policy agencies are among the actors 'who' represent women. When these frames are feminist, agencies have the ability to challenge the status quo inside the state. The more agencies take up demands from women's movement actors, the greater the expansion of state structures to include representatives of women's interests. This finding confirms the assumption that placing gendered ideas into the frame of a policy debate usually gets women's representatives a place at the decision-making table.

Reviewing the discourse in the many debates in the RNGS data, the authors found that, until the 2000s, the agencies considered women as undifferentiated with the exception of some attention to class. Movement actors spoke for groups of women, such as workers, prostitutes, or those on public assistance, but rarely explicitly noted differences in race, ethnicity, region or religion. Combing the data for what it says about diversity found little attention to intersectionality. At this point, whatever knowledge the RNGS data provides to understand questions about 'which' women are represented in state feminism is limited.[9]

In contemplating 'where' representation occurs, authors incorporate RNGS findings about the openness of policy subsystems into their thinking. They drilled

9. This is due in large part to the time period of the study – the 1970s to the early 2000s when issues of race and ethnicity were less intertwined with gender issues as they are now, particularly in the European countries in the study.

down further and found that the overwhelming importance of legislatures as locations for final policy actions suggested the need to take a closer look at women legislators. They found that when policy subsystems are closed, which occurred in over half of the debates, intervention by women legislators improved the chances for movement success. This finding illustrates that legislators and agencies should be considered as allies for movement actors as predicted by the triangle of women's empowerment model.[10] Lovenduski and Guadagnini identified the same actors in the model as active representatives, but their findings challenge the notion of linkages in the form of a triangle. Rather, they found a line linking autonomous and integrated women's movement actors to women legislators as well as a separate and converging line where agencies act independently to effect representation.

Finally, the authors contribute evidence that, with respect to both descriptive and substantive representation of women, the presence of women in legislatures is only a bare beginning. They considered how 'effective' descriptive presence of women has been; this required them to see if there is some connection between the percentage of women in the legislature with one or another measure of effectiveness, such as agency representativeness, policy content (substantive outcomes), or movement actor presence in policy making. They found none. Rather, they present persuasive evidence that it is critical actors not critical mass that provide for the most effective representation. 'Where one or more women legislators take a stand in the debate, movements are more than twice as likely to achieve both substantive and descriptive representation than when non legislators do so' (Lovenduski and Guadagnini: 189–90).

RNGS deeds: Linking theory and practice

From the beginning, RNGS researchers intended to work with those actors who directly promote women's rights in policy. The hope was that both the approach and findings about alliances between women's movement actors and women's policy agencies or state feminism, would aid practitioners and activists to pursue their agendas on behalf of gender equality and women's interests more effectively. Reflecting an 'integrated empirical feminist approach' (Mazur 2012), RNGS researchers followed the rules of the scientific method in the study design and, as a group, sought to integrate this work into activist and policy arenas thereby making a difference in women's and men's lives. Many individual members served as consultants to women's policy agencies in their countries, in effect becoming 'femocrats' themselves.[11]

10. There are different terms used to capture the links within movements and among movements, state agencies, and women in legislatures: strategic partnerships; velvet triangles; feminist advocacy coalitions. Vargas and Wieringa (1998) are often cited as the first scholars to use the triangle metaphor.

11. Australian researchers first coined the term 'femocrat' to describe the feminists in government, usually in women's policy agencies (e.g. Eisenstein 1996). Since then, it has come to mean any

Here, we present four different ways that RNGS as a group turned their words into deeds by introducing findings, frameworks, and methodologies into practitioner and policy oriented arenas and thus contributed to the push for gender equality and women's rights.[12] Examining these nine different instances of turning words into deeds provides further insight into the complex process of how scientific research can affect social and policy change through policy expertise on gender.[13]

Policy recommendations to governmental organisations

One of the most straightforward ways that researchers can influence policy is by providing expert recommendations to government agencies at all levels: local, sub-national, national and extra-national. Bureaucrats or women's group activists may solicit researchers for proposals or recommendations for specific policy actions based on their work even without asking for a report or background paper. In the RNGS cases below, two of these types of actors contacted us, as co-conveners of RNGS, to provide recommendations for a specific governmental office, based on our studies of women's policy agencies and state feminism: a bureaucrat in the European Commission for the World Trade Organization and the director of the Institute for Women's Policy Research, a women's policy think tank, for the Obama administration in the USA.

Amendments proposed to the World Trade Organization (1998)

One of the first issue-specific books in the RNGS project looked at job training policy debates. In the process of preparing the book, we held a conference at the University of Washington through the Center for West European Studies on *Women and Social Rights in the European Union: Job Training and the Global Economy*. Most of the participants were members of RNGS and presented some preliminary results. Other gender and policy experts and practitioners also participated, including a bureaucrat from the European Commission, who was a European Union Fellow at the University of Washington at the time. Thus, the conference provided a venue for experts, researchers and policy actors to discuss issues of women's rights and gender equality in the context of employment policy and job training.

One of the major findings of the RNGS job training network is that the job training subsystem is highly restricted and closed to advocates of women's rights

---

individual who works for gender equality machineries.

12. It is important to note that these are not the only policy expert activities of RNGS researchers; many individuals were consulted by their own governments, international organisations, non governmental organisations, etc., often using their country specific RNGS research to provide expert opinions and recommendations. The French expert report examined below is an illustration of one of these national level consultation processes.

13. For more on gender expertise and its impact on feminist policy formation *see* Hoard (forthcoming).

and women's policy agencies. This is particularly the case in the European context, where collective bargaining agreements set the employment policy agenda and closed neo-corporatist style tri-partite negotiations between organised labour, management and labour ministries drive policy forward. Indeed, it was in one or two of the job training debates, where women's policy agencies played the crucial 'back-up' role, in gaining women's movement success mentioned above. That is, women's movement actors and their ideas, with little leverage to enter into policy discussions and little voice in organised labour and management, were brought forward by the state-based women's policy agencies.

For the 'Eurocrat' participating at the RNGS conference on job training at the University of Washington, these insights into how to bring gender equality into trade negotiations more effectively offered important lessons for the broader international employment policy community. He saw an opportunity in Kingdon's 'policy window' (1995) to introduce these findings during the re-formulation of the World Trade Organization's Codes of Conduct and International Labor Standards. Based on what he had learned at the conference, he asked us, the conveners of RNGS, to develop several gender-focused amendments for codes of conduct in order to include specific actors to represent women's rights issues and place women's policy agencies into the negotiations of collective agreements. We submitted these amendments to the WTO by official channels through the European Commission, just six months after the conference.

IWPR recommendations to the Obama administration (2008)

In the aftermath of President Obama's election, women's groups, under the leadership of the D.C.-based women's policy think tank, the Institute for Women's Policy Research, teamed-up to call for a stronger women's policy agency presence in the US federal government. Our work with IWPR since the early 2000s (*see* below), had put the RNGS project on Director's Heidi Hartman's radar screen. She contacted us for advice on a briefing paper that was eventually presented to the Obama administration. We made the following four recommendations based in large part of the work of the USA team, Dorothy McBride and colleague Janine Parry, but also on some of the larger lessons learned from the RNGS study as a whole. The first two recommendations were adopted by the Obama administration.

1. A White House office for women's equality that is a correspondent with the Women's Bureau in the Department of Labor and other women's policy agencies in government departments.
2. An Inter Agency Cabinet Council to promote gender equity across departments.
3. Reinvigorate the Women's Bureau as the hub for coordinating the interagency work and the site for any Commission that officially brings in the full range of women's group voices into policy deliberations.
4. The adoption of the Women's Bureau model for all government departments: Agency with statutory authority, placed at the top policy-

making circles with regional offices with a citizen's advisory commission to connect to the constituencies.

Research funded by a women's policy agency

Women's policy agencies often have budgets for research to fund specific projects; in some cases they ask researchers to make specific policy recommendations based on them. In the RNGS study, 46 per cent of all agencies had research staff and/or funds to finance external research projects. At the same time, nearly 40 per cent devoted less than 15 per cent of the budget to research, and only 7 per cent had moderate or high levels of funding.

Women's rights service in France (1997–2000)

In 1997, the Women's Rights Service in the French Ministry of Employment and Solidarity awarded project funding to Amy Mazur, also Director of the French RNGS team. The French women's policy agencies, like all government agencies in France, dedicate a good portion of their operating budgets for funding research projects studies with scientific rationale but also with policy implications and recommendations. In the late 1990s, femocrats in the Service were very interested in the influence of women's policy agencies at the sub-national and local levels. France has long had an established territorial women's rights administration with regional and departmental delegations, and in the mid 1990s certain city governments created new municipal women's rights commissions. The femocrats in the Service wanted to have a more systematic study of these different levels of agencies alongside the national-level RNGS study. The research monies supported two goals: (1) the French translation of the RNGS national studies across the five policy areas; and (2) a new sub-national study of the regional, departmental and city level offices in the Provence Côte d'Azur region across the same five policy areas.[14] The final report included the study findings, a future research agenda and the following policy recommendations:

1. Increase the staff and budgets of the territorial agencies;
2. Develop a more systematic approach to mainstreaming;
3. Use the term 'gender' officially in policy documents;
4. Develop formal training for all femocrats;
5. Develop training modules on gender equality at the administrative elite training schools (Grande Ecoles);
6. Develop more specific administrative orders about gender equality policy with each individual ministry.

14. The research team included Amy Mazur, Claudie Baudino, Jean Robinson and Andrew Appleton.

Reports to international organisations

International organisations like the World Bank, the United Nations, and the European Union have increasingly taken on pivotal roles in promoting gender equality policies, women's rights, and women's participation in decision making in the global arena (e.g. Pruegl *et al.* 2012). As such, they are important forums for the articulation of gender equality issues and demands for policies as well as commissioners of gender expertise. For many of these international organisations, expert reports with recommendations are the lifeblood of their policy deliberations; they provide the informed opinions that serve as the background and foundation for larger policy proposals about gender equality. We present two instances where we filed such reports based on RNGS research: the first for a United Nations Expert Group Meeting on Women's Political Participation and the second for a Background Paper for the 2012 World Development Report of the World Bank.

RNGS results presented at United Nations EGM (2005–2006)

In 2005, the Division for the Advancement of Women of the UN contacted RNGS as part of planning for an Expert Group Meeting in Addis Ababa, Ethiopia, on 'Equal Participation of Women and Men in Decision-making Processes, with Particular Emphasis on Political Participation and Leadership'.[15] This EGM was an extension of the international women's rights policy process that the Women's World Summit in Beijing in 1995 had set in motion. The RNGS conveners responded to the call. Amy Mazur presented a working paper for the Expert Group Meeting and provided the DAW organisers with a list of experts from RNGS' growing network of associates who also had knowledge to contribute to the EGM.[16] Mazur along with Shirin Rai (Warwick University and a RNGS associate), acted as rapporteur and put together a common report of all of the experts at the meetings in Ethiopia. She later presented the final report to the UN Commission on the Status of Women and to the NGO forum held at the same time as the Commission meeting in New York City.

The report assessed the factors that contribute to increasing women's representation and placed gender equality mechanisms at the center of any strategy

15. The expert group meeting format is a major instrument of the UN to bring experts together to present their research and to write collectively a common report from that presented research and produce a series of policy recommendations to the UN. An EGM typically takes 3–4 days and the final report is presented to the United Nations through formal channels. For the EGM reports, including the RNGS report and the final report to the United Nations go to http://www.un.org/womenwatch/daw/egm/eql-men/index.html.

16. RNGS also compiled a list of over 100 associates who had some link to the study and/or activities of women's policy agencies. The RNGS contact list is available on request.

to promote women's descriptive and substantive representation. The experts also argued that in order to 'go beyond numbers' to promote gender equality effectively in policy outcomes, there needed to be a combination of critical actors, and critical structures – effective women's policy agencies – at critical junctures. Thus, the RNGS view of women's policy agencies as important sites of representation was an integral part of the final report and recommendations. Two series of recommendations were finally made: (1) for increasing the number of women in decision making; and (2) for enhancing the impact of women's increased presence in decision making.

Background paper for world development report (2012)

The World Bank commissioned us to prepare a background paper on the design and effectiveness of gender equality mechanisms for the World Development Report in 2012, which was to have a significant gender component.[17] We focused on how to take the RNGS findings and apply them to understanding women's policy agencies outside of the West. The first part of the paper presented the findings. It assessed the usefulness of the RNGS measurement tools for research in countries outside the west along with a set of questions that must be considered in designing such a tool. We concluded with a list of conditions that, in various combinations, may lead to agency success and policy recommendations for designing gender machineries in the western democracies.

The second part of the paper offered a critical analysis of published work on gender machineries in developing countries. Based on a systematic inventory of the literature on these structures it showed the extent to which we have credible evidence that documents if, how and why gender machineries have been important and effective 'institutional channel[s] for gender policies and guidelines for the State'. The report concluded with a presentation of policy recommendations intended to promote more systematic studies of gender machinery performance. Thus in this case, more than conventional recommendations for government action, the suggestions focused on a new research agenda and methods to advance that agenda, in large part based on the RNGS approach. The background paper was used in Chapter Eight, 'Pathways to Reform' of the World Development Report.

Policy practitioner/activist dissemination and networking

In this last category of transposing words to deeds, we focus on more informal links between research and practice through women's groups, policy practitioners, and individual citizens. Across all four of these networking and disseminating activities, RNGS researchers tried to bring the lessons learned from their research to inform a more practical approach to promoting women's rights and gender equality.

---

17. Go to the RNGS website for a copy of our background paper.

IWPR Collaborations (2005)

A big part of our work with this women's policy think tank was to bring our research findings to practitioners and activists who could use what we had learned in their own political work. We began getting to know the team at IWPR in the early 2000s and had talked about possible collaborations with their research – a major part of their own policy and lobbying work (http://www.iwpr.org/). The IWPR policy conferences are an exemplar for bringing academics, activists and practitioners together to talk about women's policy issues. They saw our project as a way to bring more international focus to their mostly US-based activities. Thanks to our common goals and the support of their leadership, we hosted a daylong conference on the RNGS study, *Government Allies for Gender Equality: A Transatlantic Dialogue*, as part of the 8th Annual IWPR International Policy and Research Conference, June 2005. Thanks to NSF and other government funding we were able to bring fifteen RNGS researchers to present their findings at an informal poster session and to network with the over 600 attendees. We also brought femocrats in from different countries to discuss what makes for successful state feminist action. All in all it was an important moment for RNGS scholars and for scientific pursuits more generally to have an informal setting where policy practitioners and academics could meet and informally talk about their work.

Practitioner Meeting on RNGS- Belgium Research (2008)

A day-long workshop was held in Brussels with similar goals to the IWPR mini conference: to bring RNGS research to more applied settings. The RNGS Belgium team came together to discuss how its findings could help to promote women's rights in Belgium; members from the Belgium women's council attended and actively participated. They commented on how useful the RNGS approach to studying policy debates to identify women's movement participation and the presence of their ideas could be as a tool for assessing their own work and to validate it with various policy actors. We realised at this meeting that RNGS findings and lessons could be very useful to activists and practitioners and that we should consider how to better disseminate those findings to a broader audience outside of traditional academic publication venues.

User's Guide (2011)

With this goal of dissemination in mind from the Belgium meeting, we developed a pamphlet with tips for individual concrete action to promote women's rights and gender equality based on the RNGS study and findings, 'How do you make gender equality mechanisms (GEMS) work? Lessons from RNGS.'[18] The guide includes a summary of how 'GEMs can make a difference' through their back-up role, a list

18. For an electronic copy go to the RNGS website. We are also happy to send you as many hard copies as you would like!!! Just contact us.

of tools to evaluate and assess GEMs, as well as a list of 'best practices'. We have sought to distribute the guide as widely as possible by targeting many different women's policy agency staff as well as academics and activists with women's groups. We welcome feedback on the guide's usefulness.

Women's World Conference Networking: Does Research on State Feminism Travel? (2011)

From the beginning, the RNGS research project focused on postindustrial democracies rather than non-Western countries. At the same time, we and others have long been interested in exploring the ways the state feminism approach might be useful to scholars who are interested in studying women's policy offices in transitional regimes. Our work on the World Bank report allowed us to reflect in a systematic and formal way about this challenge. Over the years we had collected names of experts and others interested in this question, in case we might have an opportunity to bring people to discuss moving beyond the West.

Thanks to a tip from Melissa Haussman, one of our RNGS issue leaders, we found the Women's Worlds Conference in Ottawa in 2011 to be that long awaited opportunity. We offered a half-day workshop that attracted 19 scholars and activists from 10 different countries. We used our World Bank background paper as a major touchstone for discussing how to approach gender equality mechanisms across the globe from both a policy and research perspective. This group agreed to build a loose network through a leadership team of individuals from Thailand, Sub Saharan Africa and North America called 'Going Global with State Feminism' to help regionally based groups pursue coordinated research on women's policy agencies.[19] Time constraints and workloads have prevented the group from going beyond this initial launching phase; but it may be brought back on line in the near future, and of course if you are interested, feel free to contact us.

Conclusion

The RNGS project, in many ways, exemplifies the oeuvre and values of Joni Lovenduski; indeed, she has been a major architect of and contributor to its varied facets. The RNGS study has built from and made contributions to various theory-building efforts that Joni has pursued throughout her career and intersects with most of them. Gender and public policy, feminist institutionalism, gendering political science, comparative politics and cross-national analysis, state feminism and representation are all research contributions made by both Joni and RNGS as a whole. The way in which RNGS has taken seriously the complex and time-consuming process of transposing research findings into practice and political action, resonates with the importance the broader, empirical feminist community places on transposing words into deeds.

19. All workshop materials are on the RNGS website.

References

Chappell, L. (2006) 'Comparing Political Institutions: Revealing the Gendered "Logic of Appropriateness"', *Politics and Gender*, 2 (2): 223–225.

Eisenstein, H. (1996) *Inside Agitators: Australian femocrats and the state*, Philadelphia: Temple University Press.

Hoard, S. (forthcoming) 'Does gender expertise matter? Toward a theory of policy success', Palgrave.

Kingdon, J. (1995) *Agendas, Alternatives and Public Policies*, New York: Harper Collins.

Lovenduski, J. and Guadagnini, M. (2010) 'Political Representation', in D. E. McBride and A. G. Mazur (eds) *The Politics of State Feminism: Innovation in comparative research*, Philadelphia: Temple University Press, pp.164–192.

McBride, D. E. and Mazur, A. G. (2010) *The Politics of State Feminism: Innovation in comparative research*, Philadelphia: Temple University Press.

— (2008) 'Women's Movements, Feminism and Feminist Movements', in G. Goertz and A. Mazur (eds) *Politics, Gender and Concepts: Theory and methodology*, Cambridge: Cambridge University Press, pp. 219–43.

Mazur, A. G. (2012. 'A Feminist Integrative and Empirical Approach in Political Science: Breaking down the glass wall', in H. Kincaid (ed.) *Oxford Handbook of the Philosophy of Social Science*, Oxford: OUP, pp. 533–58.

Pringle, R. and Watson, S. (1992) 'Women's Interests and the Post Structuralist State', in M. Barrett and A. Phillips (eds) *Destabilizing Theory: Contemporary feminist debates*, Cambridge: Polity Press, pp. 53–73.

Pruegl, L., Caglar, G. and Zwingel, S. (eds) (2012) *Feminist Strategies in International Governance*, London-New York: Routledge.

Vargas, V. and Wieringa, S. (1998) 'The Triangle of Empowerment: Processes and actors in the making of public policy for women', in G. Lyclama à Nijeholt, V. Vargas and S. Wieringa (eds) *Women's Movements and Public Policy in Europe, Latin America, and the Caribbean*, New York: Garland, pp. 3–23.

Vignette – Women and the State: Re-gendering our institutions

Baroness Howe

Elspeth Howe, Baroness Howe of Idlicote was awarded her life peerage in 2001, she was one of the first British 'People's Peers'. Her husband is the British Conservative party politician, Geoffrey Howe, Baron Howe of Aberavon; the couple each hold their peerages in their own right. She has served on many British public bodies, including as deputy chair of the Equal Opportunities Commission (1975–1979), on the Department of Employment's Working Group on Women's Issues between (1992–1997) and she chaired the Broadcasting Standards Commission (1993–1999). Baroness Howe has been witness to and a participant in the changing role of women in the British State; she reflects on what progress has been made and where there is still work to do.

The first Hansard Society Women at the Top Report – which I Chaired was published in 1990: it identified the 'formidable' barriers that women faced in public life. These included structural barriers, working practices, and above all, attitudes that prevented women from reaching senior positions in the public and private sectors. There was indeed a 'glass ceiling'. Discrimination was widespread – direct and overt; and indirect and disguised. For politics, the Report recommended a Speaker's Conference to consider the ways in which Parliament, and party practices and procedures, place women at a real disadvantage; that political parties should scrutinise their own policies and practices, and eliminate those that serve to hinder the progress of women; and that women Life Peers should be created to ensure fair representation.

Fifteen years later, the fourth Hansard Society Report *Changing Numbers, Changing Politics*, co-authored by Joni Lovenduski, was focused more narrowly than the 1990 report, with analysis of developments in the political sphere, and an exploration of the impact these women MPs had had. As I made clear in my foreword, some significant progress had been made in the intervening period, with women MPs comprising nearly 20 per cent of the total membership of the House of Commons by 2005, and with women's representation in the Scottish Parliament and National Assembly for Wales after the first devolved elections higher, at 40 per cent and 50 per cent respectively. I made it clear too that justice demands that political inequality between women and men should be addressed.

The 2005 Report argued that much of the relative improvement in women MPs' presence at Westminster between 1990 and 2005 reflected changes in the legislative framework within which politics takes place. The Labour Party's use of All Women Shortlists, first used in 1997, and, then since 2005, was legally permitted by the Sex Discrimination (Election Candidates) Act which was passed in 2002. This law initially allowed political parties to use such equality measures until 2015; whilst later legislation, the Equality Act 2010, extended this provision until 2030. I concluded that the authors had made the most persuasive presentation yet of the case that only All Women Shortlists will result in significant and lasting change; that merely using the language of equality or promoting equality, perhaps through special training or financial assistance, does not guarantee that women candidates will be selected for winnable seats, and hence that the numbers of women MPs will not necessarily increase. I was, then, certainly not against what the Labour Party did in 1997. I noted too, back in 2005, that not all of the UK's political parties had sought to take advantage of this. This remains true today: both the Liberal Democrats and the Conservatives continue not to take up the opportunities provided by the Sex Discrimination (EC) law.

In 2008–10 a Speaker's Conference called for in that first *Women at the Top* report, was established under Gordon Brown's premiership. It would once again review the obstacles that women, and other groups, face in achieving equality in politics. Some, but by no means all, of its recommendations have been introduced since. As many of these made clear, it is critical to report and monitor outcomes in politics (and business for that matter).

As far as political oversight of businesses' equal opportunity practices and their approach to ensuring that women of equal ability progress to top jobs in their organisation is concerned, there has been some progress. We do now have a situation where all the political parties realise that in a world market we need to maximise each individual's potential.

So what is now required of companies is that as well as selecting all their entrants on a sex equality basis, they must plan the expected route and support for their high flier entrants. The Davies Report – Women on Boards (2011) requires a yearly progress report of those intended for company top jobs, and though the plan is to achieve an equal number of top job opportunities in companies for women as well as men in this way, if this doesn't succeed, then legislation to achieve this will be introduced.

As far as my own work in the Lords is concerned, certainly my background in equal opportunities, continues to influence my activities there but not, of course, exclusively. I was the first Deputy Chairmen of the Equal Opportunities Commission from 1975–1979, and although in 2001 when appointed to the Lords as a Cross Bench Peer, I had been Chairman of the Broadcasting Standards Commission since 1993, it was my experience of working for women's equality that equally underlay my nomination for the Upper House. But my interest began even earlier than that. Women's inequality was made real to me by the knowledge that women who had worked for the national interest in both World Wars (manning the factories) and supported in these roles by state provision of childcare, were pushed back into the home once the men returned from the battlefield. Later experience with the Conservative Party highlighted the then current views of Tory women who felt that women seeking parliamentary selection should be – at home looking after their children. However, I was one of a growing number who took up women's rights within the party. And travelling with my husband whilst he was Foreign Secretary (1983–1989) gave me the opportunity to see progress in other countries – particularly in the USA.

Let me end with a comment on what still remains an important issue. Women's career choices still depend on the kind of careers advice young women receive. This was a problem when I was at the EOC and still is. Young women need to know of choices beyond hairdressing and secretarial work. They need to be made aware too of the financial consequences of certain career choices – and indeed of the country's shortages, and what's available in their own area. And engineering remains far too dominated by men! I'm glad to say a few more young women are now entering that profession, but there is room for many more. So please, from now on far better trained careers advisors for girls!

Chapter Seven

The Critical Mass Theory in Public and Scholarly Debates

Drude Dahlerup

> Women have gained the right to vote, and possess de jure equality, in nearly all Member States of the United Nations. However, despite forming at least half the electorate in most countries, they continue to be underrepresented as candidates for public office. In 1995, approximately 10 per cent of members of national assemblies across the world were women (*Beijing Declaration and Platform for Action*, Article 182) and even fewer women held positions in the government. These figures fall short of reaching the target of having 30 per cent of women in positions at decision-making levels by 1995 endorsed by the Economic and Social Council. The figure of 30 per cent forms the so-called 'critical mass', believed to be necessary for women to make a visible impact on the style and content of political decision-making process.
>
> (UN Division for the Advancement of Women, DAW, 2005[1])

Introduction

All over the world one can hear the argument, that 'it takes a certain number or percentage of women in politics, *a critical mass*, to make a difference'. An increase to 30 per cent women is often pointed out as the minimum requirement, as in the UN statement above. Frequently, it is argued that a correlation between the numbers or rather the share of women in political assemblies and women 'making a difference' has been proved 'by research'. But is this true?

This article will scrutinise the critical mass argument in the scholarly debates, and at the same time analyse how the critical mass argument, in spite of scholarly reservations has spread among those advocating an increase in women's political representation ever since the 1980s. During the last decades it has moreover been instrumental to the rapid spread of electoral gender quotas all over the world (Dahlerup 2006a; Krook 2009). It is no coincidence that 30 per cent is the most

1. Concept paper for the expert meeting on 'Equal participation of men and women in decision-making processes', Addis Ababa, Ethiopia, 24–27 Oct. 2005.

commonly used candidate quota percentage, be it quotas by law or party quotas adopted by individual political parties (www.quotaproject.org).

The political use of the critical mass 'theory' is an outstanding example of the close, yet complex links between gender research and gender equality policies. No doubt, feminist scholarship (publications, speeches at political conferences, counselling) has been important, may be more important that we have previously realised, for the actual increase in women's representation in many countries.[2]

The analysis of the public debate reveals that the argument of a critical mass is most commonly being used under two circumstances. Firstly, and most importantly, as an argument for increasing the number of women in political assemblies to a substantial level. Secondly, women politicians have frequently made used of the critical mass argument when defending themselves against the critique, predominantly from feminist organisations, that they have not make enough of a difference after they have been elected. Women politicians have defended themselves by arguing that one cannot expect them to make major changes, as long as they are only a small minority in the elected assemblies – adding that this has been proved 'by research'.

Critique of women politicians for not making a difference, has, however, also been expressed publicly by commentators, who are in fact sceptical about a gender perspective in politics, and who do not see women's under-representation as a problem worth discussing. Why campaign to elect women, if they do not make any difference? Gender is not important, it is argued.

Consequently, it is highly relevant to look closer at the alleged link between women's share of the political assemblies and the difference they make once elected. It will be argued in this article, that even if the critical mass argument appears to be primarily a prediction about what will happen once women's representation exceeds a certain crucial threshold, it has mostly been applied to the opposite situation, when women's representation amounts to *less than 30 per cent*. In its historical context, the critical mass argument should be interpreted as an attempt to shift the focus from women's alleged lack of qualifications in politics to a critique of the conditions women meet when entering the political arena in small numbers. It points to the inequality embedded in the political norms and culture, which in most countries developed before women had access to the political arena.

One crucial question is *what differences* are expected from a growing number of women in politics. It will, however, be argued that the critical mass argument seems to be strategically most effective in building broad advocacy coalitions, when it is *not* specified what 'difference' more women in politics will make. This problem is so to speak left to the future after the critical mass of women has been obtained.

Within the expanding research field of gender and politics, the critical mass theory has been the object of numerous interesting discussions, but little empirical testing. In 2002, Studlar and McAllister state that the idea of a critical mass

2. Joni Lovenduski's work in the United Kingdom is an excellent example of this.

constitutes more of a theoretical expectation than a demonstrated effect (2000: 234). Manon Tremblay calls it a 'dogma' (2006: 502) and Joni Lovenduski talks about an 'underdeveloped concept' (2001). Karen Beckwith and Kimberly Cowell-Meyers state that the critical mass theory is both problematic and under-theorised in political science (2007).The actual increase in women's representation in a number of countries over the last decades, with thirty-eight countries having passed the 30 per cent threshold by summer 2014 (www.ipu.org) has actually improved the possibilities of operationalising and testing what ought to be labelled the critical mass *hypothesis*, rather than the critical mass *theory*.

This chapter first looks at the origin of the critical mass hypothesis before discussing the Scandinavian legacy, being the first area with more than 30 per cent women in parliament and local councils. The normative claim for why women should make a difference is then discussed and three areas are selected for special scrutinising of the debate and possible testing of the critical mass hypothesis: changes in workplace culture; policy changes; and finally, changes in women's numerical representation, a less discussed field in the critical mass discussion. The chapter then addresses the surprising revival of the critical mass argument, namely in the more neo-liberal coloured discussion, which has followed after the extraordinary Norwegian law demanding a 40–60 per cent quota for both sexes in the boards of the biggest public and private companies.

The origin of the critical mass hypothesis

The concept of a critical mass is borrowed from nuclear physics, where it refers to the smallest amount of fissile material needed for a sustained nuclear chain reaction, in general terms an irreversible take-off into a new situation or process.

By analogy, the term critical mass has been used since the 1980s in gender and minority research within the social sciences about an expected qualitative change, a turning-point, which may be an irreversible take-off into a new situation, following an increase in number or percentage of those under-represented or out-numbered. It makes a difference whether women, and in a similar way, blacks or immigrants, constitute a small or a large minority in an organisation or assembly (Dahlerup 1988a).

But is it possible to make such an analogy from physics to social life? In physics, the concept of a critical mass is applied to processes, which takes place in isolated entities or rooms. In social science there is hardly any entity which does not have at least some interaction with its surroundings. Consequently, the analogy has its limitations.

Today, the term critical mass is being used in many other contexts as well, as about diffusion of innovations or even as a name for regular bicycle protest events, which have spread all over the world, since Ted White's film *Return of the Scorcher* from 1992 showed, how in the crowded Chinese traffic, bicyclists would queue up at unregulated intersections until the backlog reached a 'critical mass', at which point that mass would move through the intersection!

Moss Kanter's theory

The first scholarly use of the concept of critical mass in political science research on gender and politics was inspired by organisational theory, not least by the American sociologists, Rosabeth Moss Kanter's (1977) research on 'women' and 'blacks' as minorities in organisations. Without using the concept of a critical mass, Kanter makes the point, that '[t]he life of women in the corporation was influenced by the proportion in which they found themselves' (1977: 207). Moss Kanter identified four types of group on the basis of different proportional representation of socially different people, be it women and men or blacks and whites: the *uniform group* or organisation, the *skewed group* (with a minority of no more than 15 per cent, which often functions as 'tokens', and have 'only woman' status, and become 'symbols of how-women-can do') and the *tilted group* in which the efficiency of the minority increases and it is becoming strong enough to begin to influence the culture of the whole group, and alliances between minority group members become a possibility. The previous 'tokens' have turned into a 'minority'. The ratios for the tilted group is not clear in the book, in the text defined as 65:35, in the tables, however, from 15 to 40. Finally in the *balanced* group, defined as 40:60 and down to 50:50) the gender or race becomes less important than other structural and personal factors (Kanter 1977: ch.8, for various interpretations *see* Dahlerup 1988a, 2006b; Mateo-Díaz 2005; Childs and Krook 2006, 2008).

The foundation of Moss Kanter's reasoning is that within their human similarities, there are differences in culture and behaviour between the minority and the majority group, not by birth (biological arguments being otherwise the most common at that time) since differences, Kanter argues, can better be explained by 'roles and situations' (1977: xiii). The majority in an organisation places its mark on the organisational culture, which gives the minority many kinds of difficulties. The problems for women in the corporations derive from women's minority position, not from being women. Other minorities, such as blacks, will encounter the same problems, she argues.

With her work, Kanter pointed to important dynamics for minorities within organisations, even if one may argue that the cultural and social position of specific groups in society in general cannot be disregarded: the successful careers of the small group of male nurses illustrate this point. And the working conditions and salaries of women workers in the textile industry were always very poor, in spite of women being the majority of the workers, or may be even because of this gender distribution. However, Kanter's contribution was important because she directed the attention to what happens within the organisations and institutions at what she labels 'the intermediate level' (1977: x).

The critical mass argument has been transferred into political life on the basis that politics is also a workplace with its own internal rules, norms and practices. Women were newcomers, even intruders, when during the first many decades after enfranchisement the elected women were few, under 10 per cent in most old Western democracies (Dahlerup and Leyenaar 2013). The theory of a critical mass and minority theory is focusing on identical problems (Lovenduski 2001).

Mercedes Mateo-Díaz has criticised the extrapolation of the findings from the corporations to the political arena, not least because the symbolism (perceptions, identifications) is much stronger when it comes to the act of representation. Mateo-Díaz also criticises the assumption that changing working conditions for women will lead to substantial differences in policies (2005: 119 f). Following the same line, a distinction is here made between women politicians' *ability* to perform their task as politician the way they want, feminist or not feminist (the working conditions) and their *commitment* to work for gender equality (the policy dimension) even if the two perspectives are not unconnected (Dahlerup 2006b).

The Scandinavian legacy

Marie Wilson, head of the White House Project, a nonpartisan organisation in New York that works to elect women to all levels of office, sets that 'critical mass' bar higher, at 33 per cent. That's closer to women's percentages in legislatures in Scandinavian nations, which have typically led the world in working toward gender equality (interview www.womensenews.org, Dec.27, 2012).

The small Nordic countries inhabit a special position in the critical mass debate, since they were the first to pass the 30 per cent threshold. In general, the Nordic countries are well-known globally for their early and high representation of women in politics, which combined with the general positive picture of the Scandinavian welfare state as being particularly 'women friendly' no doubt has contributed to the general idea, that many women in politics will make a substantial difference (Haavio-Mannila *et al.* [1983] 1985; Lovenduski 1986; Bergqvist *et al.* 1999; Freidenvall *et al.* 2006).[3] However, in the first decades after women's enfranchisement around World War 1, women's political representation in the Nordic parliament and local councils, with the exception of Finland, remained very low to the great disappointment of those women's organisations that had worked hard for women's right to vote and to stand for election. It was not until after World War 2 that the number of women in the elected assemblies slowly began to rise in all Nordic countries.

Figure 7.1 illustrates how the substantial increase in women's representation in the Nordic countries came with the 1970-80s, a period of extensive feminist mobilisation in Scandinavia as in most parts of the Western world. At the end of the 20th century, only five countries in the world had actually passed the 30 per cent threshold, among them four Nordic countries: Finland in 1983, Norway in 1985, Sweden in 1986, Denmark in 1990, and the Netherlands in 1992. In the 1980s and 90s such a high women's representation was outstanding.

The scientific study of gender and politics, originally labelled the study of 'women and politics' soon developed into a substantial research field within Nordic academia, and several comparative Nordic projects have been issued, financed by

3. Scandinavia usually refers to Denmark, Norway and Sweden, while the Nordic countries cover these three countries plus Finland and Iceland. Here the terms are used interchangeably.

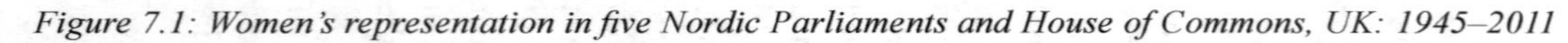

Figure 7.1: Women's representation in five Nordic Parliaments and House of Commons, UK: 1945–2011

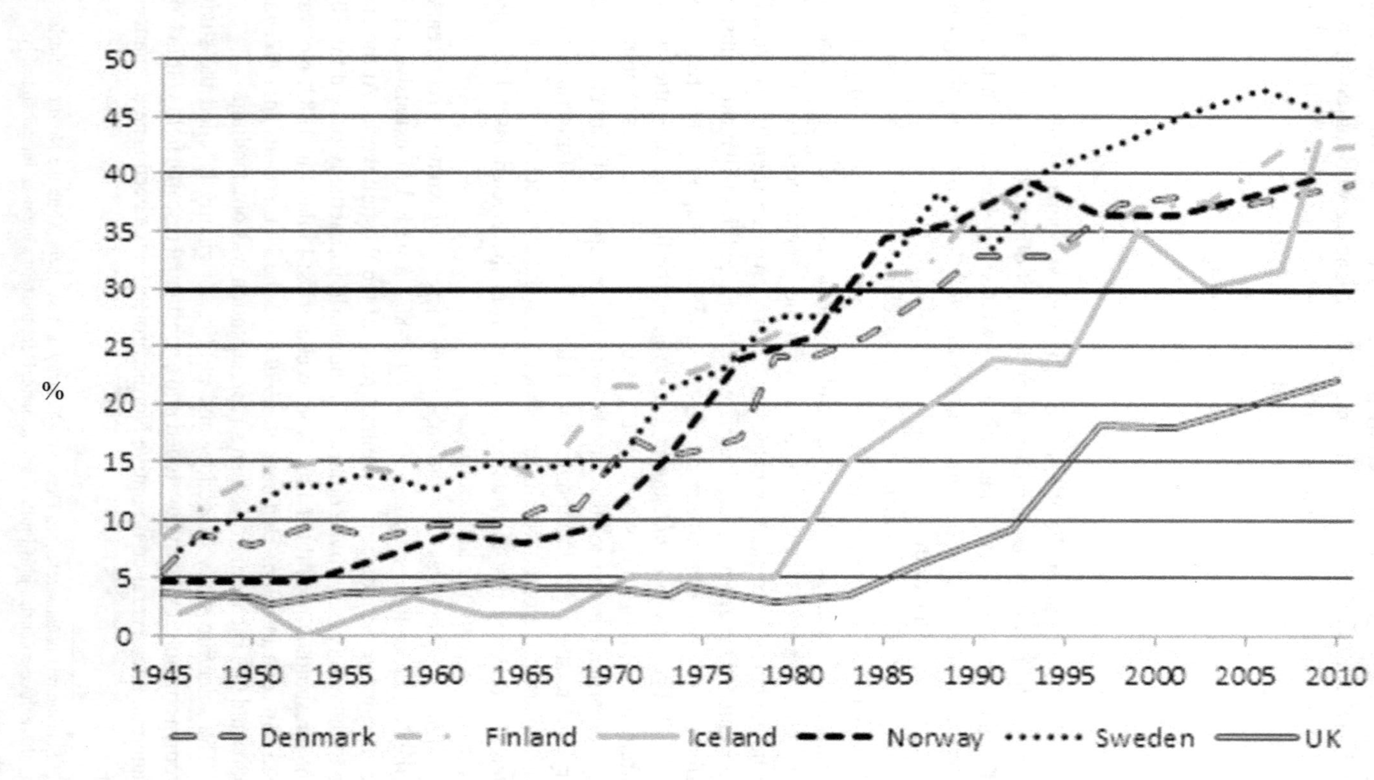

Sources: Kön och Makt i Norden, del 1 landrapporter; Statistics Norway, http://statbank.ssb.no/statistikkbanken/ ; European Parliament (2011)

the Nordic Council of Ministers (Haavio-Manilla *et al.* [1983]1985; Bergqvist *et al.* 1999; Niskanen and Nyberg 2009; Niskanen 2011). In the Nordic countries the interaction between feminist researchers on the one hand and feminist politicians and feminist movements and organisations on the other hand has been and still is intense, may be with a highpoint in the 1980s. The feminist discourse at the time was one of strong critiques, not of gains obtained: critique of male dominance which forced women to be politicians 'on the premises of men'; and strong critique of the fact, that the higher up in the hierarchy, the fewer women (the law of increasing disproportions) (Haavio-Manilla *et al.* 1985). One may argue that this strong critique also by feminist research has been conducive to changing male dominance in Nordic politics.

Many reforms were carried through during this period in a process of policy diffusion between the Nordic countries: free abortion on demand; split taxation and the removal of all other legal provisions, which made the man the head of household; part-time workers (mostly women) became entitled to unemployment benefit; the establishment of public gender equality agencies; public gender equality plans; extended public day care and equal treatment and equal pay provisions, first in the collective agreements, and later in legislation because of EU directives.

Consequently, there were many good reasons to start researching the thesis of the importance of the size of the minority in Scandinavian politics. In one of the first articles in political science, which made use of the critical mass theory, entitled 'From a small to a large minority: women in Scandinavian politics' (Dahlerup 1988a) I discussed the theory of a critical mass against Scandinavian experience with 20–30 per cent women in parliament and local councils. Was there any scientific evidence supporting the theory of a substantial change, now women had passed the 30 per cent threshold? This 1988-article argued that in order to answer this question, it is necessary to specify different dimension of political life that could be expected to change into a qualitatively new situation with more women in politics:

Dimension of possible change with a critical mass of women in parliament:

1. Changes in the reaction to women politicians
2. Changes in the performance and efficiency of the women politicians
3. Changes in the social climate of political life (the political culture)
4. Changes in the political discourse
5. Changes of policy (the political decisions)
6. Increase in the power of women (the empowerment of women) (Dahlerup 1988a: 283–84).

While the first dimension relates to the attitudes towards women performing political roles, the second and third dimension deals with the working conditions for women politicians. Dimension four, changes in the political discourse, points to the tone of the debates in the political assemblies, but touches also upon the discourses on women and gender equality in society in general. Dimension five concerns what most feminist advocates would see as most important, namely changes in public policy. Dimension six covers changes in the overall power or lack of power of women in society and in politics.

The general argument of the 1988-critical mass article was that in relation to most other dimensions than those dealing with the political workplace, critical acts seems more important than critical mass when it comes to human beings. Most importantly is 'the willingness and ability of the minority to mobilise the resources of the organisation or institution to improve the situation for themselves and the whole minority group' (1988a: 296). However, as Mercedes Mateo-Díaz critically states, the critical act perspective is not really embedded in Kanter's workplace perspective (Mateo-Díaz 2005: 122).

In the 1980s it was, however, difficult to find research on women in Nordic politics, which could support the critical mass hypothesis. Firstly, this was because of the general difficulties in isolating the effects of the sheer numbers of women from other influential factors and secondly, because the critical mass hypothesis requires studies over time, before and after the 30 per cent, which were not available at that time, as women in politics was a relatively new research area.

In a rare survey, the European Commission showed a general decrease from 1975 to 1983 and again to 1987 in the number of voters who 'had more confidence in a man than a woman as their member of parliament' (dimension one). The difference between female and male voters was minor compared to the huge variations between the countries, with more German and Italian voters being against a female representative, and much fewer in Denmark, which also held the highest number of women in parliament (Dahlerup 1988a: 286).[4] Speaking to dimension two, surveys among local politicians from both Sweden and Norway in the 1980s revealed that more female than male local politicians were dissatisfied with their own performance as politicians and felt they lacked personal influence in politics. Yet, there was only a slight or no gender difference in drop-out rates from local politics. These results were not correlated with different levels of women's representation in the municipalities (Wallin and Bäck 1981; Hellevik and Skard 1985). Interviews with Nordic women politicians in the 1980s showed awareness among women politicians of all political colours, especially among those in national politics, that the main problem was not women's alleged shortcomings, but barriers in the male dominated political culture. This no doubt contributed to the Nordic success in increasing women's representation to a world-wide high during the 1970-90s. But the evaluations about the advantages of a large number of women could differ:

> Of course one has to behave as naturally as possible and not make a fuss about oneself, but find one's place as one of them. But I feel more comfortable when

4. This survey was conducted by the European Commission among its member states in the 80s. Consequently, Denmark was the only Nordic country included.

> there are some women. I do not know why. I had the feeling that the men in a way built a wall around themselves and their clever economic thoughts (Interview with Elsi Hetemäki-Olander, vice chair and MP for the Conservative Party in Finland, in Dahlerup 1985, in English in Dahlerup 1988a: 287).

> I felt – embarrassing to admit – that it was pretty comfortable (being the only women in the local council). It gave me some advantages. Because the men had not so much to contribute with, had in fact no knowledge or experiences concerning the political issues I took up. So I felt I had some success with these issues (children's and women's issues). I was in fact the only one who knew anything about these issues [...] they would never have reached the political agenda without me (Gerd Forsell, Swedish Cons).

Later, she was elected to the County Council with more women:

> It is a positive difference, when you are many women and if you share perspectives. And if you really push for certain issues together. Then it is a tremendous advantage to be more women. But it is a dammed disadvantage, if in a mixed assembly of both women and men, the women do not believe that their female values have any significance (Interview with Swedish Gerd Forsell (Cons.) in Dahlerup 1985: 72).

In a survey among women's organisations and equality committees within all political parties in the five Nordic countries (WOC Survey 1984) all these women's organisations, except for one, answered in the affirmative to the following question: 'Do you believe that more women in politics will lead to change in what issues are brought forward?' However, many of them added: 'if there are a sufficient number of women, since the few women cannot make much of a difference'. Some argued that such changes have already occurred (Dahlerup 1988b: 292). This shows that the idea of the importance of the size of the minority was already part of the Nordic debate on women's political representation in the 1980s.

Were women in Scandinavian politics showing an increased commitment to gender equality and women's issues once their number grew (dimension 5)? It is hardly possible to draw this conclusion, because even if there were many feminist actions in the Nordic parliaments in the 1980, also across party lines, a large portion of the very few female parliamentarians in the 1920s and 30s actually worked for women's issues and gender equality. The Nordic countries have a long tradition, although with variations in strength, for informal cross-party collaboration among women politicians working for gender equality issues. Not in formalised women's caucuses, but sometimes even in a coordinated action, women politicians would raise new issues in their respective party factions in an attempt to persuade their male colleagues. To get women's issues and gender equality policies integrated into party platforms and government programmes as general political issues has been the strategy of Nordic feminists (Sainsbury 1993). However, this rather successful strategy makes it even more difficult to scrutinise the effect of the growing number of women politicians in Scandinavia than in less strong party systems.

The travel of the story of the critical mass

A Google search in 2013 on critical mass theory shows not only an extensive scholarly debate about the theory, but also an extensive use of it in public debate. In a Spanish translation, the 1988-article has circulated in Latin America (Dahlerup 1993). This is an example of how a new idea can travel around the world, when useful in various political contexts. For in spite of the scholarly reservation about the critical mass theory expressed in the 1988-article and other articles that followed, and in spite of the argument of Child and Krook that the two classic works of Kanter and Dahlerup 'have largely been misread – and thus misconstrued [...] with crucial implications for subsequent research on the relation between women's descriptive and substantive representation' (2008: 726) *the story* of the critical mass theory, e.g. the travelling of the argument around the world constitutes an interesting research subject in its own right (Dahlerup 2006b).

Should women make a difference?

What are the normative claims behind the wish that women shall make a difference? And what if women politicians do not turn out to make a difference, yes may be even explicitly do not want to make a difference as *women* politicians?

These questions should be placed within normative political theory on women's political representation. When women began to press for access to public life, they were faced with what Carole Pateman has labelled *Wollstonecraft's dilemma* named after one of the first feminist writers, Mary Wollstonecraft (1759–1797). It was taken for granted 'that for women to be active, full citizens they must become [like] men. But if, on the other hand, women were to retain their experiences and qualities, so that they were an integral part of their citizenship, women would remain marginalised' (Pateman 1989:14).

The arguments, which were used by the suffrage campaigns and later by advocates of more women in politics, reflect this dilemma. Firstly, according to the *justice argument*, women should be granted suffrage and later representation as a natural right, today expressed in terms of human rights. Under this perspective, women do not have to prove whether they are similar to or different from men, or if they will make a difference. But secondly, the demand for suffrage and, later, for increased or equal representation have also been based and still are, on *the experience argument*; as long as men and women live so different social lives, the experiences of (various groups of) women should not be excluded from political decision making. According to a third type of argument, *the interest argument*, less commonly used though, there is a conflict of interest between men and women regarding many political issues, and consequently men cannot represent women. For instance, why do we still have a gender gap in salary in favour of men in spite of decades of equal pay provisions and EU-directives? May be men do not really take an interest in equal pay?

While the two latter arguments consider representation as a means to make a difference, the justice argument, frequently used also by other under-represented or excluded groups, looks upon representation as a goal in itself, what we today would label symbolic representation (Kraditor 1965; Dahlerup 1978; Hernes 1982; Philips 1995).

In recent debates on women's representation, a fourth and a fifth argument are heard: *the utility argument*, according to which the society should make use of all talents in society, has gained in importance in newer discussions. It is a waste to exclude talented people for leadership positions because of their gender, skin or ethnicity. We will return to the utility-argument in connection with the new use of the critical mass argument in the most recent discussions about quotas for women in the steering boards of public and private companies. The last of the newer argument to be mentioned here is *the democracy argument*: if parts of the population are de facto excluded from influence, the political system will lack democratic legitimacy. In Iris Marion Young's words: 'The normative legitimacy of a democratic decision depends on the degree to which those affected by it have been included in the decisions-making processes and have had the opportunity to influence the outcomes [Iris Marion Young argues further, adding] on equal terms' (2000: 5–6, 23).

The European Women's Lobby has made use of a similar argument about democratic legitimacy in their 2008 campaign for *gender parity* in politics. Their argument gained extra strength because they placed it within the general discourse about the 'democracy deficit' of the European Union institutions:

> No Modern European Democracy without Gender Equality [...] The current under-representation of women in most elected assemblies in Europe, including in the European Parliament, is a serious democratic deficit threatening the legitimacy of European institutions and political parties (www.womenslobby.org).

The conclusion is that there is no one argument that unites all advocates for gender equal representation, apart from the argument that women are being de facto excluded (Dahlerup 2011). The critical mass hypothesis, however, seems predominantly to rest on the experience argument and the difference of interest argument, but as we shall see, even the neo-liberal utility discourse can make use of the critical mass argument.

The demand for gender parity in politics does not necessarily presuppose that all women have the same interests and demands, if one, as Young, takes a more dynamic approach to representation based on a model of deliberative democracy. Then the inclusion of women is primarily a question of democratic legitimacy. Young strongly argues against seeing the inclusion of women as a kind of interest representation. She argues that representation is a dynamic relationship, not a substitution or identification (2000)[5].

---

5. This could also be seen as an argument against Judith Butler, who has criticised the feminist movement and feminist theory for seeking political representation based on an assumed existing common identity (Butler1990/99: 3).

A. Critical mass and change in the political workplace culture

> In 1993, a Member of Parliament missed a vote in the Canadian House of Commons while she was searching for a women's washroom. Shortly afterward, the large men's washroom off the lobby of the chamber was converted into separate facilities for men and women. It has been suggested that Parliament will change as more women are elected. Research indicates that to have a significant impact on the culture of an organisation, women must occupy at least one-third of the available space – the target referred to as the 'critical mass of women'. It would be expected, then, that Parliament might become a more women-friendly environment when Canada approaches that critical mass – which brings us back to the question of electing more women to Parliament. (Julie Cool, Library of the Canadian Parliament, Publ. No 05-62Em 2010).

Today, a considerable amount of the scientific literature on gender and politics discusses how to reformulate the critical mass hypothesis in order to make it apt for empirical testing. In the following, this newer discussion of the critical mass hypothesis is scrutinised within three selected dimensions or areas: 1) Changes of the workplace culture; 2) Change of policy (substantive representation); and 3) Acceleration in women's numerical representation (descriptive representation).

In this quotation above from the Canadian parliament, the critical mass hypothesis is used concerning the situation of women in the *political workplace*. The workplace perspective was the focus of Moss Kanter's classic article, although her focus was on minorities, be it women or blacks in big corporations. The arguments behind the critical mass hypothesis in this field is that as a small minority women become tokens or proxies to those holding power positions in the parties, and that the few women are turned into representatives of Woman, and if they fail, women as a category are seen as a failure in politics. Further, Kanter argues, people from the minority tend to be unable to form coalitions, since it is a looser strategy to associate yourself with others from the minority.

From a methodological point of view it is, however, difficult to distinguish the effect of the increasing number of the minority on the political workplace culture from other important factors of change, some of which might have contributed to the enhanced female representation. Nevertheless, it is too early to dismiss the relevance of the size of the minority in organisations. Comparative studies over time or between units, for instance municipalities in one country with different levels of women's representation, is a relevant research strategy.

The critical mass hypothesis, it is most important to observe, has been very instrumental in exposing a critique of the conditions women politicians meet in male dominated political institutions. In this way, the massive critique of women politicians' alleged lack of qualifications and lack of adaption to the established norms has being exchanged with a critique of the established institutions themselves, as in the following quotation.

> When a liberal politician, Jutta Zilliacus, in the 1970s was appointed as the first woman ever to the board of the public radio in Finland, the newspapers wrote about 'poor Jutta', since it was well-known that the board used to make their decisions while in the Sauna! But she threatened to join the gentlemen in the sauna, if the decision making was not returned to the meeting room, and once she actually entered the sauna, as the only one wrapped in a towel. That helped, she reported! (Dahlerup 1985: 303).

There is a long tradition in gender and politics research to investigate the barriers women politicians meet in the political workplace, using a variety of methodologies: observations, surveys, discourse analysis, analysis of institutional practices; as well as statistical analyses of gendered drop-out rates, on promotion and issue specialisation according to gender. In investigating the gendered effects of the political culture and practices, the research may adopt an *institutionalist perspective*, looking for inequality that is embedded 'in the walls', that is the formal and informal norms and practices of the political institutions. The researcher may also address the issue from an *actor oriented perspective*, looking at how politicians, individually or in groups, act to comply or protest against oppressive norms. Since Moss Kanter's classic article, new perspectives such as those of gender performativity, doing and undoing gender, have developed as important research fields, mostly in organisational research, but most recently also in political science (Butler 2004; Puwar 2004; Kelan 2010). Old dilemmas for women in politics have been given new theoretical bearing as in the discussion of the costs paid by women politicians if they – in order to adapt in a hostile surrounding – try to 'undo' their gender, which sometimes might lead to undoing themselves and their humanity, it is argued (Kelan 2010).

In practical life, the political workplace has no doubt been subject to substantial changes over time. Many political parties have deliberately altered their structure and way of working after pressure from women's groups within the parties. The very negative perceptions of women as politicians from earlier times ('women belong to the home') have slowly changed in the old democracies and in many other places on the globe, however, still dominant in some regions and in some parties (Dahlerup and Leyenaar 2013). Stereotypes and confinement to a few policy issues also limit the room of manoeuvre of politicians of national minority or immigrant background in Europe. The *numbers* combined with the *time* passed since the newcomers entered political life no doubt play a role.

The idea of a specific tipping-point attached to a specific number or share of women in an assembly must no doubt be discharged under the workplace perspective. But there may be critical episodes, a heated debate or a sudden increase in women's representation after a campaign against women's under-representation, which can become formative moments, e.g. leading to enduring changes of the male coded political culture. Further, the relevance of the size of the minority cannot be dismissed, but in fact seems more important concerning workplace norms, than concerning changes of policies, since the organisational perspective directly involves gendered perceptions, gendered codes and actual sex segregation of tasks and positions in political life.

Two concepts of political effectiveness

Anne Marie Goetz has developed a conceptual framework for research on what she labels 'women's political effectiveness', defined as 'the ability to use "voice" to politicise issues of concern to women' (2003: 29). Alternatively, one could prefer to talk about the effectiveness of politicians in a different way, open to any kind of agenda that individuals or group of women politicians may want to pursue, being feminist or not. It seems relevant to make a distinction between on the one hand the problems all members of a minority meet in their ability to perform their task as politicians the way they want, because they are a minority and may be newcomers to the political scene (minority representation, newcomers) and on the other hand the resistance those politicians meet, if they are committed to pursue a feminist or gender sensitive agenda. Historically, these two perspectives are interlinked, but they are not identical.

Gender-sensitive parliaments

Today, several international organisations work to promote what has been labelled 'gender-sensitive parliaments'. The Inter-Parliamentary Union, IPU, describes the objectives for such a programme in the following statement:

> A gender-sensitive parliament is one in which there are no barriers – substantive, structural or cultural – to women's full participation and to equality between its men and women members and staff. It is not only a place where women can work, but also one where women want to work and contribute. […] A gender-sensitive parliament is therefore a modern parliament; one that addresses and reflects the equality demands of modern society. Ultimately, it is a parliament that is more efficient, effective and legitimate (Inter-Parliamentary Union 2012a).

This discourse of gender-sensitive parliaments reflects the shift away from women's alleged shortcomings, to demand reforms of the political institutions in order to make them more inclusive. The point is that women politicians must be able to perform their task, the way they prefer, without prejudice, practical barriers or harassment and without being excluded from the most influential settings because of their sex. The first women elected to parliaments usually worked hard to adapt to the rules, which were made before women had gained access. Eventually, however, the critique of the political workplace from a gender perspective increased. This also included a new critique of traditional masculinity in politics – 'politics as a football game!' In terms of practical consequences of this critique, several parliaments have developed support systems to especially help women politicians, like kindergardens for the children of politicians, stylists and hairdressers for MPs in a rush, change of meeting hours, ban on night meetings and on sexist language.

However, research shows that politics in general is still male coded, even if substantial changes have taken place in many countries. In the Swedish parliament with, at that time, 48 per cent women, a cross-party initiative of women parliamentarian filed a complaint to the speaker about sex discrimination in the parliamentary committees. They argued that women are still exposed to certain 'male domination techniques', as for instance not being listened properly to by their male colleagues. The speaker took the complaint very seriously and initiated several reports and surveys to investigate the problem (Jämställt? Röster från riksdagen 2010). So even if numbers count, in interaction with other factors, all barriers for women politicians are not automatically removed by a substantial increase in their numbers.

B. Critical mass and policy change

> When the number of women MPs doubled (to 18 per cent) after the 1997 election, much was expected of them. Since 1997 the key question about having more women in politics has been what difference they have made. Sometimes this has been a hostile question, asked by those observers whose distaste for women's presence in this once male bastion is palpable. The new Labour women MPs were frequently criticised in the press as nothing more than lobby-fodder and many were pilloried for adhering to party discipline in the House of Commons, criticism that reached its peak in the first session of Parliament when benefits to single mothers were cut and Labour women voted with their party (Lovenduski 2001: 755).

Policy change constitutes the core of critical mass thinking: when the share of women in political assemblies exceeds a certain threshold, then, and first then, can women politicians begin to make a difference. It is a hypothesis about a specific *turning-point*. By analogy to nuclear physics one additional assumption at play is that of a *continuous change* towards more gender equal policies with no going back to previous stages.

The prediction or the wish that a large minority of women will start making a difference may refer to different aspects of political decision making: changing the political agenda; gendered political priorities and preferences leading to new political initiatives; or changes in the horizontal sex segregation (i.e. in parliament committees); and finally, of course, in changes in legislation. Mateo-Díaz (2005:161) states that the critical mass hypothesis is made on the basis of differences in terms of attitudes between men and women, but this seems too narrow a perspective.

It is relevant to make a distinction between women politicians' *ability* to make a change (the workplace perspective, *see* the previous section) and their willingness or *commitment* to make change in a specific direction, here in supporting gender equality issues (the policy perspective). The critical mass discussion often diffuses these two perspectives.

Women politicians have, ever since enfranchisement, been criticised by the feminist movements for not being feminist or not sufficiently feminist (Dahlerup 1988a: 292). This critique can be illustrated by the following sharp statement from a representative of the feminist movement from more than hundred years ago:

> I believe that the greatest danger for feminism is not that no women get elected at all, or maybe only a few. The greatest danger is that only such women are elected that we cannot consider our representatives because they have absolutely no understanding of the idea of feminism. Surely this will often be the case if we leave it to the political parties to decide which women to nominate for election [...] (statement from 1915 by Gyrithe Lemche, a Danish feminist leader around the time of women's enfranchisement; in Dahlerup 1988a: 292).

The commitment and the ability or opportunities might be interlinked, as in this quotation from a female and feminist MP, representing the Norwegian Labour Party: 'If you talk feminism, the problem is not just that they do not listen to you, but if you are listened to, then I feel it gives you bad marks: Here she goes again!' (in Dahlerup 1985: 198). It is, however, part of the Nordic legacy that the very same female politician in spite of the reported resistance to her feminist initiatives, nevertheless became a cabinet minister in the 1980s at a very young age.

Defined primarily as a question of increased commitment to gender equality and an increased willingness of a larger number of women politicians to identify themselves as special representatives of women voters when they become a large minority, the critical mass hypothesis, with or without adhering to a specific turning-point, shares some of the ideas – and the same problems – of what in newer research is labelled the relation between 'descriptive' and 'substantive' representation of women, as discussed in Chapter Three in this volume.

Is it possible to define 'women's interests', e.g. interests that all women irrespective of location, class, ethnicity, age, sexual preferences etc. share? Can conservative women, socialist women and young queer feminists agree on anything? Yes, says the feminist movement, and points to the theoretical perceptions of the patriarchal system, and to specific policies such as violence against women and, women's representation. Some researchers prefer to rely on subjectively defined differences between men and women on interests and attitudes (Celis 2006; Mateo-Díaz 2005) others look at legislative behaviour and contact with women's organisations (Hernes 1987; Franceschet and Piscopo 2008) while others develop theoretically founded definitions that are sensitive to diversity among women, but also state some common ground (Wängnerud 2009; Beckwith 2012).

In the public debate, and even in research, one meets many more or less vague terms like 'women friendly' legislation (Hernes 1987); 'the promotion of women's interests', 'accountable to women', 'gender sensitive politics', 'women's political effectiveness' (Goetz 2003); and 'strategic gender interests' (Waylan 1994). In the public debate and in international declarations, as argued above, such lack of clarification might be conducive to consensus-building, as when all governments of the world were to agree on the wording of the relatively radical Platform for Action, adopted at the UN Fourth World Conference on Women, Beijing 1995. But for the scientific discussion about the possible effects of a critical mass, one needs relevant conceptual tools of analyses. The subject requires a comparative *approach*, comparative over time and/or between comparable units with different levels of women's representation. Here are some examples:

Women in US State legislatures

In her study of the relationship between the percentage of women in 12 US state legislatures and their policy priorities at several points in time in the 1980s, Sue Thomas, concludes that women in states with a higher share of female legislators 'introduce and pass more priority bills dealing with issues of women, children, and families than men in their states and more than their female counterparts in low representation legislatures'. She adds, however, that an organised women's caucus can have the same effect even without 15–20 per cent women in the state legislature (1991: 958).

Women in Swedish municipal councils

Studying the budgets at the local level in Sweden, Wängnerud and Sundell (2012) found some effect of the gender composition of the city council in terms of differences in budget spending among municipalities, but only as one factor among many other factors, not least left party dominance. Other studies working with one indicator or a broader spectrum of issues have found that a substantial increase in women representation at one point in time has led to changes in the political agenda and in perceptions of women's agency in politics (*see* for instance Childs 2001; Lovenduski 2005).

Women in New Zealand's parliament

Sandra Grey has made a textual analysis over time of parliamentary debates on three topics: child care, pay equity and parental leave. She did find some support for a critical mass hypothesis: Once female MPs moved from being a token to a 'minority group' in the New Zealand House of Representatives in 1984, the amount of debates on issues such as child care and parental leave were increasing, and female politicians claimed a greater stake in these debates. Agenda setting is, however, Grey states, not identical to policy outcome (Grey 2006:497). Similar results have been found in other studies of other countries. But are such agenda chances evident in New Zealand and in other democracies due to rising numbers of women in the national legislature alone, Sandra Grey critically asks? Her conclusion is that 'the critical mass is only useful if we discard the belief that a *single proportion* holds the key to all representation needs of women and if we discard notions that *numbers alone* bring about substantive changes in policy processes and outcomes' (2006: 492, emphasis added). Instead Grey advocates a more complex joint-effect model.

Plenty of research has found differences in female and male politicians' policy priorities, even when controlled for party affiliation. In her comprehensive analysis on the critical mass hypothesis and gender gaps in female and male MPs specialisation, policy areas and role identifications, based on interview data, Mercedes Mateo-Díaz (2005) compares attitudes among members of parliament in several European countries in 1996, and – especially relevant for the critical mass discussion – analyses the result of a repeated surveys among Swedish MPs over a time span of several decades (*see also* Wängnerud 2000). Mateo-Díaz's analysis results in four categories: issues with non-significant gender differences, issues for which gender differences are constant, issues where gender differences are decreasing and finally those with increasing gender differences over time (2005: 164f.). This analysis opens up for a more dynamic conceptualisation of the critical mass perspective.

Based on survey data among voters, Ronald Inglehart and Pippa Norris (1999) identify three historical evolutions: the first stage is called the *orthodox or traditional* gender gap, where women are more conservative than men. In the second stage, the convergence assumption, the gender gap in attitudes seems to disappear. In the third stage, the modern gender gap or the *realignment assumption*, women tend to vote more for Left-wing parties than men, following, among other things, their position on the labour market.

Transferring this trend among the voters to the parliamentary arena, Mateo-Díaz adds a fourth stage, *a new convergence*, where the gender gap is vanishing, because men and women more and more live the same lives and gender role socialisation is weakened (Mateo-Díaz 2005: 159–60). Also Lena Wängnerud found a *narrowed gender gap over time* in the Swedish parliament (2009).

Indirectly contrasting the critical mass hypothesis, Mateo-Díaz backs the convergence assumption with an additional argument: as the number of women politicians increase, the probability of attaining a higher socio-demographic and ideological diversification in parliament increases as well (2005:160). Others have in a similar way argued that as the number of women politicians increase, the group may grow more diverse (Childs and Krook 2008: 730). These assumptions are, however, not backed by empirical data. No doubt, the diversity among women politicians in Western democracies has increased recently in terms of ethnicity and openly expressed sexual preferences. But on the other hand, this is most probably not the case in terms of class and ideology. Ideologically, political parties move towards the middle (catch all parties). Moreover, the class differences between the few women elected in the interwar period and far into the 1950s were enormous, compared to modern Western parliaments, where a growing share of the MPs – female as well as male – come from middle class jobs in the public sector, while working class MPs have become increasingly rare.

A diminished gender gap in parliament might in fact be an effect of the very influx of women in politics, leading to a change of the agenda and the priorities of both male and female politicians, and of the political parties, which now include issues like public child care, pay inequality and violence against women in their programmes and policies. Making a difference is not the same as staying different (on this 'difference fallacy', *see* Dahlerup 2006b: 517–18). While the theory of increased diversity contradicts the critical mass theory, the argument that women politicians have substantially influenced the politics of their male colleagues and the parties, gives some support to the critical mass hypothesis, yet, makes it even more complicated to demonstrate empirically.

Several conclusions can be drawn from this short discussion related to policy change: no specific *turning-point*, a critical mass of women of say 25–30 per cent can be identified. That does not imply that an increase in women's political representation is unimportant, as several comparative studies have documented. Further, no *constant change* towards more gender equality policy can be identified with a growing number of women politicians. To take the example of the Nordic countries: here the feminist commitment among women politicians was more widespread in the 1980s, and in some of the countries also in the 1990s, than in the new millennium in spite of a higher number of women in political assemblies. An alternative and more complex thesis is that a supportive *Zeitgeist*, a strong feminist mobilisation in civil society and a comprehensive public debate over feminist issues and gender equality seem to be the most important factors for feminist awareness and inclinations to act on gender equality of female as well as male politicians (*their feminist commitment*) and the percentage of women in the political assemblies is just one factor in a complex picture.

It is time to move beyond the critical mass assumptions, when public policy is concerned. In *State Feminism and Political Representation*, Joni Lovenduski appropriately states, that while increasing women's descriptive representation may lead to the inclusion of women's concerns, it is only one of the several ways of enhancing women's (substantive) representation (2005: 5). After all, as rationally stated by Lovenduski, 'feminising politics is like many other political processes'(2005:180). Sarah Childs and Mona Lena Krook propose a shift in the central research question from '*when* women make a difference' to '*how* substantial representation of women occur' 2008:734). Karen Beckwith and Kimberly Cowell-Meyers rephrase the theoretical question from the critical mass debate in this way: what are the conditions that govern the ability of women legislators to make a difference? (2007: 553). To the question of opportunities or 'abilities', this article adds the 'commitment': What are the conditions that govern the commitment and interest of women politicians – and some male politicians as well – in making a difference by initiating and supporting gender equality policies? As an additional suggestion, this article recommends studies of under which historical conditions, and over which political issues, large coalitions of women's organisations and groups have been formed and with what effect.

C. Critical mass and the acceleration in women's numerical representation

Does obtaining a critical mass of women in politics lead to further increase, maybe even an acceleration in women's numerical representation above the 30 per cent? This is the third dimension to be discussed in this article. Maybe surprisingly, this is, as Studlar and McAllister point out, a less-explored dimension of the critical mass concept (2002: 233). It is also almost impossible to find a quotation in the public debate, which makes use of the argument that a critical mass of women, say 30 per cent, is needed for further acceleration of women's numerical representation. May be that would be too provocative!

Why should there be such a link? A structural explanation could be that with more than 30 per cent women, old prejudices against women as politicians have been removed, and a new parity-democracy norm established. An actor-oriented explanation could be that with a the growing number of women politicians, more women will obtain influential positions in the recruitment processes of the political parties (the opportunity) and that they will tend to recruit other women (the commitment) either as a matter of gender identification or as a temporary move in order to change male dominance in politics.

Analogous to the situation in nuclear physics, the critical mass assumption on the numerical increase could be translated into at least two hypotheses: firstly, a *continuous increase* after say 25–30 per cent has been obtained, which implies the idea of irreversibility. Secondly, *acceleration* in women's representation is expected. Both hypotheses can quite easily be tested.

In old democracies, which granted women the right to stand for election before and around World War 1, it took many more years and more elections to overcome the ten per cent barrier, than to go from 10 to 25 per cent (Dahlerup and Leyenaar 2013: Table 11.1). The main increase took place following the large feminist mobilisations in the 1960-80s, however with some delay, for instance in the United Kingdom (Lovenduski 2013). After this, however, we saw no acceleration, and most recently there have even been examples of *stagnation* over several subsequent elections, also in countries with high women's representation like Denmark and the Netherlands. Yet, Icelandic women's representation sky rocketed as the result of a strong feminist reaction to the financial crisis, resulting in 43 per cent women in parliament and a women prime minister (Styrkársdóttir 2013). In Sweden, however, women's representation recently dropped after the entrance into parliament of an anti-immigration party with, by Swedish standards, very few women in their parliamentary party (3 out of 20).

Drastic *falls,* however, that is a decrease of more than 10 per cent units in one election, have been very rare in the old democracies, unlike the decrease in the parliaments of Central and Eastern Europe after the collapse of the Soviet Union (Matland and Montgomery 2003; Galligan *et al.* 2007). On a world scale, in one fourth of all elections to lower or upper houses in 2012, women's representation actually fell; it stagnated by 7 per cent; and actually increased in as many as two thirds (68 per cent) of the elections (IPU 2012b).

In a statistical analysis based on data from twenty industrialised democracies over a period of half a century, Studlar and McAllister found little cross-country evidence that having a critical mass of women legislators is a substantial contributing factor to either female representation *levels* or *changes* in those levels (2002: 247). Their conclusion, that gains in women's representation in old industrialised democracies have been incremental rather than a critical mass accelerating the election of women, is supported by other research. Rather than an effect of an increased number of women in politics, the remarkable increase in women's representation during the 1980s and 90s should be seen as an effect of the strong feminist mobilisation of the 1960-80s, which reached inside the political parties, especially parties on the left, and made them nominate more women in winnable seats (Lovenduski 2005; Freidenvall *et al.* 2006; Dahlerup and Leyenaar 2013). In conclusion, neither the thesis of an acceleration nor that of a continuous increase following a passing of the critical mass threshold can be substantiated.

Critical mass or gender parity?

Most recently, a more ambitious demand for gender balance or gender parity, i.e. 50–50 or 40–60 per cent women and men in political assemblies is replacing the demand for a critical mass of women. This happens first and foremost in countries which already have obtained a high representation of women, while the critical mass argument is still being used in countries and organisations with low women's representation. Many international declarations now entail parity as the goal.[6] The UN Beijing Platform for Action from 1995 is somewhat contradictory in that it demands a 'critical mass of women leaders', yet, at the same time demanding 'equal participation' and 'equitable distribution of power and decision-making at all levels'.

However, the critical mass argument has, perhaps surprisingly, been reactivated in the new debate on quotas for women in *company boards*. The under-representation of women in business is now being discussed world-wide, following the Norwegian law, which was the first to establish the rule of minimum 40 per cent and maximum 60 per cent of both sexes on the boards of the biggest companies, public as well as private. After Norway, Spain, France, Italy and probably soon also the European Union will follow the Norwegian example. The quotation below shows how the critical mass argument is being used for this new area:

Women on company boards – a revival of the critical mass argument:

> The magic number became known as the 30 per cent solution, the idea being that once women reached a Critical Mass in an organisation, people would stop seeing them as women and start evaluating their work as managers. This theory was originally developed more than 40 years ago by Harvard sociologist Rosabeth Moss Kanter in her book *Men and Women of the Corporation.*
>
> Fifteen years after the Beijing Declaration, Norway is the only country to have progressed towards this goal via legislation – championed by someone who definitely doesn't meet the profile of a typical feminist. Norwegian politician Ansgar Gabrielsen is a Pentecostal Christian, and an archetypal alpha-male businessman. His reasons seem logical and resource driven.

6. Examples are the European Women's Lobby demands 'parity', and the Southern Africa Development Community (SADC) which sets of 50 per cent target for 2015 in its 2008-declaration.

> 'What's the point in pouring a fortune into educating girls, and then watching them exceed boys at almost every level, if, when it comes to appointing business leaders in top companies, these are drawn from just half the population – friends who have been recruited on fishing and hunting trips or from within a small circle of acquaintances?' he says. 'It's all about tapping into valuable under-utilised resources. (Nicki Gilmour, founder and CEO of theglasshammer.com, January 21, 2010. Accessed March 10, 2013).

The critical mass hypothesis is, as the quotation illustrates, seen as a valid argument in the discussion about gender quotas for the boards of the biggest companies, an arena, where women are grossly under-represented at the same time as more and more women enter business at a high level. The quotation also illustrates the use of the *utility-argument*, discussed above. Increasing the number of women is based on the argument, here shown through a quote from the Norwegian minister, Ansgar Gabrielsen (Cons.) who proposed the law, that society and the companies should not waste the talents of women. Increasing women's representation is considered *useful*. Moving from a justice argument or a feminist argument of conflicts of interests between women and men to a utility-argument matches the present neo-liberal discourse, especially in the business world. Addressing women in business, Nicki Gilmour from *the gkasshammer* goes on asking: 'How to build a Corporate Critical Mass Solution'. This supports the argument of this article that the critical mass argument is first and foremost being considered most useful in situations, where women have not yet reached a representation of 30–35 per cent.

Conclusion

For students of gender and politics the critical mass hypothesis represents a real challenge, since it touches upon many key aspects of theories of representation and democracy. Since as many as thirty-eight countries having now passed the 30 per cent threshold, at least once, the opportunities of testing the hypothesis empirically have increased substantially. There is, however, no reason to start from scratch again.

Two aspects of the critical mass hypothesis can be eliminated from the start. The physics analogy has its limitations, since human beings are not like particles. Consequently, the effect of a critical mass cannot be understood as something that happens in a *closed room*, disconnected from what happens outside, here outside the political assembly. Further, there is no *automatic* effect of a certain gender proportion, since political change in general involves acts and actors. 'No one ever said it would be automatic. No one ever said it was inevitable', Joni Lovenduski maintains (2012: 90).

A further specification follows from the analyses of this chapter. It is time to leave the idea of a specific *turning-point*, or tipping-point, irrespective of it being set at 25, 30 or 33 per cent. It seems inappropriate to work with a dichotomy: looking for effects before and after a certain numerical level or change of level in women's representation. Studlar and McAllister ask the relevant critical question, whether there is supposed to be a single level that has universal application, or should we look for different levels in different types of democracies (2002: 234) – and in semi-democratic countries, one could add.

This conclusion does not imply, that there are no turning points in history, no critical points or formative moments (Hughes and Paxton 2008; Dahlerup and Leyanaar 2013). On the contrary. But to take advantage of a larger number of women in political assemblies, *critical actors* (Childs and Krook 2009) performing *critical acts* are needed (Dahlerup 1988a). Numbers do count, especially in politics. Of the three dimensions scrutinised in this article, the politics-as-a workplace seems most interesting from a critical mass perspective, following Moss Kanter's more sociological research perspective.

The main problem of the critical mass hypothesis is the difficulties in distinguishing the effect of an increasing number of women in politics from all the other factors at play, including the factors which contributed to the increase in the first place. However, the recent previously unseen leaps in women's representation by the use of quota regulations – like Senegal going from 22 to 43 per cent overnight, Algeria from 8 to 32 per cent, and Timor-Leste from 28 to 38 per cent women, all in one election during 2012 opens up interesting new research on the effect of a sudden, substantial increase in women's share in the political assemblies.

In the public debate, however, the critical mass argument has no doubt made a difference. This article has shown how critical mass, since the 1980s has been, and is still, globally important for the advocacy of increasing women's representation, and thus it should be. In spite of scholarly reservations about the validity of the critical mass hypothesis it should nevertheless be studied for what it is: an important global discourse. The research agenda could encompass among other themes, the discourses, the diffusion of arguments, the effect on women politicians under different levels of representation and, not least, the persuasive capacity of the critical mass argument: who outside feminist circles really wants women in politics to make a difference?

Should feminists give up on critical mass?, Sarah Childs and Mona Lena Krook ask. Their answer is a 'Contingent Yes' (2006). In another article the same authors argue that later scholars have 'largely misread – and thus misconstrued' the classic works of Kanter and Dahlerup, which introduced critical mass thinking in organisational and political life (2008:726). That is probably true, but may also be a consequence of the exploratory character of these first contributions in the 1970s and 80s. However, as it has been argued here, many stakeholders may not have been so interested in further clarification.

For the public debate and for those who argue for a critical mass of women in politics, the strategic value of the critical mass argument, this article has argued, seems to be bigger, when the question of what difference women would make once a larger minority is left to the future. The likelihood of forming broad coalitions for changing women's historical under-representation across party cleavages, class, age, ethnic background and various types of advocacies for women and various feminist ideologies seems to increase when the key argument is the de facto exclusion of women, combined with an elusive hope of change when more women are elected.

References

Beckwith, K. (2012) 'Plotting the Path from One to the Other: Women's Interests and Political Representation', Paper for the conference 'Identity, Gender and Representation: Empirical Analysis of Representation of Women's Interests', Texas A&M University, February 24–25, 2012.

Beckwith, K. and Cowell-Meyers, K. (2007) 'Sheer numbers: critical representation thresholds and women's political representation', *Perspectives on Politics* 5 (3): 553–65.

Bergqvist, C. *et al.* (1999) *Equal Democracies? Gender and politics in the Nordic countries*, Oslo: Scandinavian University Press. Published 1999 in a Scandinavian edition: *Likestillte demokratier? Kjønn og politikk i Norden,* Oslo: Universitetsforlaget.

Butler, J. (1990) *Gender trouble: Feminism and the subversion of identity*, New York: Routledge.

— (2004) *Undoing Gender*, London: Routledge.

Celis, K. (2006) 'Substantive representation of women: the representation of women's interest and the impact of descriptive representation in the Belgian parliament (1900–1979)', *Journal of Women, Politics and Policy* 28 (2): 85–114.

Childs, S. (2001) 'In their own words: New Labour women and the substantive representation of women', *British Journal of Politics and International Relations* 3 (2): 173–90.

Childs, S. and Krook, M. L. (2006) 'Should feminists give up on critical mass: a contingent yes', *Politics & Gender* 2 (4): 522–530.

— (2008) 'Critical mass theory and women's political representation', *Political Studies* 56: 725–36.

— (2009) 'Analysing women's substantive representation: from critical mass to critical actors', *Government and Opposition* 44 (2): 125–45.

Dahlerup, D. (1978) 'Women's entry into politics: the experience of the Danish local and general elections 1908–20', *Scandinavian Political Studies* 1 (2–3): 139–62.

— (1985) *Blomster & Spark. Samtaler med kvindelige politkere i Norden*, Stockholm: Nordisk Ministerråd.

— (1988a) 'From a small to a large minority: women in Scandinavian politics', *Scandinavian Political Studies* 11 (4): 275–98.

— (1988b) *Vi har ventet længe nok. Håndbog i kvinderepræsentation.* Handbook in women's representation, issued in Danish (1988) Icelandic (1988) Swedish (1989) Norwegian (1989) and Finnish (1990), Nordisk Ministerråd.

— (1993) 'De una pequena a una gran minoría: una teoría de la 'masa crítica' aplicada el caso de las mujeres en la política escandinavia', *Debate feminista* Year 4 (8).

— (2006a) *Women, Quotas and Politics*, London and New York: Routledge.

— (2006b) 'The story of the theory of critical mass', *Politics & Gender* 2 (4): 511–22.

— (2011) 'Engendering representative democracy' in S. Alonso, J. Keane and W. Merkel (eds) *The Future of Representative Democracy*, Cambridge: Cambridge University Press.

Dahlerup, D. and Leyenaar, M. (eds) (2013) *Breaking Male Dominance in Old Democracies*, Oxford: Oxford University Press.

Franceschet, S. and Piscopo, J. M. (2008) 'Gender quotas and women's substantive representation: lessons from Argentina', *Politics & Gender* 4 (3): 393–425.

Freidenvall, L. *et al.* (2006) 'The Nordic Countries: An incremental model', in D. Dahlerup (ed.) *Women, Quotas and Politics*, London: Routledge.

Galligan, Y. *et al.* (2007) *Gender Politics and Democracy in Post-Socialist Europe*, Opladen & Farmington Hills: Barbara Budrich Publishers.

Goetz, A. M. (2003) 'Women's Political Effectiveness: A conceptual framework', in A. M. Goetz and S. Shireen Hassim (eds) (2003) *No Shortcuts to Power: African women in politics and policy making*, London: Zed Books, pp. 29–80.

Goetz, A. M. and Shireen Hassim, S. (eds) (2003) *No Shortcuts to Power: African women in politics and policy making*, London: Zed Books.

Grey, S. (2006) 'Numbers and beyond: the relevance of critical mass in gender research', *Politics & Gender* 2 (4): 492–502.

Haavio-Mannila, E. *et al.* (1985) *Unfinished Democracy: Women in Nordic politics*, Oxford: Pergamon Press. First published 1983 in a Scandinavian edition: *Det uferdige demokratiet. Kvinnor i nordisk politikk*, Oslo: Nordisk Ministerråd.

Hellevik, O. and Skard, T. (1985) *Norske kommunestyrer – plass for kvinner?*, Oslo: Universitetsforlaget.

Hernes, H. (1982) *Staten – kvinner ingen adgang?* Olso: Universitetsforlaget.

— (1987) *Welfare State and Woman Power: Essays in state feminism*, Vojens: Norwegian University Press.

Hughes, M. M. and Paxton, P. (2008) 'Continuous change, episodes, and critical periods: a framework for understanding women's political representation over time', *Politics & Gender* 4 (2): 233–64.

Inglehart, R. and Norris, P. (1999) 'The developmental theory of the gender gap: women's and men's voting behavior in global perspective', *International Political Science Review* 21 (4): 441–63.

Inter-Parliamentary Union (2012a) *Plan of Action for Gender-Sensitive Parliaments*, Geneva.

— (2012b) *Women in Parliament in 2012:The Year in Perspective*, Geneva.

Jämställt? Röster från riksdagen (2010) *En uppföljningsrapport* by G. Upmark and L. Freidenvall, 2011/12:URF1. Stockholm: The Swedish Parliament.

Kanter, R. M. (1977) *Men and Women of the Corporation*, New York: Basic Books.

Kelan, E. K. (2010) 'Gender logic and the (un)doing gender at work', *Gender, Work and Organizations* 17 (2): 174–94.

Kraditor, A. S. (1965) *The Ideas of the Woman Suffrage Movement 1890–1920*, New York: Doubleday.

Krook, M. L. (2009) *Quotas for Women in Politics: Gender and candidate selection reform worldwide*, Oxford: Oxford University Press.

Lovenduski, J. (1986) *Women and European Politics: Contemporary feminism and public policy*, Sussex: Wheatsheaf Books Ltd.

— (2001) 'Women and politics: minority representation or critical mass? *Parliamentary Affairs* 54: 743–58.

— (2005) *Feminizing Politics*, London: Polity Press.

— (2012) 'Drude Dahlerup and Feminist Political Science' in L. Freidenvall and M. Micheletti (eds) *Comparisons, Quotas and Critical Change*, Department of Political Science, Stockholm University.

— (2013) 'United Kingdom: Male Dominance Unbroken?' in D. Dahlerup and M. Leyenaar (eds) (2013) *Breaking Male Dominance in Old Democracies*, Oxford: Oxford University Press.

— (ed.) (2005) *State Feminism and Political Representation*, Cambridge: Cambridge University Press.

Mateo-Díaz, M. M. (2005) *Representing Women? Female legislators in West European parliaments*, Essex: ECPR Monographs.

Matland, R. A. and K. A. Montgomery (2003) *Women's Access to Political Power in Post-Communist Europe*, Oxford University Press.

Niskanen, K. (ed.) (2011) *Gender and Power in the Nordic Countries – with focus on politics and business*, Oslo: NIKK Publications 2011:1.

Niskanen, K. and Nyberg, A. (eds) (2009–10) Kön och makt i Norden, *Vol I-II, Nordic Council of Ministers*, Tema Nord 2009:569, 2010:525.

Pateman, C. (1989) *The Disorder of Women: Democracy, feminism and political theory*, Cambridge: Polity Press.

Phillips, A. (1995) *The Politics of Presence*, Oxford: Clarendon Press.

Puwar, N. (2004) *Space Invadors: Race, gender and bodies out of place*, London: Berg.

Sainsbury, D. (1993) 'The Politics of Increased Women's Representation: The Swedish case' in J. Lovenduski and P. Norris (eds) *Gender and Party Politics*, London: Sage.

Sawer, M. (2000) 'Parliamentary representation of women: from discourses of justice to strategies of accountability', *International Political Science Review* 21 (4): 361–80.

Studlar, D. T. and McAllister, I. (2002) 'Does a critical mass exist? A comparative analysis of women's legislative representation since 1950', *European Journal of Political Research* 41: 233–53.

Styrkársdóttir, A. (2013) 'Iceland: Breaking Male Dominance by Extraordinary Means', in D. Dahlerup and M. Leyenaar (eds) (2013) *Breaking Male Dominance in Old Democracies*, Oxford: Oxford University Press.

Thomas, S. (1991) 'The impact of women on state legislative politics', *Journal of Politics*, 53: 958–76.

Tremblay, M. (2006) 'The substantive representation of women and PR', *Politics & Gender*, 2 (4): 502–11.

Wallin, G. and Bäck, T. (1981) *Kommunalpolitikerna*, Report 8, Kommunalpolitiska forskningsgruppen DsKn:18.

Wängnerud, L. (2000) 'Representing Women', in P. Esaiasson and K. Heidar (eds) *Beyond Westminster and Congress: The Nordic experience*, Columbus: Ohio State University Press, pp.132–54.

— (2009) 'Women in parliaments: descriptive and substantive representation', *Annual Review of Political Science* 12: 51–69.

Wängnerud, L. and Sundell, A. (2012) 'Do politics matter? Women in Swedish local elected assemblies 1970–2010 and gender equality in outcomes', *European Political Science Review* 4 (1): 97–120.

Waylan, G. (1994) 'Women and democratisation: conceptualizing gender relations in transition politics', *World Politics* 46 (3): 327–54.

Young, I. M. (2000) *Inclusion and Democracy*, Oxford: Oxford University Press.

Web sites:

— www.womenslobby.org – European Women's Lobby.

— www.ipu.org The Inter-Parliamentary Union's website on women's political representation worldwide

— www.quotaproject.org – global quota web site operated by International IDEA, Stockholm University and the Inter-Parliamentary Union.

Vignette – The Story of Critical Mass: Women at Westminster

Jackie Ashley

Jackie Ashley is a highly regarded British journalist and broadcaster. She is currently a columnist with the *Guardian* Newspaper and presenter of BBC Radio Four's 'The Week in Westminster'. She has worked for BBC television's 'Newsnight', she was ITN's Political correspondent (1986–1999) and the political editor of the *New Statesman* (2000–2002). She has written frequently and powerfully on women and politics and has been observing politicians at close quarters since the 1980s; as such she's ideally situated to comment on what difference women politicians make.

We have come a long way since the "Betty women". Betty was the name given by one old style Tory MP to every one of the small number of women MPs at Westminster back in 1987 – because they all looked the same. An astonished Gillian Shepherd, former Tory Cabinet minister, couldn't quite believe what she was hearing when she first entered the house and was addressed as Betty.

They were indeed different times. Back then I was lobby correspondent, working for ITN. When I became pregnant in 1989, I was horrified to be told by my boss that several Tory MPs had asked that I didn't appear in the lobby, because my burgeoning bump was offensive to them.

25 years on, life at Westminster is much easier for both female politicians and female journalists, even if the dream of parity between men and women remains just that. We have our second female Home Secretary, have had a female Foreign Secretary and I believe that in years to come there are several good candidates for Chancellor: Labour's Rachel Reeves, Liz Kendall and Stella Creasy, along with the Conservatives' Andrea Leadsom, Charlotte Leslie or Harriet Baldwin. And certainly the bookies favourite to be the next Labour leader is Yvette Cooper. The Lib Dems, along with UKIP, of course, have some way to go when it comes to women's representation.

More women MPs have helped changed the atmosphere at Westminster, but have equally changed the focus of debates. The great influx of female MPs came in 1997, with 120 women in total, up substantially from before. Without so many women it is unlikely that Parliament would have got to grips with many issues, from domestic violence to the unfairness in women's pensions, to female genital mutilation and equal pay.

And women do things differently. Many of the women MPs interviewed as part of a groundbreaking study by Boni Sones, Margaret Moran and Joni Lovenduski in 2004 said they hated the yaa-boo atmosphere of the Commons chamber, particularly at Prime Minister's Questions.

They also hated the casual sexist abuse thrown about the chamber, such as Barbara Follett's revelation that when women stood up to speak, the Tory MPs opposite would cup imaginary breasts and say 'melons' as they spoke.

But as the years have passed, the sexist behavior was exposed and certainly some male MPs have started to behave better. The new intake of women MPs on both sides of the House are a feisty lot, who seem much less ready to put up with any nonsense, and it is cheering to see younger, immaculately turned out women take on the early ministerial and shadow ministerial roles. I tend to think that a decade or so earlier they would simply have been patronised.

I must give a mention here to Margaret Hodge, the Labour chair of the Public Accounts Committee, who has refused to be told (and believe me, they have tried) that she mustn't harass ministers, officials, large companies and the rest too harshly when they appear before her committee. Hodge has given a roasting to many, from chief executives to top civil servants, for failing to do their jobs properly, and has exposed some real scandals, including the failure to pay much tax by companies like Google and Starbucks. How many male chairs would have done that?

For all the male clubs and drinking groups at Westminster where the 'real' decisions are taken, women have managed to join together too, to support and encourage each other. There is a strong sisterhood among the female MPs on Labour's side, and the Conservatives' 'Women to Win' campaign has ensured that many of their candidates have come into politics together.

Cross party co-operation on certain issues is not unknown, and the women MPs are often in touch with female journalists and academics, who can usefully work together to bring an issue to the fore. Academics, like the excellent Joni Lovenduski, produce the statistics and research; MPs raise the questions in Parliament and the journalists can then push a good story. Labour's Commission on Older Women, set up by Harriet Harman and Fiona McTaggart is a good current example of how the different roles fit together.

As to the future though, the picture is far from rosy. Experts who have studied the polls and the early selection of candidates suggest that the number of women at Westminster could well go down after 2015. We know what that means: women becoming marginalised again, having to fight to get their voices heard and it being "normal" to have only a handful of women in the cabinet. So it's up to all of us, academics, journalists and MPs to keep up the pressure, to make sure that Westminster represents the whole nation, not just the male half of it.

Chapter Eight

Gender and Political Recruitment

Meryl Kenny

This chapter takes stock of the research on gender and political recruitment, revisiting and assessing the impact of the dominant framework used in the literature, Pippa Norris and Joni Lovenduski's (1995) supply and demand model – which proposes that the outcome of particular parties' selection processes for women's descriptive representation are the combined result of the supply of available candidates and the demands of party selectors. It highlights the ways in which the supply and demand model has been taken forward in new directions for theorising about gender and political recruitment and concludes by reflecting on the legacy of this seminal work for subsequent generations of gender politics scholars and for electoral politics more broadly.

Understanding political recruitment: The supply and demand model

Work on candidate recruitment and selection explores how and why people become politicians, studying the critical stages through which individuals move into political careers. Candidate selection is the main activity of political parties, where political access is traditionally controlled by a series of 'gatekeepers' (*see* Gallagher and Marsh 1988). While there are some exceptions to this statement – most notably in the case of the United States – in most countries, political parties have exclusive control of the candidate selection process, determining the overall composition of the legislature and structuring electoral choice (Norris and Lovenduski 1995: 2). Thus, the candidate selection process is a crucial intermediary stage for prospective female candidates: in order to stand for office, women must not only select themselves to run, but must also be selected by political parties.

Norris and Lovenduski can be described as early new institutionalists in their approach to theorising the political recruitment process; combining an analysis of the wider institutional and political context with a micro-level analysis of candidate and selector attitudes (*see* Norris and Lovenduski 1995: 11; Norris 1997: 8–9). In doing so, they identify three broad levels of the political recruitment process. The political system – incorporating the legal system, electoral system and party system – sets the general 'rules of the game'. Within this context, parties are the central gatekeepers and their decisions are shaped by factors such as party organisation, ideology, formal party rules and informal norms and practices. Operating within these broader political and party contextual settings are the factors which most directly influence the political recruitment of individuals – the resources and motivations of prospective candidates as well as the attitudes of gatekeepers.

In Norris and Lovenduski's model, the outcome of particular parties' selection processes can be understood in terms of the interaction between the *supply* of candidates wishing to stand for political office and the *demands* of party gatekeepers who select the candidates. In seeking to explain the social bias evident in most legislatures, Norris and Lovenduski explicitly integrate gender into the dynamics of supply and demand. On the supply side, due to wider systemic factors such as the public/private divide, the sexual segregation of the work force, and patterns of gender socialisation, we might expect aspiring female candidates to have less time, money, ambition, and confidence than their male counterparts. Alternatively, the effect of gender on the selection process can be seen as a product of demand, either through direct, indirect or imputed discrimination (Norris and Lovenduski 1995: 106–108; *see also* Childs *et al.* 2005; Lovenduski 2005). In cases of direct discrimination, party selectors make judgments of potential candidates on the basis of characteristics seen as common to their social group, rather than as individuals – for example, asking gender discriminatory questions in the selection process. In instances of indirect discrimination, gendered assumptions of what makes a 'good candidate' discriminate against women – for example, privileging candidate criteria primarily associated with men and masculinity. Finally, in cases of imputed discrimination, party selectors make positive or negative judgments of potential candidates on the basis of the anticipated reaction of the electorate to a particular social group – for example, assuming that women lose votes.

Importantly, supply-side and demand-side factors interact at each stage of the political recruitment process; for example, potential applicants may decide not to come forward because of anticipated failure or perceived discrimination in the selection process. However, while supply-side and demand-side factors do interact, Norris and Lovenduski argue that they are analytically distinct, clearly differentiating between supply-side factors which inhibit women from applying to be a candidate, and demand-side factors, which affect whether or not they are accepted by selectors after they decide to run for office (1995: 108).

'If only more women came forward...'

Subsequent research in the gender and politics field has largely focused on establishing which set of factors is more important in explaining women's descriptive under-representation. Those who advocate supply-side explanations suggest that the outcome of the selection process reflects the supply of applicants aspiring to a political career. Factors such as resources – time, money, experience – and motivational factors – ambition, interest, confidence – influence who decides to run for office. This line of argument is frequently used by political parties, who often claim that they would like to select more women, but that not enough are coming forward (*see* for example Evans 2011; Sanbonmatsu 2006).

Somewhat surprisingly, Norris and Lovenduski (1995) suggest that supply-side factors at the time of the 1992 UK general election offer the most plausible explanation for the social bias of the House of Commons. Drawing on findings from the 1992 British Candidate Study, they acknowledge that the selection process demonstrates social bias towards young, white, well-educated, male professionals, but conclude that this bias largely reflects the pool of eligible applicants for political office. In terms of the effects of gender, they do find some inter-party differences, suggesting that supply-side factors are more important for Conservative women, while demand plays a bigger role in the Labour Party (Norris and Lovenduski 1995: 116). Ultimately, however, they argue that supply-side factors are more persuasive than demand-side factors in explaining women's descriptive under-representation at Westminster, suggesting that if more women came forward, more would be selected (Norris and Lovenduski 1995: 248).

Supply-side explanations are also particularly prevalent in the United States, where the gate-keeping powers of parties are weaker than in parliamentary democracies (but *see* Niven 2006; Sanbonmatsu 2006). In this context, a notable recent study by Jennifer Lawless and Richard Fox (2005) finds that women in American politics are substantially less likely than men to consider running for office or to put themselves forward as candidates. Drawing on the Citizen Political Ambition Study – which consisted of surveys of 'eligible' candidates in the occupations that usually precede a career in American politics as well as in-depth interviews – they hypothesise that this gender gap in political ambition is linked to several factors, including patterns of gender socialisation. Ultimately, they argue that the gender gap in political ambition is driven largely by women's greater aversion to campaigning, gender gaps in perceptions of qualifications and electoral viability in which women – despite sharing similar qualifications and experiences with their male counterparts – are less likely to perceive themselves as 'qualified' to run and hold office, and lower levels of party recruitment for women than men (*see also* Moncrief *et al.* 2001).

Accounts that emphasise the importance of supply-side factors have resulting implications for strategies to increase women's descriptive representation (*see* Lovenduski 2005; Childs 2008; Krook 2010a). Political parties can use a range of measures to increase women's political presence. As Lovenduski (2005) defines these: equality rhetoric involves the public acceptance of women's claims and can be found in party platforms, manifestos, and speeches. *Equality promotion* attempts to bring more women into politics through measures such as training, financial assistance, soft targets, and other initiatives. And *equality guarantees* use strategies such as party or legislative quotas to secure places for women candidates. Thus, if supply-side explanations are perceived to be more important in explaining women's under-representation, equality rhetoric (for example, encouraging women to come forward) and promotion initiatives (for example, training sessions or financial resources to cover personal expenses) should theoretically encourage greater numbers of women to run for office. In other words, the assumption is that 'the impetus for change must come from women themselves' (Krook 2010a: 159). As Norris and Lovenduski (1995: 248) note, however, these sorts of changes are unlikely to make more than a 'modest difference in the short term', resulting in only small gains in women's descriptive representation (similar conclusions are reached by Lawless and Fox 2005). Still, increases in the available supply of women candidates – however modest – may highlight resistance to women candidates and also draw attention to the need for stronger equality measures in order to increase demand (Lovenduski 2005: 92).

The limiting power of demand

However, while most feminist scholars recognise that supply-side factors play a role in the recruitment process, research in the field has increasingly focused on demand-side explanations of women's descriptive under-representation. Political parties select their candidates on the basis of both formal and informal criteria – for example, a candidate's political experience, abilities, or personal qualities. In doing so, they may take 'information short-cuts' to make quick judgments about candidates they do not know well, which can take the form of direct, indirect or imputed discrimination against certain types of candidates (Norris and Lovenduski 1995: 14, 107).

Examples of this approach are particularly prevalent in the large body of literature on women's descriptive representation at Westminster, the UK Parliament, where gender politics scholars have increasingly argued that the central problem for British political parties is one of demand rather than supply (*see* for example Shepherd-Robinson and Lovenduski 2002; Childs *et al.* 2005; Ashe *et al.* 2010; Evans 2011). In highlighting the limiting power of demand, despite increases in the supply of female candidates, these studies arguably correct a previous bias in the field towards supply-side explanations. Much of the early literature on gender and political recruitment in Britain stressed the importance of supply-side factors in explaining women's political under-representation, relying in large part on selectorate self-perceptions. For example, John Bochel and David Denver's (1983) study of Labour Party selectorates found that a majority of the selectors interviewed were supportive of the idea that more women should be selected as candidates. From these findings, they concluded that there was little evidence of prejudice or discrimination against women in the selection process, and that if more women came forward, more would be selected (*see also* Bristow 1980). The assumption, then, was that the 'real problem' lay elsewhere (Lovenduski and Norris 1989: 537): that women were reluctant to come forward not because of anticipated failure or perceived discrimination in the selection process, but because of wider societal or cultural factors, including patterns of gender socialisation.

As Norris and Lovenduski (1995) point out, accounts that rely largely on selectorate self-perceptions are highly problematic (*see also* Lovenduski and Norris 1989). Party selectors may say they want more women in office, but in practice, may evaluate female prospective candidates unfavourably. Thus, subsequent work in this area has sought to gather reliable evidence of whether discrimination occurs in the selection process, generally by incorporating interviews with prospective women candidates on their experiences and perceptions of direct, indirect or imputed discrimination (*see* for example Norris and Lovenduski 1995; Shepherd-Robinson and Lovenduski 2002; Evans 2011; Childs and Webb 2012). This is accompanied by the acknowledgement that perceptions of discrimination do not necessarily constitute definitive proof. Still, even if these perceptions are 'erroneous, or a rationalisation of failure', they still may play an important role, for example, by discouraging some female candidates from coming forward (Norris and Lovenduski 1995: 130; *see also* Evans 2011: 94–95).

Through this work, these scholars have altered both academic and popular perceptions of the 'problem' of women's under-representation in British politics and have kept the pressure on political parties to implement equality measures to address the issue of women's legislative recruitment. For example in 1998, following the (partial) implementation of all-women shortlists (AWS) by the British Labour Party for the 1997 General Election, Joni Lovenduski and new MP, Maria Eagle published an influential Fabian pamphlet which argued that there was 'no evidence to suggest that the culture of the party [had] changed in favour of selecting women' (Eagle and Lovenduski 1998: 29). They argued that the problem of women's under-representation in the Labour Party was one of demand, rather than supply, with selectorates still unwilling to select women in seats where they were not required to do so. Ultimately, they concluded that party selectors would only select women in high enough numbers to 'make a difference' if they were compelled to implement equality guarantees (Eagle and Lovenduski 1998: 10).

Similarly, Laura Shepherd-Robinson and Joni Lovenduski's (2002) Fawcett Society report following the 2001 General Election, found that British political parties were 'institutionally sexist', meaning that gender bias was entrenched and well-established in the parties in terms of personnel, practices, and outcomes. Drawing on both interviews and focus group evidence, the report found that the key factor explaining low levels of women's political representation in the House of Commons was a lack of demand on the part of candidate selectors and that both incidences of direct and indirect discrimination were widespread in all of the parties. Women candidates reported that they were judged on a different basis than men and also reported numerous examples of overt discrimination, ranging from gendered assumptions regarding women's traditional roles to explicit sexual harassment. Reinforced by a number of recent in-depth studies of British political parties (e.g. Evans 2011; Childs and Webb 2012), as well as a series of academic and policy-oriented publications tracing trends in women's political recruitment to the House of Commons over time[1] (*see* for example Lovenduski 2001; Campbell and Lovenduski 2005; Childs *et al.* 2005; Campbell and Childs 2010; Ashe *et al.* 2010), these interventions have popularised the arguments for increasing women's descriptive representation and have been used as important campaigning tools for women in parties and in civil society.

Beyond Britain, additional case study and comparative evidence also points to parties as the main barriers to increases in women's representation. Miki Caul Kittilson's (2006) comparative study of women's political presence in Western Europe focuses exclusively on demand-side factors, starting from the point that the key mechanism for increases in women's parliamentary presence is the political party. Meanwhile, Susan Franceschet (2001) finds that women are marginalised in Chilean political parties by a number of gendered factors, including a lack of

1. As well as for devolved elections to the Scottish Parliament and National Assembly for Wales (*see* for example Russell *et al.* 2002; Mackay 2003; Mackay and Kenny 2007; Kenny and Mackay 2011, 2013; McAllister and Cole 2014).

access to the informal party networks that male politicians enjoy, which are crucial for campaign financing and for obtaining winnable seats. Similarly, Rainbow Murray's (2010) study of French political parties concludes that the privileging of male attributes by party selectors and the prioritisation of men for key positions in local and national office are key factors in explaining women's political under-representation in the French National Assembly.

This is not to suggest that the literature is no longer concerned with supply-side factors or that there are no issues with the supply of women candidates – for example, the diversity of women standing for office (Childs and Webb 2012: 73). Rather, the literature increasingly recognises that party demand can help determine supply, putting pressures for change on political parties (rather than on prospective women candidates) and highlighting the need for special measures to ensure that women are selected. Equality guarantees – that is, gender quotas in the form of reserved seats, party or legislative quotas – '*require* an increase in the number or proportion of particular parliamentarians and/or make a particular social characteristic a *necessary qualification* for office' (Ashe *et al.* 2010: 459; cf. Lovenduski 2005; original emphasis). As such, equality guarantees create an artificial demand for women candidates, which may subsequently lead to increases in supply. However, comparative studies point to important variations in gender quota measures in both form and effect, with some measures producing large increases in women's descriptive representation and others resulting in stalling or decreases in the number of women parliamentarians (*see* Krook 2009; and Krook and Norris' Chapter Nine in this volume). This suggests that quotas are institutionally constrained and that the presence of these measures may not in itself be sufficient to dramatically 'shift the dynamics of demand' (Krook 2010a: 161; *see also* Lovenduski 2005)

Beyond supply and demand?

While the supply and demand metaphor is widely used by political parties and gender politics scholars, several recent studies have questioned whether the model remains a convincing framework for the study of gender and political recruitment (*see* for example Krook 2010a, 2010b; Kenny 2011, 2013; Ashe and Stewart 2012). These critiques point to two underlying problems in the original model, as well as subsequent applications of the framework. First, they argue that the model underestimates the extent to which gender norms shape and distort the dynamics of supply and demand. While the original model does attempt to integrate gender into the recruitment process, Norris and Lovenduski (1995) see gender as one of many factors that influence the dynamics of supply and demand. This perspective sits somewhat at odds with both previous and later work on gender and political recruitment, including Norris and Lovenduski's own, which highlights the structural barriers constraining potential female candidates and the discriminatory effect of masculinist norms which pervade the candidate selection process. For example, in their earlier work, Lovenduski and Norris challenge the assumption that demand-side selection criteria are gender-neutral, simply distinguishing between 'good' and 'bad' candidates on the basis of 'merit'. Instead, they call for a critical interrogation of the model of the 'ideal candidate', which they argue favours the stereotype of a white, male, professional: '...both the way in which the role of the candidate is defined and the candidate qualities sought tend to penalise many women' (Lovenduski and Norris 1989: 559). Similarly, Jenny Chapman's (1993) analysis of selection practices for local government candidates in Scotland finds that in each of the main political parties, the typical profile of female candidates resembled that of 'losing men'. Women candidates, as a group, were less likely to possess the attributes associated with 'winning' candidates.

Building on these insights, recent studies point to the need to go beyond discrimination at the individual selector level, arguing that 'lack of supply is partly a function of subtly gendered demand' (Murray 2010: 46). While there are no standard or universally recognised qualifications to be selected to run for office, formal and informal candidate requirements such as party service, resources, and experience strongly influence who decides to run for office and shape the supply of candidates along gendered lines. Prospective female candidates, then, face what Chapman (1993) refers to as the 'scissors' problem: they are less likely to possess the appropriate 'qualifications' for office, and, in turn, concerns over the appropriateness of their qualifications may prevent them from running for office altogether (*see also* Lovenduski 1993: 12).

One example of such an approach can be seen in Murray's (2010) study of candidate selection in France. In her examination of party selection criteria, Murray finds that while none of these criteria are overtly gendered, many of the qualities sought were more prevalent in men than women, resulting in a lower supply of female candidates. For example, women were less likely than men to be well known within the party (for example, through holding prominent positions at the local level), they were less likely to be active within the party, and they had reduced access to leadership positions (Murray 2010: 64–67). Meanwhile, studies of candidate selection in Scotland and the UK point to how the prioritisation of subjective and gendered criteria such as 'localness' by party selectors can serve to discriminate against women candidates (Kenny 2011, 2013; Childs and Webb 2012; *see also* Lovenduski 1993). Others point to how the demand for female candidates is shaped by the 'gender identities' of party selectors (Krook 2010a: 163), with women additionally disadvantaged by the fact that most candidate selectors are male (*see* for example Niven 1998; Kittilson 2006). In a study of US party chairs, for example, David Niven (1998) finds that male party elites generally list stereotypically masculine characteristics when asked to describe a 'good candidate'. These research findings highlight the pervasive ways in which gendered norms and practices shape the demands of candidate selectors, suggesting that elites may be more likely to select male candidates, even as women enter politics in higher numbers.

The second criticism of the supply and demand model centres on the institutional dynamics of the model. While the supply and demand model attempts to systematically theorise the interconnections between the institutions of political recruitment, applications of the framework sometimes oversimplify the dynamics of the selection process. Norris and Lovenduski (1995) stress the institutional complexities of the model, highlighting the ways in which the dynamics of supply and demand interact with each other and with wider systemic and political factors. As such, they advocate the necessity of understanding the political recruitment process 'in a comprehensive model, rather than relying upon simple deterministic and monocausal explanations' for representative outcomes (Norris and Lovenduski 1995: 194). However, these nuances are often lost in subsequent applications of the model. For example, while Norris and Lovenduski highlight the interaction between supply and demand-side factors, most research in the field focuses on establishing which set of factors is more important in explaining women's descriptive under-representation, the supply of available candidates, or the demands of party selectors.

As Ashe and Stewart (2012) point out, studies that focus only on supply-side or demand-side factors can only provide partial explanations of women's descriptive under-representation. Demand-side focused studies might overlook issues of under-supply, while, more likely, supply-centred studies risk underplaying the role of gatekeeper discrimination. Thus, the authors argue that investigating both supply and demand is necessary to identify why some candidates succeed in moving through the selection process, while others do not. In addition, Ashe and Stewart find that most work in the field takes only a partial look at the recruitment process rather than adopting a multi-stage analysis (from application to election), which inhibits researchers from identifying the precise stages at which under-representation begins to occur (2012: 690). As such, the authors adopt a more holistic 'diagnostic approach' to assess women's descriptive under-representation in British Columbia (BC) – involving stage-by-stage supply and demand testing – and argue that the lack of women participating in the election stage of the BC recruitment process is due to gatekeeper discrimination at the selection stage.[2]

Yet, as already highlighted, while it is important to investigate both supply and demand, research evidence increasingly privileges demand-side explanations. In highlighting the limiting power of demand, these accounts arguably correct an assumption of equal weighting between supply and demand and point to how these factors interact in ways not necessarily anticipated by the original model (*see* Murray 2010; Kenny 2011, 2013; Childs and Webb 2012). As discussed above, parties may select their candidates on the basis of subtly gendered criteria, which shapes the available supply of female candidates and may also result in women self-selecting themselves out of the process. In addition, attempts to reform the political recruitment process – through innovations such as gender quotas – can result in an increase in the number of female candidates, but the impact of such measures ultimately depends on the willingness of political elites to implement and enforce these policies (*see* for example Kittilson 2006). Again, this is not

2. In contrast, they find that for ethnic minority candidates, discrimination occurred at the selection stage in the centre-left New Democratic Party and at the application stage in the centre-right Liberal Party.

to say that supply-side factors are not still important, but rather signals a greater convergence in the field around two main points of agreement: first, that party demand shapes supply, and second, that there are generally sufficient numbers of women candidates to be selected for winnable seats or places, if political parties choose to do so (Childs and Webb 2012: 73; *see also* Ashe and Stewart 2012).

Thus, given that the 'political market' is profoundly shaped and distorted by gender norms, it is unlikely to produce equilibrium between the forces of supply and demand (Krook 2010a: 161). As such, several recent studies emphasise the importance of recognising multiple directions of causality in the political recruitment process, highlighting how the different levels of the political recruitment process interact with each other in complex and interlocking ways (*see* for example Krook 2009, 2010a, 2010b; Kenny 2011, 2013; Childs and Webb 2012). A notable example of this sort of approach is the work of Mona Lena Krook who attempts to reformulate the key features of the supply and demand model into a feminist and institutionalist framework (Krook 2009; 2010b). In doing so, she adopts a broader conception of 'institutions' – consistent with that used by new institutionalists – to include both the formal and informal 'rules of the game' that shape human interaction (*see* for example North 1990). Krook (2009: 43–47) begins by arranging the factors that influence the political recruitment process into different causal categories, distinguishing between the *systemic*, *practical*, and *normative* institutions that affect patterns of women's descriptive representation. *Systemic institutions* refer to the formal features of the political system, including electoral rules, ballot structures, district sizes and number of political parties. *Practical institutions* include formal and informal party practices of political recruitment, encompassing both formal and informal requirements for candidacy. And *normative institutions* are the formal and informal principles that define the means and goals of recruitment, including definitions of equality and representation found in electoral laws, party statutes, public speeches, political ideologies, and so on.

Krook argues that more attention should be given to the causal role of *institutional configurations* – that is, how the systemic, practical and normative institutions of political recruitment fit together in reinforcing and conflicting ways to determine patterns of women's descriptive representation. Indeed, most studies of women's political recruitment do acknowledge the role of multiple institutions in shaping representative outcomes, albeit often implicitly (Krook 2010b: 711; *see also* Krook 2009). Norris and Lovenduski (1995), for example, identify the electoral system as a key systemic factor shaping patterns of political recruitment. Yet, they also point out that more proportional electoral systems are neither necessary nor sufficient conditions for increased levels of women's descriptive representation (Norris and Lovenduski 1995: 194). In other words, while systemic variables like electoral systems may set the 'rules of the game' in which selection decisions take place, their effect is mediated by other political and institutional factors. This is accompanied by the recognition that particular institutional configurations 'may operate not only across but also within countries' (Krook 2010b: 712), which has shifted the focus away from static percentages of women in national parliaments to look at inter-party variations in levels of women's descriptive representation (*see* especially Caul 1999; Kittilson 2006). In drawing attention to the importance of institutional interconnections, as well as timing, sequence, and context, these sorts of approaches allow for a more nuanced framework that moves beyond applications of supply and demand as a straightforward interaction model.

Gender, institutions and political recruitment

Building on these developments, the supply and demand model remains a compelling framework for the study of gender and political recruitment, albeit with some critical refinements. First, applications of the model need to recognise that it is 'embedded in a wider gendered context' (Childs and Webb 2012: 73; *see also* Kenny 2013). In this view, gender cannot simply be conceptualised as one of many factors that affects the dynamics of supply and demand, manifested, for example, at the individual level through direct or indirect discrimination by party gatekeepers. Rather, an integrative approach is needed that involves 'recasting the candidate selection process in terms of the gendered institutions that may inform the calculations of potential candidates and political elites' (Krook 2010b: 711). Feminist theoretical and empirical work on gender and institutions suggests that gender relations are cross-cutting, that they play out in different ways in different types of institutions and on different institutional levels, ranging from the symbolic level to the 'seemingly trivial' level of interpersonal, day-to-day interaction, where the continuous performance of gender takes place (Kenney 1996: 458; *see also* Lovenduski 1998; Kenny 2007). Thus, gendered interactions at the individual level in the political recruitment process take place within a framework of formal and informal party rules and practices which are shaped and structured by masculinist gender norms, as well as a wider context of systemic and structural barriers which have a differential effect on men and women as institutional actors (Kenny 2011: 24).

Viewing the political recruitment process through a gendered lens also requires 'fine-grained descriptions of gendered environments accompanied by explanations of how gender constrains or enhances agency and affects stability and change' (Lovenduski 2011: xi). This requires a more thorough examination of the internal and gendered dynamics of political parties. As several recent studies have noted, parties are both the main barriers and the key actors for increasing women's political presence and are in need of further attention by gender politics scholars (Lovenduski 2005: 137; *see also* Kittilson 2006; Threlfall 2007; Murray 2010; Bjarnegård 2013; Kenny 2013). Parties are also gendered organisations, in that they are historically dominated by men and are characterised by traditional (and often unacknowledged) conceptions of gender relations that generally disadvantage women. As Lovenduski (2005: 56) reminds us: 'If parliament is the warehouse of traditional masculinity [...] political parties are its major distributors'. Thus, integrating gender into the dynamics of supply and demand requires a closer look at political parties as the central (and gendered) organisations at the heart of the political recruitment process.

Second, applications of the supply and demand framework need to recognise multiple directions of causality, rather than assume a straightforward interaction model. Political recruitment studies that emphasise the role of institutional configurations (Krook 2009) or 'nested' institutions (Kenny 2013) have the potential to bring us a step forward in this regard, highlighting how the interaction of particular institutions may help or block the selection of women candidates. This allows us to better theorise the interconnections between different political institutions – whether systemic, practical, or normative – in the recruitment process (interconnections that political actors have to negotiate) and also between political and non-political institutions. It also provides greater analytical leverage in explaining why reforms aimed at the political recruitment process such as gender quotas succeed in some contexts, yet fail in others.

The political recruitment process is shaped not only by ongoing interactions with already existing institutions, but also by gendered institutional legacies of the past, which can result in tensions and contradictions. For example, informal masculinist party traditions may undermine the introduction of new formal innovations such as gender quotas, limiting possibilities for reform and change in the political recruitment process (Lovenduski 2005; Bjarnegård 2013; Kenny 2013). Thus, by recognising that the political recruitment process has an embedded and often hidden gender dimension which can be carried forward through institutional legacies and through ongoing interactions with surrounding institutions (Mackay 2009), we can provide a more dynamic account of how the institutions of recruitment and selection change over time, which also acknowledges the ways in which 'old' gender practices, norms, and expectations can serve to dilute the impact of gender equality reforms.

This approach requires that gender politics scholars allow for and, indeed, seek elements of complexity in their empirical accounts of the political recruitment process (cf. Lowndes 2005). As Krook notes, placing a central importance on institutional configurations and causal combination places necessary limitations on prediction and prescription with regards to recruitment (2009: 224). Supply and demand factors operate within a broader institutional and political context and are subject to different spatial and temporal constraints; thus, while many of the possible explanations for women's descriptive under-representation are widespread phenomena, 'few are universal' (Lovenduski 2005: 46; *see also* Norris and Lovenduski 1995: 110). The task for researchers, then, is to carry out 'a fine grained analysis that seeks to identify *what aspects* of a specific institutional configuration are (or are not) renegotiable and *under what conditions*' (Thelen 2003: 233; original emphasis).

Conclusion

Work on gender and political recruitment has shed considerable light on the 'shadowy pathways' prior to election (Norris 1997: 8). Continuing the pioneering early work of Pippa Norris and Joni Lovenduski, contemporary research in this area suggests that women's descriptive under-representation is the combined result of: (1) the supply of prospective female candidates willing to stand for office; and (2) the demands of party gatekeepers who select the candidates. Norris and Lovenduski's 1995 supply and demand model represents a key turning point in the field – in that it is one of the first and only attempts to systematically theorise the gendered and interactive dynamics of the political recruitment process – and it continues to be the dominant framework used by gender politics scholars as well as a popular metaphor used by political parties in justifications of their selection practices.

Much of the research on gender and political recruitment has attempted to establish which set of factors – supply-side or demand-side – are more convincing in explaining women's descriptive under-representation. Yet, the relative importance of supply-side factors has been increasingly downplayed in favour of demand-side explanations. Work in the field overwhelmingly highlights the limiting power of demand, despite increases in the supply of available female candidates, and increasingly demonstrates that there are usually enough women for political parties to select, if they are willing to do so. This shift in focus, in turn, has important implications for reform strategies, putting pressures on political parties to implement equality guarantees – including party and legislative gender quotas – to ensure that women are selected and elected. Backed by detailed empirical evidence, critical actors in feminist political science – including Joni Lovenduski and other leading gender politics scholars – have been a key force for change in these debates, altering both academic and popular perceptions of the 'problem' of women's under-representation and bolstering the campaigning efforts of women in political parties and in civil society.

Norris and Lovenduski continue their path-breaking work and have influenced a second (and third) generation of gender politics scholars who have provided further insights into the interactive and gendered dynamics of supply and demand. Building on these developments, work on gender and political recruitment must continue to be attentive to gender norms and legacies and to institutional interconnections, exploring the ways in which the gendered institutions of political recruitment interact with each other in dynamic and often contradictory ways over time. In order to unravel these complexities, additional in-depth research is needed in the form of fine-grained case-by-case analysis, as well as comparative research. These kinds of studies are likely to generate a range of new insights into the 'secret garden' of candidate selection and recruitment, contributing to a wider understanding of the dynamics of supply and demand.

References

Ashe, J. and Stewart, K. (2012) 'Legislative recruitment: using diagnostic testing to explain underrepresentation', *Party Politics* 18 (5): 687–707.

Ashe, J., Campbell, R., Childs, S. and Evans, E. (2010) '"Stand by your man": women's political recruitment at the 2010 UK general election', *British Politics* 5 (4): 455–480.

Bjarnegård, E. (2013) *Gender, Informal Institutions and Political Recruitment,* Basingstoke: Palgrave Macmillan.

Bochel, J. and Denver, D. (1983) 'Candidate selection in the Labour Party: what the selectors seek', *British Journal of Political Science* 13 (1): 45–59.

Bristow, S. (1980) 'Women councillors – an explanation of the under-representation of women in local government', *Local Government Studies* 6 (3): 73–99.

Campbell, R. and Childs, S. (2010) '"Wags", "wives" and "mothers"...but what about women politicians?', *Parliamentary Affairs* 63 (4): 760–777.

Campbell, R. and Lovenduski, J. (2005) 'Winning women's votes? The incremental track to equality', *Parliamentary Affairs* 58 (4): 837–853.

Caul, M. (1999) 'Women's representation in parliament: the role of political parties', *Party Politics* 5 (1): 79–98.

Chapman, J. (1993) *Politics, Feminism and the Reformation of Gender*, London: Routledge.

Childs, S. (2008) *Women and British Party Politics: Descriptive, substantive and symbolic representation*, London: Routledge.

Childs, S. and Webb, P. (2012) *Sex, Gender and the Conservative Party: From Iron Lady to kitten heels*, Basingstoke: Palgrave Macmillan.

Childs, S., Lovenduski, J. and Campbell, R. (2005) *Women at the Top 2005: Changing Numbers, Changing Politics?*, London: Hansard Society.

Eagle, M. and Lovenduski, J. (1998) *High Time or High Tide for Labour Women?*, London: Fabian Society.

Evans, E. (2011) *Gender and the Liberal Democrats: Representing women?*, Manchester: Manchester University Press.

Franceschet, S. (2001) 'Women in politics in post-transitional democracies: the Chilean case', *International Feminist Journal of Politics* 3 (2): 207–236.

Gallagher, M. and Marsh, M. (eds) (1988) *The Secret Garden: Candidate selection in comparative perspective*, London: Sage.

Kenney, S. J. (1996) 'New research on gendered political institutions', *Political Research Quarterly* 49 (2): 445–466.

Kenny, M. (2007) 'Gender, institutions and power: a critical review', *Politics* 27 (2): 91–100.

— (2011) 'Gender and Institutions of Political Recruitment: Candidate selection in post-devolution Scotland', in M. L. Krook and F. Mackay (eds) *Gender, Politics and Institutions: Towards a feminist institutionalism*, Basingstoke: Palgrave Macmillan, pp. 21–41.

— (2013) *Gender and Political Recruitment: Theorizing institutional change*, Basingstoke: Palgrave Macmillan.

Kenny, M. and Mackay, F. (2011) 'In the Balance: women and the 2011 Scottish Parliament elections', *Scottish Affairs* 76 (Summer): 74–90.

— (2013) 'When is contagion not very contagious? Dynamics of women's political representation in Scotland', *Parliamentary Affairs* Doi: 10.1093/pa/gss109.

Kittilson, M. C. (2006) *Challenging Parties, Changing Parliaments: Women and elected office in contemporary Western Europe*, Columbus, OH: Ohio State University Press.

Krook, M. L. (2009) *Quotas for Women in Politics: Gender and candidate selection reform worldwide*, New York: Oxford University Press.

— (2010a) 'Why are fewer women than men elected? Gender and the dynamics of candidate selection', *Political Studies Review* 8, 155–168.

— (2010b) 'Beyond supply and demand: a feminist-institutionalist theory of candidate selection', *Political Research Quarterly* 63 (4): 707–720.

Lawless, J. L. and Fox, R. L. (2005) *It Takes a Candidate: Why women don't run for office*, New York: Cambridge University Press.

Lovenduski, J. (1993) 'Introduction: the Dynamics of Gender and Party' in J. Lovenduski and P. Norris (eds) *Gender and Party Politics*, London: Sage, pp. 1–15.

— (1998) 'Gendering research in political science', *Annual Review of Political Science* 1: 333–356.

— (2001) 'Women and politics: minority representation or critical mass?', *Parliamentary Affairs* 54 (4): 743–758.

— (2005) *Feminizing Politics*, Cambridge: Polity Press.

— (2011) 'Foreword' in M. L. Krook and F. Mackay (eds) *Gender, Politics and Institutions: Towards a feminist institutionalism*, Basingstoke: Palgrave, pp. vii-xi.

Lovenduski, J. and Norris, P. (1989) 'Selecting women candidates: obstacles to the feminization of the House of Commons', *European Journal of Political Research* 17 (5): 533–562.

Lowndes, V. (2005) 'Something old, something new, something borrowed…', *Policy Studies* 26 (3): 291–309.

McAllister, L. and Cole, M. (2014) 'The 2011 Welsh general election: an analysis of the latest staging post in the maturing of Welsh politics', *Parliamentary Affairs* 67(1): 172–190.

Mackay, F. (2003) 'Women and the 2003 Elections: keeping up the momentum', *Scottish Affairs* 44 (Summer): 74–90.

— (2009) 'Institutionalising "New Politics" in Post Devolution Scotland: "Nested Newness" and the Gendered Limits of Change', Paper presented at the European Conference on Politics and Gender, Queen's University Belfast, 21–23 January.

Mackay, F. and Kenny, M. (2007) 'Women's representation in the 2007 Scottish Parliament elections: temporary setback or return to the norm?', *Scottish Affairs* 60 (Summer): 25–38.

Moncrief, G. F., Squire, P. and Jewell, M. F. (2001) *Who Runs for the Legislature?*, Upper Saddle River, NJ: Prentice Hall.

Murray, R. (2010) *Parties, Gender Quotas and Candidate Selection in France*, Basingstoke: Palgrave Macmillan.

Niven, D. (1998) 'Party elites and women candidates: the shape of bias', *Women and Politics* 19 (2): 57–80.

— (2006) 'Throwing your hat out of the ring: negative recruitment and the gender imbalance in state legislative candidacy', *Politics & Gender* 2 (4): 473–489.

Norris, P. (ed.) (1997) *Passages to Power: Legislative recruitment in advanced democracies*, Cambridge: Cambridge University Press.

Norris, P. and Lovenduski, J. (1995) *Political Recruitment: Gender, race, and class in the British Parliament*, Cambridge: Cambridge University Press.

North, D. C. (1990) *Institutions, Institutional Change and Economic Performance*, Cambridge: Cambridge University Press.

Russell, M., Mackay, F. and McAllister, L. (2002) 'Women's representation in the Scottish Parliament and National Assembly for Wales: party dynamics for achieving critical mass', *Journal of Legislative Studies* 8 (2): 49–76.

Sanbonmatsu, K. (2006) *Where Women Run: Gender and party in the American states*, Ann Arbor, MI: University of Michigan Press.

Shepherd-Robinson, L. and Lovenduski, J. (2002) *Women and Candidate Selection in British Political Parties*, London: Fawcett.

Thelen, K. (2003) 'How Institutions Evolve: Insights from comparative historical analysis' in J. Mahoney and D. Rueschemeyer (eds) *Comparative Historical Analysis in the Social Sciences*, Cambridge: Cambridge University Press, pp. 208–240.

Threlfall, M. (2007) 'Explaining gender parity representation in Spain: the internal dynamics of parties', *West European Politics* 30 (5): 1068–1095.

Vignette - Gender and Political Recruitment: 'How Can You Get the Best Person For the Job When the Best Person Hasn't Even Applied?'

Dame Anne Begg MP

Dame Anne Begg MP is a British Labour Party politician. She was first elected to the House of Commons in 1997, she serves on the All Party Group on Equalities and was previously its chair, since July 2010 she has chaired the Work and Pensions Select Committee. In 2011 she was appointed Dame Commander of the Order of the British Empire (DBE) for services to disabled people and to equal opportunities. Anne Begg argues powerfully for equality guarantees using her own experience of being selected through a Labour party all-women-shortlist and her observations of the disadvantages faced by women candidates.

'We want the best person for the job', is the most common reason given for not implementing any form of positive action to improve women's representation. To which my retort is always, 'How can you get the best person for the job when the best person hasn't even applied?'

Of course there are other answers such as the inbuilt discrimination at interview or selection, or the biases inherent in the qualities and experience being looked for at application stage. But for me, despite being an active member of a Trade Union and the Labour Party, being an MP was not in my 'life plan'.

Who in their right minds would want to be an arrogant, pompous, venal, out of touch, sleazy MP? Yup, I had all the same prejudices as everyone else. Nor did I want to enter a world of late nights, constant travelling, boorish behaviour and bullying. I didn't think that someone like me from a very ordinary working class background who had lived my whole life in the North-East of Scotland would either be welcome or fit in. I was also a Labour Party member in an area where Labour coming in third was regarded as a good result!

So what changed? If the Labour Party hadn't adopted All-Women Shortlists in half of their winnable seats ahead of the 1997 election I wouldn't be an MP today. Not because I wasn't capable of doing the job, or didn't have the qualifications – I clearly am and did. It was because I was prejudiced against the job.

It took the party members in a winnable constituency 40 miles away from where I lived to persuade me to enter the selection process. Without the All-Woman Shortlist, I wouldn't have been approached. Plenty of local men were willing to put themselves forward so in an open selection the CLP wouldn't have done any 'head-hunting'.

So addressing the supply side through creating a demand for women candidates is just as important as removing the inherent discrimination in selection processes if we are to achieve a more diverse Parliament.

The routes into elected politics are varied and are often different for men and women. It often depends on what event moves someone from being merely interested in politics to become actively involved. For me it was being the Union rep during the teachers' industrial action in the mid 1980's.

For other women, it might be the lack of nursery provision in their area, or the threatened closure of a local hospital which turned them into campaigners and helped politicise them. These should have been exactly the qualities selection panels were looking for, but without the 'right' connections in the political party then either they couldn't get on the short-list or no-one encouraged them to think of themselves as potential candidates. That's assuming they were members of a political party – but probably no one had suggested this either. It wasn't an urban myth that some local Labour parties wouldn't accept 'outsiders' as members saying that the Party was full. And anyway, if they had been campaigning against something being introduced or scraped by the Council they were seen as trouble makers. Heaven-forbid that anyone seeking elected office wanted to change things!

That's why gender equality, and equality in general, is essential in other walks of life. We have come some way but we still aren't good at talent spotting able candidates and fostering them.

The experience of the Scottish Parliament is illustrative of how difficult it can be to maintain gender balance, and the necessity to get buy-in from all political parties to achieving it in the first place. The results of the first election to the Parliament flattered to deceive because Labour was the largest party and had used positive action – a twinning and zipping system – to make sure half of its MSPs were women. However, the other parties did not follow suit so the overall gender balance in the Parliament was only 40 per cent. Since then, the numbers of Labour MSPs have been slashed to be replaced by mainly male SNP MSPs. A new Parliament which started with such promise appears to be going backwards.

Judging by the reaction from the Tory women during the debate we held on the anniversary of the publication of the Speaker's Conference report on parliamentary representation, there is no appetite for legislative sex quotas in UK elections which would be the only way of overturning the huge in-built bias against women in the Commons in less than a decade.

However, the Commons' Chamber today looks very different from 1996 or indeed from after the 1997 election; there are more MPs who are women, more from black and minority ethnic communities or have a disability. These MPs are not yet in the proportions found in the general population but Parliament's reflection, while slightly distorted, resembles the population of our country more than it has ever done before.

Chapter Nine

How Quotas Work: The Supply and Demand Model Revisited

Pippa Norris and Mona Lena Krook

In this chapter we apply and extend Norris and Lovenduski's Supply and Demand model to the case of elections to the European Parliament. We operationalise the supply and demand model with systematic multilevel evidence drawn from the European Parliamentary Election Study 2009. We find that women candidates did not observe any negative experience of sex discrimination; perceived largely similar levels of gatekeeper support and they had slightly more financial resources for campaign spending. Women candidates also had similar, or marginally greater, political experience across a range of offices and organisational networks, educational qualifications and more worked in the public sector. Furthermore, women and men were equally politically ambitious in their future career goals. However, the results of the analysis suggest that gender quotas shape the demand-side support offered for women by gatekeepers. In countries with gender quota policies, selectors face incentives and penalties in their choice of candidates on party lists. In this context, selectors (particularly party officials) provide more encouragement for potential female nominees. Countries using quota policies also attract a greater supply of women candidates who are well-qualified and experienced.

Around the globe only thirty-three countries have achieved the 30 per cent target for women in decision-making positions set by the 1995 Beijing Platform. Progress over time has proved slow and erratic. The standard yardstick, used for the UN Millennium Development Goals, is the proportion of women elected to the lower or single house of parliament. Around the world, today women are roughly one in five legislators.[1] This figure has doubled since the mid-1990s but nations and global regions have experienced significant retreats as well as advances, frustrating the hopes of progressive reformers (Matland and Montgomery 2003; Saxonberg 2000). This is not simply a problem which will gradually be overcome through the process of human development expanding opportunities for women in literacy, education, and the paid workforce. Within the European Union, all relatively affluent post-industrial societies, women constitute on average 26 per cent of members of parliament (MPs) and senior ministers in government, 28 per

1. Inter-Parliamentary Union. *Women in National Parliaments: Situation as of 31 December 2012.* http://www.ipu.org/wmn-e/world.htm

cent of judges in the European courts, 30 per cent of top civil servants in national governments, and 32 per cent of members of regional assemblies.[2] As depicted in Figure 9.1, recruitment is a winnowing process from ordinary citizens to the apex of power, with a shrinking pool at each step, like a game of musical chairs. The European Parliament (EP) reflects these challenges; in 2009 women constituted roughly one third of the candidates and one third (35 per cent) of the members (MEPs) elected to this body. This pattern disguises substantial contrasts across EU member states, however (*see* Table 9.1); women are almost two-thirds (61 per cent) of MEPs from Finland, and half the delegates from Estonia and Slovenia, compared with less than one fifth of the MEPs from the Czech Republic and Luxembourg. Among the laggards, Malta displays the poorest record, returning an all-male delegation to the parliament.[3]

As the previous chapter by Meryl Kenny laid out, Norris and Lovenduski's supply and demand framework for understanding political recruitment has had considerable influence on the study of gender and politics over the last two decades (Norris and Lovenduski 1995). As Kenny notes, it has been subject to some criticism of its conceptualisation and reach – for example, does it apply more widely across a broad range of contemporary societies, such as those in Latin America or in other transitional democracies (Field and Siavelis 2008; Hazan and Rahat 2010; Siavelis and Morgenstern 2008a; Siavelis and Morgenstern 2008b)? Nonetheless it continues to be widely cited as an analytical framework or organising metaphor used to identify and weigh the core components in political recruitment in many countries. Thus in recent years it has been employed to explain such diverse phenomenon as, for example, provincial elections in British Columbia and Canadian parliamentary candidates (Ashe and Stewart 2012; Cheng and Tavits 2011), the recruitment of mayors in Belgium (van Liefferinge and Steyvers 2011), women candidates in Chile (Franceschet 2005), and the implementation of gender quotas in the German Länder (Davidson-Schmich 2006). Similar 'push-pull' models have also been used to analyse such diverse phenomenon as patterns of population migration and the recruitment to top management in the private sector (Kirkwood 2009). Yet, it is worth asking whether the original supply-and-demand framework is still relevant today, over and above already identified criticism,[4] given the growing state regulation of the recruitment market for elected office and the rapid diffusion of gender quota policies. Indeed, it can be argued, quite rightly, that we need to go beyond the standard neo-classical supply-and-demand model (Kenny 2011; Krook 2010).

---

2. European Commission. Women and men in decision-making, third quarter 2012. http://ec.europa.eu/justice/gender-equality/gender-decisionmaking/database/highlights/index_en.htm
3. European Commission. Women and men in decision-making, third quarter 2012. http://ec.europa.eu/justice/gender-equality/gender-decisionmaking/database/highlights/index_en.htm
4. For example, given changes in British political parties, such as the use of direct primaries, is the model still helpful to understand the political recruitment process at Westminster?

Table 9.1: Women in the European Parliament, 1979–2009

		1979	1984	1989	1994	1999	2004	2009	Trends
FI	Finland					44	43	62	
EE	Estonia						50	50	
SI	Slovenia						43	50	
DK	Denmark	31	38	38	44	38	43	46	
FR	France	22	21	23	30	40	45	46	
SE	Sweden					41	47	45	
NL	Netherlands	20	28	28	32	35	48	42	
IE	Ireland	13	13	7	27	33	38	42	
PT	Portugal			13	8	20	25	41	
ES	Spain			15	33	34	26	41	
DE	Germany	15	20	31	35	37	33	38	
SK	Slokavia						36	38	
BE	Belgium	8	17	17	32	28	33	36	
HU	Hungary						38	36	
RO	Romania						29	36	
EU	**ALL**	**16**	**18**	**19**	**26**	**30**	31	35	
CY	Cyprus						0	33	
LV	Latvia						33	33	
BG	Bulgaria						44	33	
EL	Greece		8	4	16	16	29	32	
AT	Austria					38	28	32	
UK	United Kingdom	14	15	15	18	24	26	32	
LI	Lithuania							25	
IT	Italy	14	10	12	13	11	21	22	
IT	Italy						38	22	
PL	Poland						15	22	
CZ	Czech Republic						21	18	
LU	Luxembourg	17	50	50	50	33	50	17	
MT	Malta						0	0	

Source: http://www.europarl.europa.eu/aboutparliament/en/00622bc71a/Distribution-of-men-and-women.html

Figure 9.1: The sequential recruitment process in the European parliament

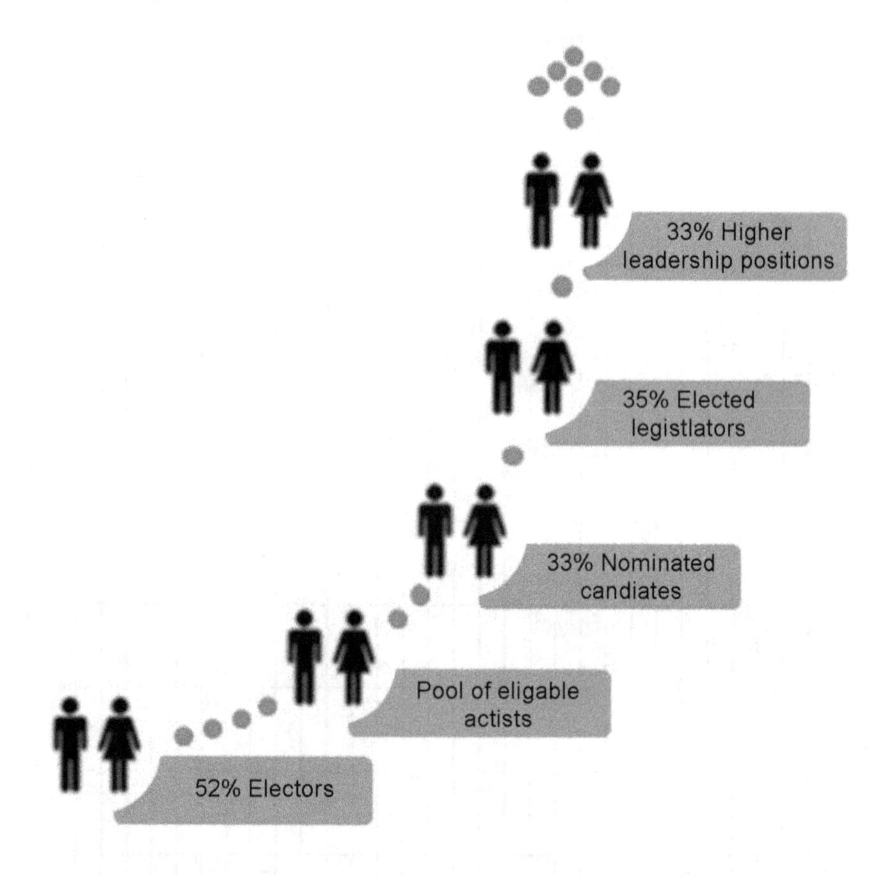

Until the early-1990s, in Western democracies the recruitment of political candidates for elected office was usually regarded as a private process governed primarily by internal party rules, procedures, and constitutions, and only loosely regulated by the state. Gatekeepers were largely free to nominate whomever they wished as their standard-bearers, within constitutional requirements for matters such as the minimal legal age and national citizenship of eligible parliamentary and presidential candidates. Traditionally it was thought that political parties should be free to nominate their own candidates, with voters determining who was returned to office. Since the early-1990s, however, the internal processes and functions of political parties have become increasingly subject to constitutional and legal regulation (van Biezen and Borz 2012; Van Biezen and Piccio 2013), including through the adoption of gender quota policies.

An extensive body of research has sought to explain the growing popularity of these policies worldwide and to determine their consequences (Childs 2004; Dahlerup 2006; Kittilson 2006; Krook 2009; Swers 2002; Thomas 1995; Towns

2010). Gender equality policies are implemented through three mechanisms: (i) the use of reserved seats for members of parliament, (ii) legal statutes affecting candidate lists for all parties, with different types of enforcement mechanisms and penalties for non-compliance, or (iii) procedural rules governing internal recruitment procedures and outcomes, adopted by specific parties within each country (Krook 2009). The substantial literature suggests that gender quotas are usually most effective when they are designed to fit the type of electoral system, where ranked candidate lists alternate by sex ('zippered'), where enforceable mechanisms penalise non-compliance, and where the target level set for any gender quotas are fairly generous (Dahlerup 2006; Krook 2009).

What impact do these regulations have? For a simple benchmark, we can compare the proportion of women elected to the European Parliament in June 2009 by the type of gender quota in use in each member state, without any controls. Hence women were on average around 35 per cent of MEPs in states with no gender quotas, 33 per cent of MEPs in states where at least one party adopted a gender quota in its rulebook, and 38 per cent in states with legal gender quotas applying to all parties. This modest (3-percentage point) gap between legal and no-quota states is slightly smaller in size to that observed using similar comparisons in national parliamentary elections.[5] This simple yardstick may be misleading and the effects spurious, however, since many other factors may be driving both the success of women in gaining elected office and also the willingness of countries and parties to adopt legal quotas, such as the existence of egalitarian cultural attitudes in Nordic and Mediterranean European societies.

More rigorous within-country studies have sought to evaluate the effect of gender quota policies by comparing the proportion of women members of parliament immediately 'before' and 'after' implementing new quota policies (Norris 2008). By comparing 'inputs' and 'outputs', both methods essentially treat the series of steps within the interior recruitment process, and thus the supply of women nominees and the attitudes of gatekeepers, as a classic 'black-box': focusing on the combined effects of supply and demand, rather than disaggregating these steps (Ashe and Stewart 2012). But how do quota policies actually achieve their intended goals? The underlying mechanisms within the 'black box' remain poorly understood and under-conceptualised. It is important to understand these linkages, however, not least because some quota policies have proved far more effective than others.

To further these goals, in this chapter we theorise that the implementation of gender quotas as formal institutional rules is similar to government regulation of many other sectors, such as financial markets, environmental emissions, or private health care. Quota regulations have the potential capacity to alter both supply (women's willingness to run for office) and demand (the constraints and incentives facing gatekeepers). For example, in countries such as Belgium,

5. *See* Figure 5. D. Dahlerup *et al.* (2011) Electoral gender quota systems and their implementation in Europe, Brussels: European Parliament's Committee on Gender Equality.

France, and Slovenia, laws regulate the composition of party lists for the European Parliament. Selectors have to include a specified proportion of women in 'zippered' (alternating) rank position in party lists; otherwise lists will be legally disqualified for ballot access. In this context, gatekeepers have strong incentives to encourage women nominees, and eligible women activists are more likely to come forward to pursue these expanded opportunities. Other types of institutional rules, notably the type of proportional or majoritarian electoral system, have long been regarded as central to the operation of recruitment markets (*See* for example McAllister and Studlar 2001). Growing regulation of the recruitment process within political parties can be expected to have heightened the importance of institutional rules.

Building upon Lovenduski and Norris's earlier analytical supply-and-demand framework of political recruitment, therefore, we theorise that gender quota regulations could affect the nomination of candidates through demand or supply (as depicted in Figure 9.2). One plausible argument is that gender quota regulations could strengthen the incentives for gatekeepers to nominate women candidates (on the *demand-side*), through reinforcing egalitarian social norms and also raising the costs of non-compliance. Gatekeepers therefore want to pull more eligible women onto their lists of candidates. It is also possible, however, that quota regulations could encourage more women activists to pursue legislative careers (on the *supply-side*), through expanding their opportunities for success and reducing the risks of running for office. From this perspective, the expression of political 'ambition' is not a fixed and unchangeable social psychological attribute, learnt through role models in the early socialisation processes. Instead previously-suppressed drives respond rationally to the calculation of success. Elected office involves certain potential benefits, such as the status and power associated with leadership positions in public service, but also major costs for candidates, not least the time and energy demands of campaigning, the risks of career-breaks and opportunity displacement costs from other employment sectors and, in some cases in highly traditional cultures, even the threat of violence and intimidation facing women. Gender quota policies have the capacity to alter the rational calculation of costs and benefits in pursuing political careers. Lastly, of course, both effects could also operate simultaneously in an interactive process, for example if party gatekeepers actively seek out women activists to nominate as candidates, and if this process encourages suppressed female ambitions among those who may have previously felt that they had no chance of succeeding against the odds.

Core propositions

The theoretical framework advanced here generates several testable propositions when predicting how the effects of gender quota policies will differ, as shown in Figure 9.2. The quasi-experimental treatment concerns the type of gender quota policies used in each country for elections to 2009 elections to the European parliament. The effects of these policies are examined by classifying EU member states most simply into those using (1) legal, (2) party, and (3) no gender quotas. In most European countries, the types of gender quota policies used for national

Figure 9.2: How types of gender quota policies effect the nomination of women

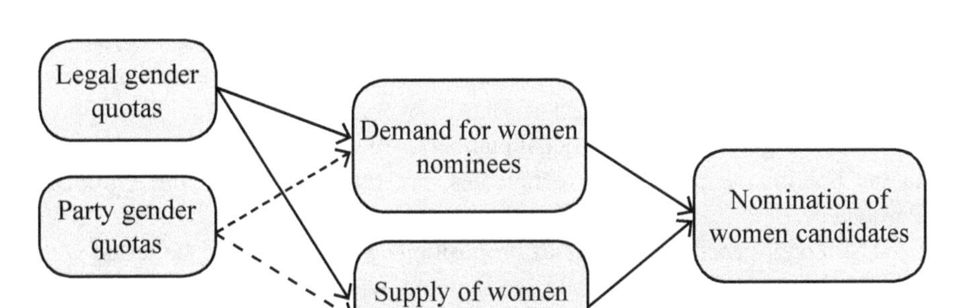

parliamentary elections are also used for all other levels of election, although there are some exceptions to this rule (Dahlerup and Freidenvall 2009; Kantola 2010). For these contests, six states such as Belgium, France, and Poland employed legally-binding quotas affecting the composition of candidate lists used by all political parties (with or without effective enforcement mechanisms and egalitarian levels). Another seventeen member states, such as Germany and the Netherlands, used party gender quotas implemented through internal rules in some parties but not all. Other states, such as Bulgaria and Latvia, did not employ any measures. Although there remain important differences in both levels and types of implementation, the use of gender quotas by each member state is operationalised in the models as a simple ordinal scale (none = 0, party quotas = 1, legal quotas = 2).

Thus we theorise that in countries where *legal gender quotas* regulate the lists of nominated candidates for all parties seeking ballot access, quotas can be expected to have the strongest impact on the demand and supply of women nominees. Party *gender quotas*, where only some (but not all) parties introduce positive action measures and 'soft' targets into their selection rules and process, are predicted to generate weaker effects on the nomination of women candidates overall in each country. These policies depend upon the formal and informal enforcement mechanisms within each party, which may be effective or relatively weak. Moreover these types of quotas are restricted to the particular parties, such as those on the left, which have chosen to adopt these measures. Lastly, societies without any statutory or party gender quotas at all function as a control group. Plausibly the number of women and men candidates may vary over time for many reasons, such as the gradual spread of more egalitarian cultural attitudes towards the role of women in public life. Therefore the contrast in women's nomination observed between countries using legal gender quota policies, and those with no gender quota policies, provide the critical test used in this study.

In deciding which aspect of the sequential recruitment process to elected office poses the greatest barriers to women, it helps to identify the sex ratios in each step (*See*, for example, Ashe and Stewart 2012). In the context of elections to the European Parliament in 2009, the fact that women constituted around one third of the nominated candidates, and approximately one third of the successfully-elected MEPs, suggests that the key hurdle is the number of eligible women activists who are *nominated*. Once they get past this hurdle, women and men candidates appear to succeed in getting elected in equal numbers. We therefore focus most attention to the nomination process for candidates, not their election to the European Parliament.

The model generates a series of propositions which can, then, be tested with the available empirical evidence to examine whether gender quota policies shape gender gaps in either the supply of eligible nominees or the demands of gatekeepers. Gender gaps in the *demand-side* decisions of gatekeepers are monitored by two main indicators: gender gaps in *gatekeeper support*, measured by the levels of the encouragement which candidates reported receiving from different types of gatekeepers when they first decided to stand (H1.1), and the *campaign resources* available to candidates, monitored by their total expenditures on personal campaigns (H1.2). The core logic predicts that in countries without gender quota policies, gender gaps should be wider across these indices. In this context, compared with men, women candidates should be observed to receive less encouragement and fewer campaign financial resources. In countries with legal quotas, on the other hand, any gender gaps are expected to diminish or even reverse. In this context, gatekeepers have stronger incentives to nominate women candidates and, once on the list, to provide the financial backing helping them to succeed. The use of two indices serves to check the robustness of the results.

On the other hand, to see whether gender quotas shape 'supply-side' factors in women's nomination to the European parliament, we predict that in countries with legal quotas, we should observe smaller gender gaps in political ambition (H2.1), as well as smaller contrasts in the political leadership experience of candidates (H2.2). Again the core logic suggests that gender quota policies should shrink gender gaps across these 'push' indices, as more women with leadership experience and political ambitions will calculate that they have good opportunities to win nominations if they step forward.

The test in our models focuses upon the size of any gender gaps observed in recruitment to the European Parliament (i.e. differences between male and female candidates), including in gatekeeper support and in the campaign resources which candidates reported receiving (on the demand side) and in leadership experience and political ambitions (on the supply side). Legal gender quotas are expected to be most effective in diminishing, or even reversing, gender gaps though the disadvantages which women nominees have traditionally experienced in either supply or demand. Party gender quotas are expected to have moderate effects. The control treatment for comparison is member states without gender quotas, where women candidates are expected to prove at a disadvantage to men in both supply and demand factors.

The European Union context

To test these propositions, recruitment to the European Parliament in the 2009 elections is examined. This comparison therefore adopts a 'most-similar' design when seeking to compare the recruitment processes across a broad range of European states. Despite important differences, contemporary European societies have relatively similar affluent post-industrial economies, sharing centuries of shared cultural roots and historical traditions prior to the Cold War era. Equal opportunity and affirmative action policies adopted by the European Union (EU) apply to all member states, providing a common normative and legal framework. Elections to the European Parliament also involve simultaneous contests for the same office, with all 27 EU member states now employing relatively similar proportional electoral systems (using either party list Proportional Representation or the Single Transferable Vote). The comparison of EU member states has the advantage of excluding several factors which confound global comparisons, such as national contrasts in the structure, size, roles, and powers of parliaments; types of electoral systems; and sharp contrasts in levels of female literacy, education and paid employment. This controls for many extraneous factors ('noise') when comparing the recruitment process across diverse nations.

Data and Evidence

Data is derived from a survey of 1,576 candidates standing for election to the European Parliament, conducted as part of the PIREDOU European Parliamentary Election Study 2009.[6] In these contests, 736 Members of the European Parliament (MEPs) were elected in twenty seven member states to represent approximately 500 million Europeans, making these the biggest trans-national elections in history. The dataset is based on interviews conducted both online and by mail, using a standardised common survey questionnaire, translated into several languages. The instrument sought to gather information about recruitment and nomination processes, political experience, campaign activities, political attitudes and values, and social and political background data. The data was weighted by sex to be representative of the candidate population standing in the 2009 elections. In the election, women were roughly one third of the candidates and of third of the elected MEPs. Gender gaps, defined as differences among women and men candidates, are described in successive tables using the pooled survey.

6. The authors are most grateful to the EES 2009, European Parliamentary Election Study 2009, Candidate Study (Full release) (www.piredeu.eu).

Analysis and results

Demand-side factors: Encouragement and support from gatekeepers

We can start by comparing gatekeeper support monitored by the level of encouragement which candidates reported receiving from a variety of individuals and groups. These actors function in a gatekeeping role, ranging from the vital but informal encouragement and help received from spouse, friends, and family, to endorsement among more formal networks of community groups and party members. When asked whether they were encouraged to stand when they first considered becoming a candidate for the European Parliament, Table 9.2 demonstrates that the majority of candidates reported receiving encouragement from national and regional party officials. Other sources of support, mentioned by roughly one quarter to one third of candidates, included spouses or partners, other family members, and community leaders.

Two findings emerge. Firstly, contrary to explanations emphasising the problem of sex discrimination or hostile attitudes towards women by gatekeepers, in fact women candidates – when compared to men –reported receiving significantly *greater* encouragement overall from regional party officials, their spouse or partner, other family members, sitting MEPs, and interest groups. *There is no evidence from this data that women reported receiving consistently less encouragement than men.* It should be noted that this data is subjective and it cannot determine whether traditional cultural attitudes influenced the actual support given to eligible women and men at earlier stages of the recruitment process. As such, sex discrimination could still have affected the broader pool of activists who sought, but failed to secure, an official position on the party ticket. The evidence is also indirect, asking candidates to report their own perceived sources of support, rather than asking gatekeepers about their own attitudes and behaviour. Nevertheless the popular claim that gatekeepers actively discourage women candidates by discriminating against them receives no confirmation from the perception of candidates for these elections.

But these observations could arise from many factors, such as the growth of egalitarian attitudes towards gender equality in elected office in European societies. To determine whether gender quota policies affect this process, the summary support index is analysed by the type of policy used in each country. The results at the bottom on Table 9.2 suggest that in states without any gender quotas, women and men candidates reported similar, or marginally greater, encouragement from gatekeepers. In countries with party and legal gender quotas, however, women reported receiving greater support overall, a significant gender gap of 5–8 percentage points. Moreover the fact that the largest gender gap in support is observable from regional party officials (rather than, say community leaders or interest groups), also suggests that gender quota policies do play a positive role in shaping attitudes among core gatekeepers.

Table 9.2: Demand-side: Gatekeeper support

	% Women	% Men	Gender gap	Coef. of Association	Sig.
National party officials	51	48	+3	.03	
Regional party officials	59	43	+16	.03	***
Spouse/partner	37	23	+14	.14	***
Other community leaders	25	22	+3	.03	
Other family members	31	21	+10	.11	***
Sitting MEP	19	14	+5	.15	***
Representative of an interest group	16	10	+4	.09	***
Retired MEP	08	05	+3	.05	
Gatekeeper Support Index by type of quota policy					
No gender quotas	32	30	+2		
Party rule gender quotas	33	25	+8		
Legal gender quotas for all parties	34	29	+5	.15	***
ALL: Gatekeeper Support Index	33	26	+7	.15	***

Note: Q38. 'When you first became a candidate for the European Parliament, did any of the following encourage you to stand? Tick all boxes that apply. …' Yes/No. % 'Yes.

The Gatekeeper Support Index sums these eight items and standardises the measurement to 100 points. The coefficient of association is measured by ANOVA, without controls. The gender gap is calculated as the mean Gatekeeper Support Index of women minus the Index of men. A positive coefficient suggests that on average women have more support than men. *** Sig .001 level

Source: 2009 European Election Candidate Study (Full Release)

Demand-side factors: Financial campaign resources

Table 9.3 examines the distribution of campaign resources, serving as a more concrete indicator of any potential demand-side sex discrimination. If male candidates enjoy greater financial resources, more help from the party, or the support of more campaign workers, this could put them as a distinct advantage over female candidates. It is often assumed that women face greater difficulties in fund-raising, and they should, therefore, have fewer financial resources available for their campaigns. Again certain counter-intuitive findings emerge from the comparison. Firstly, no statistically significant sex differences are evident in the distribution of campaign resources, except that women reported receiving a significantly higher proportion of party funds. This source is likely to provide valuable help for women's campaigns, as party donations are easier to raise than having to depend upon outside donations or private funds. In addition, overall, women spent slightly more than men (roughly 2000 Euros or 10 per cent more) on

Table 9.3: Demand-side: Distribution of campaign resources

	% Women	% Men	Gender gap	Coef. of Association	Sig.
Total financial resources used in your campaign (Euros)	22,204	20,058	+1,689	.01	
Proportion of this total from …					
…Party funds	54	48	+6	.08	**
…Donations	15	15	0	.0	
…Private funds	37	41	-4	.04	
Number of campaign workers	14	13	+1	.02	
Financial resources by type of quota policy					
No gender quotas	14,596	8,830	+5,766		
Party rule gender quotas	26,739	14,295	+12,444		
Legal gender quotas for all parties	14,710	45,104	-30,403	.01	N/S

Note: Q15, 'Thinking about your campaign budget, what would be your best estimate of the financial resources you use for your campaign (including party funds, donations, and private funds)?' Q16, 'What portion of that sum comes from the party, from donations, and from your private funds?' Q17, 'Besides yourself, how many people helped in your personal election campaign?'

The coefficient of association is measured by ANOVA, without controls. The gender gap is calculated as the mean financial resources spent by women candidates minus those spent by men. A positive coefficient suggests that women have more resources. *** Sig. 001 level; ** Sig .01 level.

Source: 2009 European Election Candidate Study (Full Release)

Table 9.4: Demand side: Who are the gatekeepers?

	% Women	% Men	Gender gap	Coef. of Association	Sig.
National party officials	41	41	0	.05	
Regional/local party officials	32	24	+8	.09	*
Party members	30	25	+5	.14	***
Non-party members	6	5	+1	.01	
Minority organisations	4	4	0	.01	
Interest groups	6	4	+2	.01	

Note: Q43: 'In your party, how important are the following groups in the selection of candidates for the European Parliament? …?' % 'Very important'.

Source: 2009 European Election Candidate Study (Full Release)

their personal campaigns, although this difference proved insignificant. When the results are broken down by the type of quota policies used in each state, however women proved to be at a substantial financial advantage in countries without any gender quotas, spending on average around 6,000 to 12,000 Euros more than men. This situation reversed in states using legal gender quotas, where women candidates spent on average around 30,000 Euros less than men. This pattern suggests that there are no consistent effects arising from the use of gender quota policies for the distribution of the campaign resources which candidates spend to help ensure their election. Therefore gender quotas appear to matter more by providing an incentive for gatekeepers (especially key party officials) to encourage women candidates to come forward, but this does not necessarily mean that women candidate are subsequently given the financial resources needed to support their election.

Demand-side factors: Centralised or localised gatekeepers

Turning to the role of gatekeepers, does the type of decision-making process matter? For example, do women do better in gaining nominations under centralised or localised recruitment processes? Table 9.4 examines perceptions of the key gatekeepers in the selection process. The national and regional party leadership clearly emerges as the most important players in this process across the pooled sample, suggesting a relatively centralised and partisan process of candidate recruitment. Ordinary party members are also seen as playing a role in this process. By contrast, outsiders such as non-party members, organisations, and groups, are not regarded as particularly important. Despite all the changes to recruitment during recent decades, the route to elected office remains a party-dominated process in Europe. The only significant sex differences which emerged concern the roles of regional/local party officials and ordinary party members, which women candidates regarded as significantly more important than men. Thus women are not more likely to have to run an 'outsider' campaign, relying upon external organisations and supporters; instead they report greater encouragement from regional party officials and that this group has an important role in the recruitment process.

Supply-side factors: The experience of candidates

To consider the role of supply-side factors, we can compare women and men's leadership experience as measured through office-holding and membership of relevant elected bodies, such as local and national government, business associations and trade union organisations, and party organisations. In many European societies, prior political leadership experience is usually seen as an important asset which potential nominees bring to the pursuit of elected office, helping to secure nominations and gain campaign support. Those who have held relevant, prior political office can be expected to have strengthened relevant organisational and speaking skills, policy knowledge, and social networks, all of which are thought to be useful for political careers. Table 9.5 demonstrates the prior leadership experience of candidates in a diverse range of roles, such as holding public office and membership of organisational groups. If women lack prior experience, they may be at a significant disadvantage when pursuing elected office.

Again the results are somewhat counter-intuitive since they demonstrate that women had significantly greater experience overall, as well as through holding leadership roles in regional representative bodies, trade unions, environmental groups and, not surprisingly, women's organisations. The only sector where male candidates enjoyed a modest advantage over women concerned business organisations, probably reflecting traditional sex segregation in patterns of paid employment. Thus the overall sex differences observed in leadership experience fail to explain women's under-representation in the European Parliament. Most importantly, when broken down by the type of gender quota policies, women candidates proved marginally less experienced than men in societies without gender quotas, whereas this modest gender gap reversed in societies with quotas, where women demonstrated *greater* overall leadership experience than men. Thus the opportunities provided by affirmative action policies do appear to influence the experience of those seeking elected office, by attracting women with more experience.

Supply-side factors: Human capital

What about the human capital and socio-economic background of respondents? Human capital refers to many assets and resources which candidates bring to the pursuit of elected office. Education is usually regarded as critical for political careers, providing the formal qualifications and cognitive and personal skills which are helpful in securing elected office. Sectors of employment may be important; traditionally many MPs are drawn from public sector professions and management. Marital status may matter as well. Marriage is conventionally seen as an electoral asset for men and women, suggesting stable social relationships, although it may be difficult for female politicians to combine demanding political careers (especially given the travel required for the EP in Brussels and Strasbourg) with primary family responsibilities, if they are responsible for primary care of young children or the elderly. Further, extensive party experience is usually regarded as an important asset in Europe, demonstrating loyalty and commitment to party selectors. Age is also relevant, due to the need to acquire experience outside of parliament, with most candidates being middle–aged. The hours per week spent campaigning during the last month of the European contest is a proxy indicator of career flexibility and the capacity to invest free time in electioneering.

The results of the comparison show that overall a few significant gender differences were observed in these varied characteristics, as Table 9.6 shows. In particular, women candidates were significantly more likely to have higher levels of formal education and to work in the public sector, both of which should be seen as an advantage for political careers. Women were also significantly less likely to be married or living with a partner; this pattern has also been observed elsewhere,

where compared with equivalent men, many women parliamentarians and indeed women world leaders are disproportionately unmarried, widowed, or divorced (Norris and Lovenduski 1995). Nevertheless there were no statistically significant observable gender gaps in age, years of party membership, household income, or time devoted to campaigning.

Table 9.5: Supply-side: Strength of leadership experience

	% Women	% Men	Gender gap	Coef. of Association	Sig.
Local/regional party organisation	85	86	-1	.02	
National party organisation	81	78	+3	.03	
Local representative body	52	50	+2	.02	
Women's organisation	48	2	+46	.57	***
Trade union	41	36	+5	.06	*
Professional association	39	39	0	.01	
Environmental group	33	23	+10	.10	***
Regional representative body	28	20	+8	.08	***
Local government	28	28	0	.02	
Religious organisation	22	26	-4	.04	
National representative body	19	19	0	.01	
Business organisation	14	20	-6	.07	**
Regional government	10	8	+2	.01	
Been a lobbyist in Brussels	7	6	+1	.03	
The European parliament	6	7	-1	.03	
National government	4	4	0	.01	
Leadership Experience Index by type of policy					
No gender quotas	21	24	-3		
Party rule gender quotas	35	29	+6		
Legal gender quotas for all parties	33	28	+5	.14	***
Summary Leadership Experience Index	34	29	+5	.04	N/S

Note: Q45) 'Can you tell us about your political experience? Are you now or have you ever been a member of any of the following bodies? ...?' Q46) 'Are you a member or do you hold or did you ever hold office in any of the following organisations...?' The Leadership Experience Index sums each of these offices and then standardises the scale to 100 points. The gender gap is calculated as the mean Leadership Experience Index of women minus the Index of men. A positive coefficient suggests that women candidates have more leadership experience than men. *** Sig .001 level; N/s Not significant.

Source: 2009 European Election Candidate Study (Full Release)

Table 9.6: Supply-side: Social background and resources

	% Women	% Men	Gender gap	Coef. of Association	Sig.
Education (High)	86	80	+6	.08	**
Household Income (Moderate to affluent)	54	55	-1	.06	
Working in the public sector	42	33	+9	.11	**
Married or living with partner	70	77	-7	.11	**
Age (means years)	46	48	-2	.02	
Years of party membership	12	12	0	.01	
Time candidate campaigned during the election	34	33	+1	.02	

Note: *See* the technical appendix for coding details. ** Sig .01 level
Source: 2009 European Election Candidate Study (Full Release)

Table 9.7: Supply side: Political ambitions

	% Women	% Men	Gender gap	Coef. of Association	Sig.
Member of the European parliament	46	44	+2	.02	
Chair of my EP party group	6	6	0	.01	
Chair of EP committee	12	12	0	.01	
Leader of a European organisation	12	10	+2	.02	
Member of the European Commission	9	9	0	.01	
Member of my national parliament	39	38	+1	.01	
Chair of a national parliamentary group	7	9	-2	.04	
Chair of a national parliamentary committee	10	12	-2	.01	
Leader of a national organisation	12	12	0	.04	
Member of my national government	20	23	-3	.01	
Political Ambition Index by type of policy					
No gender quotas	13	17	-4		
Party rule gender quotas	18	17	+1		
Legal gender quotas for all parties	16	17	-1	.01	N/S
Summary Political Ambition Index	17	17	0	.01	N/S

Note: Q47 'What would you like to be ten years from now on? Please tick as many boxes as appropriate. ...?' 'Yes'. These items were summed and standardised to create a summary 100-point Political Ambition Index. *See* the technical appendix for coding details. The gender gap is calculated as the Political Ambition Index of women minus the Index of men. A positive coefficient suggests that on average women candidates are more ambitious than men.
Source: 2009 European Election Candidate Study (Full Release)

Supply-side factors: Political ambition

The final classic supply-side factor concerns gender gaps in political ambition. Social psychological theories by Lawless and Fox (2005) emphasise the reluctance of women to run for political office in America, since they are regarded as being less motivated than men (Lawless and Fox 2005). Theories have long detected sex differences in internal political efficacy among the general public, referring to the feeling that citizens can make a difference through political channels. To monitor ambition, respondents in the candidate survey were asked where they would like to be ten years from now, using a series of multiple-choice options, such as being an MEP, chair of a party group in the European Parliament, member of their national parliament, or government minister. In theory, the more ambitious the candidate, the more they would seek to hold higher office. To generate a Political Ambition Index, offices were summed and an index of political ambition was constructed on this basis. This is only a proxy measure; for example, politicians may be very driven to succeed in only one sector or type of office, rather than generally across the board. But the flexibility to move from, say, European to national political careers may be an important indicator of the drive for power. Table 9.7 presents the results of the comparison showing no significant gender gap overall in career ambitions distinguishing women and men candidates. Thus the survey results suggest that office-holding ambition failed to distinguish European candidates by sex. When broken down by the type of gender quota policy, women appeared to be slightly less experienced than men in countries where there were no gender quotas, while this modest gender gap became insignificant in countries using party and legal gender quotas.

Conclusion

The 'supply-and-demand' framework of political recruitment to legislative office in a regulated marketplace can be used loosely as a metaphor. It can also be operationalised more precisely with systematic multilevel evidence. This helps to determine whether women are reluctant to come forward to pursue political office (for example, due to lack of ambition, interest, resources, or confidence), or whether sex discrimination by key gatekeepers means that women who seek to come forward are not nominated (for example, if women are seen by selectors as less qualified, lacking in skills, or less electable), or whether the institutional context is most important (where the structure of opportunities, set by electoral systems and legal gender quotas, regulate the incentives shaping the behaviour of the pool of eligible candidates and gatekeepers). The full model ideally requires evidence collected at all three levels: the structural rules in each country and party, the background and attitudes of the broader pool of potential candidates, and the decisions of the core party and non-party gatekeepers when selecting whom to nominate. One of the main challenges facing analysts is that evidence is often only available for one of these components, not all three simultaneously.

Determining which aspect restricts women's nomination is important for understanding the recruitment process and also because each component also has different policy implications. If the institutional structure is critical, for example, this emphasises the importance of reforming the rules of the game, such as implementing binding and enforceable gender quotas or reforming electoral systems. If the essential problem is one of the 'supply' of potential nominees willing to pursue political office, however, then effective interventions should be designed to strengthen the political ambitions, resources, and skills of excluded groups, such as through offering training, fund-raising, and capacity development programmes, and also changing deep-rooted cultural values and social roles. If the main barrier to elected office is sex discrimination by gatekeepers, however, then demand-side solutions should address equal opportunity policies in recruitment procedures and anti-discrimination training programmes aimed at changing the attitudes of selectors.

Moreover the analytical framework also helps to predict the potential consequences of the recruitment process, such as for party discipline, legislative cohesion, and democratic accountability (Field and Siavelis 2008). If demand-side factors are critical, for example, so that elected members remain accountable to central or local party gatekeepers, then they have strong incentives to be party loyalists and the parliamentary leadership such as the whips office can exert stronger control over party discipline and the party programme. If supply-side factors dominate, on the other hand, this may weaken these mechanisms, producing less cohesive parties and parliaments.

Given the nature of the candidate survey dataset, several qualifications or limitations need to be emphasised. Firstly, this study cannot determine the impact of gender quotas on the broader pool of eligibles, for example if women who wanted to pursue nominations to the European parliament received greater support from party leaders in countries with legal quotas. Further analysis is required to examine information about the party members, political activists, and other local office-holders eligible to pursue a political career in the European parliament. Secondly, this study has been conducted using the pooled sample of candidates. The evidence needs to be broken down in future research at national level, as well as ideally being combined with detailed interviews and participant observation of the process and rules used for recruitment within different parties. Thirdly, the results of the analysis are also quite sensitive to the particular coding of types of quota policies, and often there remains a fuzzy distinction between 'soft' or informal targets which parties adopt as normative standards and binding party quotas which are written into formal rule books and selection procedures. In some cases, soft targets may be observed more closely than more rigid regulations. Similarly party leaders may choose to disregard legal quotas which have weak enforcement mechanisms and few effective sanctions, whereas they may feel more constrained by party constitutions. The comparison of member states across the EU also does not include any which have adopted reserved seats for women. Thus the simple classification of types of quota policies used in this study may fail to capture the complexities of how these mechanisms work in practice. Lastly it should also be noted that the study does not control for many other factors which may be influencing the willingness of women to come forward, the decisions made by gatekeepers, and the propensity to implement gender quota policies. This includes the role of egalitarian and traditional cultures. Thus societies with the more widespread adherence to women's empowerment in public life may be most willing to adopt statutes which enforce gender equality in candidate selection, as well as having more egalitarian attitudes among party selectors and women candidates. Unfortunately the survey dataset did not include suitable items allowing us to control for the effects of gender cultures.

Nevertheless, and with these qualifications in mind, the descriptive survey evidence presented here helps to explore whether supply or demand-side factors distinguish the overall pool of women and men candidates nominated for the European Parliamentary elections. The results suggest two important findings. Firstly, among male and female candidates selected for the European parliament, the overall comparison pooled among all EU member states allowed us to observe remarkably few striking or significant gender gaps which could help to explain the relatively under-representation of women in elected office and in the European parliament. *In general, women candidates did not observe any negative experience of sex discrimination; compared with men, women candidates perceived largely similar, or even greater levels, of gatekeeper support and encouragement and they had slightly more financial resources for campaign spending. Women candidates also had similar, or marginally greater, political experience across a range of offices and organisational networks, educational qualifications and more worked in the public sector. Finally, women and men were equally political ambitious in their future career goals.*

Secondly, as well as the overall results among the pooled sample of candidates, we also explored whether there were significant gender gaps among countries which used legal gender quotas, party quotas, and those which lacked such policies. The results of the analysis suggest that gender quotas shape the demand-side support offered for women by gatekeepers. *In countries with gender quota policies, selectors face incentives and penalties in their choice of candidates on party lists. In this context, selectors (particularly party officials) provide more encouragement for potential female nominees. Countries using quota policies also attract a greater supply of women candidate who are well-qualified and experienced.* On the other hand, we detected fewer consistent differences arising from quota policies in the financial resources that women and men receive during their campaigns or in the ambitions which they express for future political office. Therefore the results of our study do help us to understand better the 'secret garden' of candidate recruitment and the 'black box' of how gender quota policies work to strengthen women's empowerment and improve gender equality in political office.

References

Ashe, J. and Stewart, K. (2012) 'Legislative recruitment: using diagnostic testing to explain under-representation', *Party Politics* 18 (5): 687–707.

Cheng, C. and Tavits, M. (2011) 'Informal influences in selecting female political candidates', *Political Research Quarterly* 64 (2): 460–71.

Childs, S. (2004) *New Labour's Women MPs: Women representing women*, London: Routledge.

Dahlerup, D. (ed.) (2006) *Women, Quotas, and Politics*, London: Routledge.

Dahlerup, D. and Freidenvall, L. (2009) 'Electoral gender quota systems and their implementation in Europe', *European Parliament's Committee on Gender Equality*.

Davidson-Schmich, L. (2006) 'Implementation of political party gender quotas: evidence from the German Lander', *Party Politics* 12 (2): 211–32.

Field, B. and Siavelis, P. (2008) 'Candidate selection procedures in transitional polities: a research note', *Party Politics* 14 (5): 620–39.

Franceschet, S. (2005) *Women and Politics in Chile*, Boulder, CO: Lynne Rienner.

Hazan, R. and Rahat, G. (2010) *Democracy within Parties: Candidate selection methods and their political consequences*, Oxford: Oxford University Press.

Kantola, J. (2010) *Gender and the European Union*, London: Palgrave.

Kenny, M. (2011) 'Gender and institutions of political recruitment: candidate selection in post-devolution Scotland', in M. Krook and F. MacKay (eds) *Gender, Politics and Institutions*, Houndmills, Basingstoke: Palgrave Macmillan.

Kirkwood, J. (2009) 'Motivational factors in a push-pull theory of entrepreneurship', *Gender in Management: An International Journal* 24 (5): 346–64.

Kittilson, M. C. (2006) *Challenging Parties, Changing Parliaments*, Columbus: Ohio State University Press.

Krook, M. (2009) *Quotas for Women in Politics: Gender and candidate selection reform worldwide*, New York: Oxford University Press.

— (2010) 'Beyond supply and demand: a feminist-institutionalist theory of candidate selection', *Political Research Quarterly* 63 (4): 707–20.

Lawless, J. and Fox, R. (2005) *It Takes a Candidate: Why women don't run for office*, Cambridge: Cambridge University Press.

McAllister, I. and Studlar, D. (2001) 'Electoral systems and women's representation: a long-term perspective', *Representation* 39 (1): 3–14.

Matland, R. and Montgomery, K. (eds) (2003) *Women's Access to Political Power in Post-Communist Europe*, Oxford: Oxford University Press.

Norris, P. (2008) *Electoral Engineering*, New York: Cambridge University Press.

Norris, P. and Lovenduski, J. (1995) *Political Recruitment*, Cambridge: Cambridge University Press.

Saxonberg, S. (2000) 'Women in East European parliaments', *Journal of Democracy* 11 (2): 145–58.

Siavelis, P. and Morgenstern, S. (2008a) 'Candidate selection and recruitment in Latin America: a framework for analysis', *Latin American Politics and Society* 50 (4): 27–58.

— (eds) (2008b) *Pathways to Power: Political recruitment and candidate selection in Latin America*, Philadephia: Penn State Press.

Swers, M. (2002) *The Difference Women Make*, Chicago: University of Chicago Press.

Thomas, S. (1995) *How Women Legislate*, New York: Oxford University Press.

Towns, A. (ed.) (2010) *Women and States*, New York: Cambridge University Press.

van Biezen, I. and Borz, G. (2012) 'Models of party democracy: patterns of party regulation in post-war European constitutions', *European Political Science Review* 4 (3): 327–59.

van Biezen, I. and Piccio, D. (2013) 'Shaping intra-party democracy: on the legal regulation of internal party organisations', in W. Cross and R. Katz (eds) *The Challenges of Intra-Party Democracy*, Oxford: Oxford University Press.

van Liefferinge, H. and Steyvers, K. (2011) 'Family matters? Degrees of family politicisation in political recruitment and career start of mayors in Belgium', *Acta Politica* 44 (2): 125–49.

Vignette – Beyond Quotas: Reflections on Parity in France

Axelle Lemaire

> Axelle Lemaire is a French socialist politician. She was elected as the Member of the French National Assembly representing the French citizens in Northern Europe in June 2012. She argues that it's time for the political class to adapt to the reality of gender equality embraced long ago by the French people.

In recent years, France has implemented several laws to encourage gender equality in politics. It started with the emblematic bill voted in June 2000 under the government of Prime Minister Lionel Jospin, which defined a legal obligation for political parties to present an equal number of men and women candidates in local, regional and European elections, and created fines for political parties who would not respect this obligation in parliamentary elections. This was a bold move made by the socialist government. The socialists argued then that the law would change political practices quicker than the political classes' attitudes would do. And it did. Although despite this encouraging legal step, elite political attitudes seem to be still lagging behind today's French society. Political parties, sometimes deliberately, choose to set aside legal requirements and pay fines rather than promote women candidates. Too often, local ambitions prevail over national equality.

The 2012 election held positive lessons for gender equality; 26 per cent of all elected Members of the new French National Assembly are women, the highest proportion on record. Although that figure reveals a strong, persistent imbalance, it also reflects a dramatic improvement compared to the 2007 women intake which stagnated at 18.5 per cent or to the even more modest proportion of 12 per cent in 2002.

The gender make-up of the benches of the French Parliament now follows party divisions in a visible and almost pictorial manner. Grey hair and bald on one side; young men and women MPs on the other. Out of 155 female MPs elected in 2012, 105 are from the Socialist Party. This was a deliberate choice made by the party, at the earliest stage of the campaign.

For the 2012 election, the Socialist Party selected 216 women to run as candidates, almost half (45.9 per cent) of all socialist candidates. Meanwhile, the conservative UMP party nominated 129 women, 25 per cent of its candidates, of whom 27 got elected. This represents a mere 13.9 per cent of their 197 MPs.

In France, Left-wing parties have made additional and constructive efforts to achieve gender parity. The political divide on this issue is clear. When I sit in Parliament and look around me, I cannot help thinking that despite the enormity of the task ahead, I am sitting on the progressive side of history.

Compared with the past, women candidates were nominated in a larger number of constituencies where they had a realistic chance of winning in 2012; 48.6 per cent of the Socialist Party's female candidates were elected, compared to 68.6 per cent of the male candidates. Meanwhile, only 20.9 per cent of women conservative candidates were elected, while 44.6 per cent of the men gained a seat; a male candidate of the Socialist Party was only 1.14 times more likely to win than a woman, whereas in the UMP this proportion grew to 2.13.

Figures also show that in 2012, women candidates proved to be better at winning seats in difficult or unpredictable constituencies than their male counterparts, a phenomenon that was underestimated by the conservative party and partly explains the smaller number of women candidates elected for the UMP. I think the French electorate is somehow more ready than politicians to change the old habits of gender politics. As far as I am concerned, the reality is that being a woman helped me in my election campaign, especially given that my constituency covers countries based in Northern Europe, where gender parity in Parliament is almost achieved: 46.7 per cent of Swedish MPs are women, 41.5 per cent of Finnish MPs or 38 per cent of Danish MPs, where Helle Thorning-Schmidt is both the first woman leading the Social Democrats and the first woman who became Prime Minister. In many aspects gender equality is more developed in the Nordic states and the French people residing in Scandinavia were certainly more willing to elect a woman in order to reflect their 'northern' or 'Nordic' values.

Old attitudes: 'Are you a journalist?'

From my personal experience, it seems that discrimination remains in the French political class but seems to be taking a more subtle format. When I work in the Palais Bourbon, I keep receiving reminders that I am a woman, an impression I do not encounter in other northern countries. I receive sexist comments about the way I dress or about my physical appearance. I was profoundly shocked to discover such practices when I got elected and went back to France after twelve years spent living in London. It can also take much less 'subtle' forms: Ministers wearing skirts have recently been whistled at by conservative MPs during Prime Minister's questions in the French Parliament.

The situation seems to be worst for mothers in today's societies. I still find it difficult to define the right balance between fighting for women's rights and putting forward my difference as a woman and a mother. As an MP I spend a lot of time travelling around my constituency and commuting between my residence and Paris. I often suffer from being away from my children and find this hectic lifestyle difficult to sustain at times, as working hours are particularly tough to reconcile with parenthood. I do have many unanswered questions: Is there a female way of doing politics? Are women less hungry for power? Was my decision to decline a ministerial offer very womanish? For now, I am ending up pleading for the opening of an on-site nursery in Parliament in order for staff and elected representatives to deal with the logistical nightmare of having to find childcare arrangements at weekends or during night sessions. That's for now.

Chapter Ten

Gendering Policy: Praxis

Joyce Outshoorn and Jennifer Rubin

Feminist engagement with policy research and practice has, over several decades, highlighted how much apparently non-gendered research, policies and interventions that focused on people in general have often in practice focused on men, and on specific groups of men. This has been true across many fields including the medical sciences, social research, and policy (British Medical Association 2008). The lack of attention to differences in experiences and outcomes for different segments of the population has led to an examination of how existing policies and interventions may specifically affect and potentially disadvantage women, ethnic minorities, and others. In gender and policy analysis the retrospective assessment of how existing policies and practices affect women and men differently has been complemented in certain areas by a more prospective gendered approach, integrating a gendered lens into the development of policy and practice by considering the particular needs of, and challenges to equality or improved outcomes. Starting with questions about whether and how women are experiencing different and worse outcomes relative to men, where women are doing well, or asking about barriers to improving their outcomes in areas in which they are not, builds in gender awareness that can inform the development of new approaches and how to implement them.

Attempts to re-gender policy has been especially visible in certain areas that have evident implications for women, and around which women themselves have campaigned for change (Lovenduski and Randall 1993).

Feminist researchers and policy practitioners have collectively offered critiques of apparently non-gendered policy, policy making, and policy outcomes. They have sought to identify who the policy actors are, what possibilities exist for a re-gendering of policy, and where and when policy-making structures and processes are most conducive to feminist intervention. There has been much discussion of what counts as 'gendered policy' and what constitutes 'gender policy'. The issues feminist activists have mobilised have also been identified; and how policy concerns are framed have been revealed. Given that dynamics of the policy making process vary by sector and issue, researchers have focused in on the policy sub-system. In this respect, feminist practitioners need to identify arguments which are likely to be attractive to policy makers in the field and can be deployed strategically to maximise the chances of feminist policy change.

The chapter consists of two sections. In its main body, traditional policy typologies – notably Lowi's – are subjected to a feminist re-reading before consideration is given to a series of feminist typologies. In respect of the latter, particular note is given to Amy Mazur's distinction between 'body politics I', which covers reproductive rights', and 'body politics II' which covers sexuality and violence against women. This distinction is useful because it maps into the distinction between 'position' and 'valence' issues. The former refers to issues in which there is no consensus about the goals and the means of a policy (e.g. abortion), whereas in the latter, people agree on the goal but not on the means (ending violence against women) (Outshoorn 1986). Htun and Weldon's typology moreover makes an analytical distinction which allows for cultural flexibility in classifying issues - including body issues - making classification an empirical exercise. The latter part of this chapter comprises a case study of gendered immigration policy in the EU. The example of EU funded migration research undertaken by a private research organisation (RAND) is discussed in order to demonstrate how employing a gendered lens improves policy analysis. In so doing, the impact of formal gender mainstreaming on EU policy analysis is traced.

Gender policies and issue classification – *Joyce Outshoorn*

Researchers working on feminist public policy generally agree that policy dynamics are, generally, highly issue specific. The constellation of interests around each issue is different, with different actors. The debates and decision making often take place in different arenas such as parliament, a ministry, a court or in a corporatist institution. Amy Mazur has stated that there is no single policy style or pattern of sectoralisation across entire sectors of gender policies, and that there are few systematic patterns in either policy profiles or styles across different types of countries (Mazur 2002). On the basis of the findings of the Research Network on Gender, Politics and the State (RNGS) project on women's movement impact and state feminism, McBride and Mazur also concluded that political dynamics vary by policy sector, but not according to typical regional classification, although some country patterns can be observed (McBride and Mazur 2010). In the Quality in Gender and Equality Policies (QUING) project, Andrea Krizsán *et al.* found issue-specific differences in several respects, such as participation of women's civil society groups and attention by authorities to their demands (Krizsán *et al.* 2010). In line with these insights, Mala Htun and Laurel Weldon, in developing their framework for comparing women's legal rights across very different political systems, made the case for the need of disaggregating gender policy issues to reveal the different policy dynamics (Htun and Weldon 2010). In the political science and policy mainstream, in the important tradition of issue-classification following from the work of Theodore Lowi, scholars have always maintained that 'politics' follows policy, i.e. that the *kind of policy* determines arenas, actors and alliances – the stuff of politics (Lowi 1964, 1972). Both the work in this tradition and in feminist public policy analysis thus point to the need of focusing on the policy subsystem for the analysis of gender issues and their outcomes.

Given the importance of policy sectors and the diversity of issues making up feminist public policy or gender equality policy[1], there is a definite need for classifying gender issues, but there is no consensus on how best to do so. In the following section current categorisations of gender issues using 'body issues' as an illustrative case study are interrogated.

The case of 'body issues'

Body issues, such as reproductive rights and (sexual) violence, have preoccupied second wave feminism since its beginning in the late 1960s, and have generally, if one combines reproductive rights with fighting violence against women, been the highest priority of women's movements over the last decades (Outshoorn 2010). A step forward in understanding the policy dynamics of body issues requires scholars to disaggregate these from the overarching concept of 'gender policy' or feminist public policy.

Why is the classification of issues important, despite the continual tension between institutionalist approaches that set out to classify issues on underlying structural cleavages, and social constructionist approaches which stress that framing contests between actors determine the type of issues? Classification is necessary for systematic comparison and the precision of concepts, but is not just an academic exercise. It is important for feminist activists, as it permits the mapping of the politics around particular issues and highlights the importance of strategic framing. Strategic framing refers to defining issues in such a way that policy actors are more likely to adopt the feminist demands. As political scientist Elmer Schattschneider maintained more than fifty years ago, at the core of any political conflict is the definition of the issue: '[...] *the definition of the alternatives is the supreme instrument of power*', the antagonists can rarely agree on what the issues are because power is involved in the definition. He who determines what politics is about runs the country, because the definition of the alternatives is the choice of conflicts, and the choice of conflicts allocates power' (Schattschneider 1960: 68 emph. in orig.). The outcome allocates control over the issue, responsibility, benefits and costs for others. For instance, political decisions in the past have given the medical profession power over abortions and power to family household heads over its female members. Framing abortion as a public health issue, or prostitution as a problem for public order, for example, will invite less opposition than if they are framed as moral issues.

---

1. Following Mazur (2002: 25) I will use the term 'feminist public policy' instead of 'gender equality policy', as it is more encompassing, notably on the point of reproductive rights and other 'body' issues. For the latter, equality is not the aim, as they are about the specificity of the female body. 'Autonomy' and 'self-determination' are generally the aim of body issues. In many countries, gender equality policies do not include reproductive rights, while violence against women is included. Htun and Weldon (2010: 208) distinguish gender equality policy and sex equality policy – the latter is a narrower subcategory of the former, not focusing on normative heterosexuality. In their article they use the two categories interchangeably (2010: 213 n.10).

In political science and policy analysis there is a vast literature on classification, but Theodore Lowi's typology has easily been the most influential in the field (Lowi 1964, 1972, 1998). What needs to be determined is how it can be put to use to classify gender issues as well as the set of issues concerning the body. Several current classifications in feminist public policy analysis single out the classification of 'body issues', and their consequences for policy dynamics: Amy Mazur's categorisation in *Theorizing Feminist Policy* (Mazur 2002), the main structures determining and reproducing gender inequality approach underlying the MAGEEQ project on policy frames and gender mainstreaming (Verloo and Lombardo 2007) and the QUING project on quality in gender and equality policies (Krizsán *et al.* 2010), the dimensions of citizenship of the Feminism and Citizenship project (FEMCIT 2007; Halsaa, Roseneil, and Sümer 2012) (FEMCIT 2007[2] and Mala Htun and Laurel Weldon's framework to compare sex equality polices (Htun and Weldon 2010). Which classification does maximal justice to body issues, treating them as a distinct category with its own specific politics?

The use of typologies

Designing and using typologies in political science is extremely common: David Collier, Jody Laporte and Jason Seawright listed no less than 100 multidimensional typologies (Collier, LaPorte and Seawright 2008: 154–5) in their overview of the topic. Typologies 'can be put to work' in 'forming and refining concepts, drawing out underlying dimensions, creating categories for classification and measurement, and sorting cases' (Collier, LaPorte and Seawright 2012: 217). Typologies can be descriptive and conceptual, but also explanatory, and can be uni- or multi-dimensional. They 'serve to identify and describe the phenomena under analysis' (2012: 218) and can be used for measurement, although Collier *et al.* do not consider measurement to be the ultimate goal. A well-drafted typology is also useful as it can help to identify a subset of cases or to synthesise one's findings (2012: 226, 227). Kevin Smith, despite pointing to the perennial problems of typologies, such as the ad hoc assignment of cases to categories, their weaknesses in prediction or explanation, and categorisations which are neither exhaustive nor mutually exclusive, still sees them as useful heuristic devices which can provide a systematic basis for comparison (Smith 2002: 218).

The central assumption of Lowi's influential typology is that *politics followed policy*, reversing the common sequence of the pluralist tradition in which policy is seen as the outcome of the conflicts and debates of the actors involved in the

---

2. MAGEEQ, QUING and FEMCIT are three European comparative projects funded by the 5th (MAGEEQ) and 6th Framework Programme (FEMCIT; QUING) of the European Union in the past decade. Full titles: MAGEEQ: Mainstreaming Gender Equality in Europe – Policy Frames and Implementation Problems: The Case of Gender Mainstreaming (2003–2005); QUING: Quality in Gender + Equality Policies (2007–2011); FEMCIT: Feminism and Citizenship – Gendered Citizenship in Multicultural Europe: the Impact of the Contemporary Women's Movements' (2007–2011).

policy process. The pluralist tradition tends to ignore the role of institutions and the policy legacies of the past that set limits to political contest and determine, to a large extent, the configuration of power among the various actors. In Lowi's analysis, institutions are central: each issue has its own political structures, process, and constellation of relations between involved actors, resulting in issue-specific processing, in a particular arena and with specific conflict characteristics. Lowi's original typology had three categories: (1) distributive, (2) regulatory and (3) redistributive policies (Lowi 1964: 688, 713).

- Distributive policy is about particular cases involving many beneficiaries receiving government money for contracts or subsidies. As the actors usually deal with a specific government department and have little to do with each other, there are many winners and few losers. It follows that the political arena is stable and its politics relatively conflict-free.
- Regulatory policy is about broad social choices to regulate individual or group behaviour. As it is clear from the outset who stands to lose or gain, and that the costs cannot be evenly divided over the whole population, Lowi argued that regulatory policy is always contested and competitive. Which groups become involved, depends on the issue at hand and the conflict is finally settled in the open arena of the legislature, which has the power to decide on such conflicts.
- Redistributive policy, concerns broad issues about the distribution of wealth, involving the rich and the poor, and the politics will follow class lines. Resistance against redistributing resources is strong, resulting in stable power structures with organisations of employers and employees. Newcomers will associate with one of the two, and actors will attempt to get government on its side. Lowi leaves open the question whether an issue can 'change' category over time (Lowi 1964: 699).

Of all the debates following Lowi (for an overview: Lowi 1998; Smith 2002), two are of concern here. First, there were many attempts to make the typology truly multidimensional, which Lowi finally settled himself by adding a fourth category, constituent policy, consisting of the constitution and the rights and rules of government (Lowi 1972, 1998). The ensuing matrix is based on two dimensions: the target of government coercion (the individual or the conflict environment), and the likelihood that government will apply its coercive powers – immediate or remote (Smith 2002: 380). Secondly, a number of scholars interested in the abortion issue debated whether it was the usual type of regulatory policy, or a particular subcategory of regulatory policy, variously called 'emotive symbolic policy' (Smith 1975), 'social regulatory policy' (Tatalovich and Daynes 1984, 1998) or 'moral policy' (Mooney 2001). Scholars here retained the basic idea that politics follows policy, but did not agree on the characteristics of the new category. These involved 'dealing with first principles', non-economic values, single issue interest groups, adjudication by courts, low barriers to participation and unwillingness to compromise (Smith 2002: 383). US scholars see a diverse range of issues falling under this category: alongside abortion as the prototypical case, issues such as prostitution, homosexuality, same-sex marriage, alcohol drugs, gambling, pornography, gun control, school prayer, affirmative action, euthanasia, movie censorship and the death penalty have all been held to belong to this category. All of these are characterised by high degrees of conflict, high 'lay' interest (one does not have to be an expert to have an opinion, making it easy to participate), many interest groups and movements, and an open political arena, the legislature. Potentially issues around the female body would fall within this category: abortion and other reproductive rights such as contraception or IVF, and sexual issues such as rape or prostitution. One can maintain that issues around violence against women are 'normal' regulatory issues, often already coded in criminal law passed by the legislature. This distinction concurs with Mazur's two types of body politics.

In earlier studies, Lowi's typology was found to have worked quite well in analysis of the politics around several feminist policy issues (Outshoorn 1995; Swiebel and Outshoorn 1998). In Dutch feminist politics, for example, distributive policy served women's movement groups by providing funding for their organisation to set up, amongst others, women's health and rape crisis centres, shelters for abused women, women's publishing houses, art galleries and film productions. As Lowi predicted, this was achieved relatively free from conflict. Many feminist issues, however, fell under regulatory policy: legalisation of abortion, child custody and access rights, rape within marriage, domestic violence, incest, pornography, prostitution, anti-discrimination legislation and childcare. In accordance with Lowi's expectations, these have been decided (with varying degrees to the satisfaction of women's movement groups) by Parliament. This arena proved open and accessible to feminists but also to high conflict, opposing interests, long and intense debates, street politics and lobbying as well as the formation of new alliances between movements, political parties and experts/academics. The best illustration of protracted conflicts is the legalisation of abortion (Outshoorn 1986) and the passing of the overarching antidiscrimination law in 1994 (Celis *et al.* 2012: 127–8), both of which lasted about twenty years. Notable too, is that some regulatory issues became redefined as distributive issues: rape, incest and domestic violence all now fall under the benefits of the welfare state. They did not require new legislation, save for rape within marriage (which did provoke conflict). Childcare, at first debated as a moral issue, has become a redistributive issue in the 2000s. For redistributive policies, feminists faced the closed and stable arena of the social partners and the strong interventionist state when trying to achieve equal pay, access to employment, fair taxation and equal treatment in secondary incomes (pensions and social security benefits). All demands were contested by the predominantly male employers' organisations and trade unions (the 'social partners') within the context of a conservative welfare state that cast women as housewives only entitled to rights and benefits through a male breadwinner. In general, redistributive issues have had the relatively poorest outcomes for women, although important gains have been made since the mid 1990s, partly due to the pressure of EU directives on equal pay, equal treatment and social security rights.

One can conclude that Lowi's typology can be put to work to sort out the politics around various gender issues. In the Dutch case, the politics around reproductive rights did not differ from antidiscrimination law even if the initial stages were in different policy subsystems, as they were decided in the same arena. However, both issues met a different line-up in parliament than the predominant left-right divide characteristic for other regulatory and redistributive policies. They activated the religious-secular cleavage in the party system, which cuts across the left-right divide, leading to virulent conflict. This provides an argument for the category of social regulatory policy when using the typology of Lowi. This category can deal with the role of religion, both as a source of values and as organised opposition to feminist body politics.

Classifications in feminist public policy analysis

How have feminist public policy analysts dealt with classifying gender policies, and more in particular, body issues? In her *Theorizing Feminist Policy*, Mazur (2002: 32) distinguished eight subsectors of feminist public policy: 'blueprint policy' (statements outlining gender policies and responsible agencies), political representation, equal employment, reconciliation of work and family life, family law, public service delivery, and two categories of body politics. 'Body politics I' covers reproductive rights, and 'body politics II' covers sexuality and violence against women. She argues that they are very different to other sectors of government action as they focus on private elements of people's lives: their bodies, sexualities and reproductive capacities (Mazur 2002: 137). In particular, they focus 'on women's bodily distinctiveness and the social construction of their sexualities' (2002: 137). Here gender equality is not the goal, but at stake is autonomy, bringing in issues of control and domination. Mazur mentions that states traditionally did not 'ensure women's autonomy in making choices about their body' (2002: 138) as they often have other goals, as controlling women's bodies for social propriety or pro-natalist goals. 'Body politics II' are about policing desire and reducing (sexual) violence against women.

Mazur grounds the distinction between the two kinds of body politics *in the distinct politics of each: they are processed in different policy subsystems* (2002: 138, my emphasis). There was also a difference in historical sequence: reproductive rights were an older second wave issue, generally arriving earlier on the political agenda and leading to policy responses long before sexual and violence issues. However, she does not specify how the category of family law is different from body politics, as it also focuses on private life and states also intervene here. While the idea behind the categorisation of Mazur is clear, i.e. each category has its own policy system dealing with specific issues, it is not clear *how* she identified the eight categories. Are there underlying dimensions of conflict or does she follow dominant feminist framings to classify?

The Mainstreaming Gender Equality in Europe (MAGEEQ) project rested on the basic idea that there are three main structures that determine and reproduce gender equality: the organisation of labour, the organisation of intimacy, and citizenship (Verloo and Lombardo 2007: 28). The threefold typology was derived from earlier work by Walby, Connell, and Verloo and Roggeband (Verloo and Lombardo 2007: 28 n.4), in which they aimed at accounting for 'patriarchy', 'sexual politics' and the 'structural unequal power relation between women and men'. In the MAGEEQ project, two structures were examined, intimacy and citizenship. From the range of issues falling under 'organisation of intimacy': sexuality, reproduction, 'private and family life' and the assumption of heterosexuality, domestic violence and family policies, three were selected for further study: domestic violence, prostitution and homosexual rights (Verloo and Lombardo 2007: 31). The QUING project, which can be regarded as the follow-up of MAGEEQ (with many of the same senior researchers) focused on four policy fields of 'core relevance' to gender and equality issues (Krizsán *et al.* 2010: 12). Alongside 'general gender equality policies', which cover the gender policy machineries and equal/antidiscrimination legislation, three issues were selected: non-employment, intimate citizenship, and gender-based violence. This choice is implicitly based on the three structures that MAGEEQ developed. In QUING, intimate citizenship was defined as 'a set of policies that regulate intimate partnerships, claims about the body, the traditional and non-traditional relationships and sexuality' (Krizsán *et al.* 2010: 12, 15). It included reproductive rights; prostitution and trafficking for sexual exploitation were included under gender-based violence. In short, in this research tradition, body issues are subsumed under the category of the organisation of intimacy, along with sexuality, family life and policies and homosexual rights. The categorisation makes no assumptions or claims about the kind of politics of each category; its purpose is to enable issue-selection to analyse the framings in the major policy texts on the issue.

A third classification was developed in the FEMCIT project, which intended to extend the concept of citizenship from the usual categories of political, economic and social citizenship to issues concerning the body and sexuality, and the intimate sphere (FEMCIT 2007). This classification led to the familiar problem that issues could not be classified unambiguously: some issues can be classified in more categories and the boundaries between the categories were not water-tight. The concept of intimate citizenship was inspired by the work of Ken Plummer and is about decisions people have to make about personal life, close relationships as well as about the body (Plummer 2003: 14). It can cover partnerships, marriage, divorce, same-sex partnership recognition, solo living, child access rights and parenting, but also sexual identities and sexual practices (including prostitution), as well as reproductive rights and sexual violence. In the original FEMCIT project design (2007) sexuality was grouped together with bodily citizenship, which included reproductive rights and violence against women. During the research the question was raised whether bodily citizenship should not be part of intimate citizenship, following Plummer. However, it could be argued that reproductive rights and freedom from violence relate directly to the concept of bodily integrity, and that bodily citizenship can be regarded as a necessary condition for the other categories of citizenship, making it a separate category. Sexualities can justifiably be part of intimate citizenship, while prostitution, which can be seen as bodily citizenship as well as sexual/intimate citizenship, can also be classified as economic citizenship (it is work) or social citizenship (social rights of sex workers) (Outshoorn *et al.* 2012, 140–41).

The final classification to be discussed here, Mala Htun and Laurel Weldon's typology to classify sex equality policy (2010: 209), takes a much broader view on classifying feminist public policy issues. Their aim is to develop a typology to compare countries on a world-wide scale, while the others were drafted on European and US cases. Htun and Weldon disaggregate gender equality into a typology of policies based on two dimensions, resulting in four different categories. The first dimension is based on the question: does the policy empower women as a status group or address class inequalities? The second dimension asks if the policy in question challenges religious doctrine or codified cultural traditions, yes or no. It follows there are four types of policies: gender-status policies that are either 'doctrinal' policies or 'non-doctrinal', and class-based policies that are either 'doctrinal' or 'non-doctrinal'. Abortion and contraceptive legality, as well as family law, are both gender-status and doctrinal policies; while gender quotas in politics and violence against women are gender-status and non-doctrinal policies. Funding of abortion and contraception are class-based doctrinal policies, while parental leave or funds for child care are non-doctrinal class-based policies. Each category has its own 'set of actors, activates different cleavages in a polity, and has distinct implications for gender relations' (Htun and Weldon 2010: 208). The authors suggest that the typology can most likely 'travel' across countries, giving the example of abortion, which is a doctrinal issue in Ireland or Italy, but not in China or Japan (2010: 210). Further empirical work will be needed to test whether the typology indeed holds in other contexts.

Htun's and Weldon's typology thus splits body issues into two categories that correspond to Mazur's distinction, and shows that at a lower level of disaggregation of issues, some aspects may be categorised differently, such as the issue of the funding of abortion. While Mazur designates family law as a separate category, in Htun's and Weldon's typology it falls under in the gender-status policy category, along with abortion and contraception legality. Following their institutionalist perspective, Htun and Weldon explicitly hold that their typology does not characterise issues on how these are framed by actors in the political process, but on how they are related to religious and political-economic structures in a certain national context (Htun and Weldon 2010: 210). The issue-type determines the type of actors who become involved, but the state context shapes actors' strategies, framing and priorities (2010: 211). Although they do not refer to the work of Lowi, their typology corresponds to his logic: politics flows from the type of issue.

Summary

The classification of issues is important because it aids systematic comparison and precise thinking about the concepts employed. It is also useful when selecting issues as cases for analysis and in unpacking the container of feminist public policy. Here Lowi's typology from mainstream political analysis, and four classifications from the feminist public policy field, looking more specifically into how they deal with 'body issues', have been re-considered. Many scholars have felt the need to add a fourth category to Lowi's typology to deal with social regulatory policies, as having a distinct pattern of politics and arena of decision making. From the Dutch example, body issues often do fall into such a category, but we have also seen that they are sometimes dealt with as distributive or redistributive issues. This is related to national differences: in well-developed welfare states body issues can be public health issues, and thus redistributive policy. This suggests that Lowi's typology requires revisiting to check out for American national and cultural bias, using 'body issues' from other states as empirical cases. This also holds for the literature on moral politics more generally, which is also based on the US with its two-party system and may, therefore, have less mileage for multi-party political systems based on the social economic and religious cleavages in society.

Of the four classifications from feminist policy analysis, the question was which classification does maximal justice to body issues, treating them as a distinct category with its own specific politics. Both Mazur's and Htun and Weldon's classification allow for such a distinction. Mazur's rationale for such a distinction is that her two types of body politics and family law have different policy subsystems in which these issues are dealt with. The split of body issues into reproductive rights and violence against women is useful, as it maps onto the distinction between 'position' and 'valence' issues. The former refers to issues in which there is no consensus about the goals and the means of a policy (e.g. abortion), whereas in the latter people agree on the goal but not on the means (ending violence against women) (Outshoorn 1986). Htun and Weldon's typology makes an analytical distinction which allows for cultural flexibility in classifying issues, i.e. body issues, making classification an empirical exercise.

The other two feminist classifications, however, subsume body issues into the category of intimate citizenship, along with family law issues, same-sex marriage or regulation of sexualities. This serves to obscure important differences between the issues. Reproductive rights and violence relate directly to the concept of bodily integrity. In liberal democracies citizens are held to have decisional autonomy over their bodies, but as Bacchi and Beasley have argued, underlying the gender neutral discourse is the gendered differentiation between the autonomous citizens who are assumed to be in control of their bodies, and those who are constructed to be controlled by their bodies (Bacchi and Beasley 2002). This dichotomy legitimated - and continues to legitimate - breaches by the state in the 'public interest' of the integrity of the body of those who are not in control. It was this dichotomy that feminists challenged and continue to challenge. Moreover, the state, in practice, delegated protection against violence towards women to male authority within the family, where it led to the control of women family members. In recent decades the hard-won feminist rights to self-determination and autonomy are being threatened by the rise of bio-power, the power of state and experts in demarcating 'healthy' and 'unhealthy' bodies (Rose 2007), a field of which the gendered dimensions are yet to be explored, and its consequences for the traditional liberal concept of bodily integrity. Along with the likely hypothesis that body issues and intimacy issues are most likely processed in different policy subsystems, this merits classifying body issues as a separate category with its own power dynamics, different to issues around partnership and family law.

Box 10.1: The EU and gender: Fundamental rights, mainstreaming gender, immigration and the Lisbon Strategy – Jennifer Rubin[3]

Equality of opportunity is one area in which the EU has been able to establish universal requirements and, in some cases, changed policy and practice.[4] The establishment of a statement of fundamental rights set out:

> the principle that individuals must be granted the same opportunities with regard to their access to certain fundamental goods (freedoms, income, welfare, employment, etc.), the concept of equal opportunities has set the legal basis for the elimination of discrimination against women in the field of employment in the EU and its member states.[5]

Equality legislation has played a role in highlighting or preventing discrimination and in putting gender on policy agendas. However, while it is an important part of achieving progress, persistent inequalities suggest that equality legislation alone may not be enough to improve women's outcomes relative to men's in many areas, and that a range of measures is likely to be needed to address ongoing hurdles to equality and improve outcomes for women. To articulate an agenda for doing so, the EU set out a 'roadmap for gender equality 2006–2010'.[6] The drive for equal treatment and improved outcomes, the rights and justice aspect of gendering policy and practice, are complemented by an explicit economic interest at EU level. According to the EU, women's economic contribution through both paid and unpaid work is integral to growth and competitiveness, and this is clearly articulated through the EU's Lisbon Strategy for Growth and Jobs.[7]

Immigration is another area where there is a greater attention to gender. In 2007 the EU's DG Employment, Social Affairs and Inclusion funded the first comparative, pan-European study of the role of migrant women in the EU labour force. Women have been migrating in growing numbers for work

3. The following section briefly notes some of the more prominent institutional attention to gender at EU level, and is followed by an example of migration research funded by the EU and undertaken by the author with a team of researchers at RAND Europe, focusing on building understanding of migrant women's outcomes in the EU. I would like to thank my colleagues Michael Rendall, Lila Rabinovich, Flavia Tsang, Constantijn van Oranje, and Barbara Janta for all of their hard work on this project and of course the EU for funding our endeavours.
4. The extent to which it is possible to articulate possible changes to policy and interventions, as opposed to a less directive highlighting of good practice and learning from elsewhere is driven by the issue of subsidiarity in Member States' relations to the EU, or the areas in which the EU has 'competence' and those where Member States retain powers.
5. Charter of Fundamental Rights of the European Union (2010/C 83/02); http://eur-lex.europa.eu/LexUriServ/LexUriServ.do?uri=OJ:C:2010:083:0389:0403:en:PDF last accessed 07/07 2013
6. http://europa.eu/legislation_summaries/employment_and_social_policy/equality_between_men_and_women/c10404_en.htm
7. http://ec.europa.eu/archives/growthandjobs_2009/

as well as for family reunification (Kofman 1999), and the EU sought to understand outcomes for women migrants to the EU, in particular with respect to their participation in the labour force.

To support this research, RAND undertook a comparative assessment of how women migrants fare in receiving countries by comparison with their male migrant counterparts, as well as by comparison with EU-born and native-born women. The aim was to inform policy and decision making with research that would allow its audience to 'better integrate the gender dimension into relevant immigration policies, and the migration dimension into gender policies' (Rubin *et al.* 2008). We provided 'an overview of the situation of women migrants in the EU labour market (and of) issues and challenges related to women migrants' integration to work in Europe' (Rubin *et al.* 2008: xvi).[8]

While concerns about women's disadvantage relative to men's in labour markets are reasonably well rehearsed in the wider gender and employment literature, there is by comparison a dearth of rigorous assessment of women migrants' outcomes relative to migrant men's, native-born women's or EU-born women's outcomes. From our analysis it appeared that migrant women in the EU in many countries face a double disadvantage, as women and as migrants, and in some cases a triple disadvantage: as women, as migrants, and as non-EU migrants:[9]

1. Women are migrating more: the share of foreign-born women in receiving countries has been rising at least at the same rate as, and in some countries faster than, has the share of foreign-born men.

8. While the research and key findings are drawn from this EU-funded study published in 2008 and based on 2005 data, findings were checked in December 2012 against 2010 data in preparation for a briefing to the Ministry of Overseas and International Affairs, Delhi. It is worth noting that there are variations across countries, and some exceptions, for example in the Nordic countries migrant women's labour market disadvantage appears to be more driven by their being migrants than by their being women.

9. Some of our key findings, discussed in detail along with the presentation of the data and analysis are in the full report: http://www.rand.org/content/dam/rand/pubs/technical_reports/2008/RAND_TR591.pdf. As we note on page xvi: The empirical results of this report are based primarily on analysis of the anonymised EU Labour Force Survey (LFS) dataset, for the year 2005. The results of our LFS analyses are initially from the 20 EU countries in 2005 for which third-country migrant women can be identified, and subsequently from the 14 EU countries whose 'foreign-born' women are primarily from movement between countries and not the reconstitution of political boundaries. Countries omitted due to unavailability of variables or adequate-sized samples to identify third-country migrants are Finland, Germany, Ireland, Italy and Malta. Countries omitted due to reconstitution of political boundaries are the Baltic countries (Estonia, Latvia and Lithuania), Poland and Slovakia. A major advantage of the year 2005 for our study is that the EU LFS in that year included an *ad hoc* module on 'Reconciliation between Work and Family Life'. Because we find that migrant women are much less likely than are native-born women to combine employment with having young children, this module offers especially useful insights into a gendered analysis of migrant women's labour-market challenges and outcomes.

2. Migrant women are working more: for the most part women also make up a growing proportion of the foreign-born labour force.
3. Migrant women and migrant men often have similar levels of education: for example, similar proportions of migrant women and men have high levels of education.
4. In this context of the growing presence of women migrants, and specifically of women migrant workers, there are important gender differences in outcomes. In particular, migrant women face poorer outcomes relative to migrant men: migrant women have between 18 per cent and 45 per cent lower rates of labour force participation in the first five years after arrival than their migrant male counterparts.
5. Integration into the host countries helps but does not eradicate the effect; in other words, this deficit in labour force participation diminishes over time but persists.
6. Migrant women are disadvantaged in the EU labour force not only in relation to their migrant male counterparts, but also in relation to native and EU-born women: migrant women face higher levels of unemployment than native and EU-born women (and this is true across all educational levels).
7. Migrant women also face higher levels of involuntary part-time employment, saying more frequently than either native-born women, EU migrant women or their male counterparts that they would like more working hours.[10]
8. Migrant women are much more likely to be in jobs that are not commensurate with their skills than their native-born female or male migrant counterparts.
9. Migrant women are much more likely to be highly concentrated in low-paid and insecure employment and occupations, such as the domestic and care sector.

Taking a gendered lens to immigration policy suggests, then, that improving outcomes for women migrants may require specific interventions that take account of interrelated factors associated with their gender status and their migration status. Not only should interventions take account of the specificity of the challenges faced by women as migrants and as women, it is also important to note that no one intervention or programme on its own is likely to be effective against the complex mix of challenges. Interventions

10. Though this finding is pre-recession and only re-checked shortly after the onset of the recession and may be affected by the rising numbers of unemployed in many Member States.

traditionally associated with bringing more women into the labour force, such as increasing availability of childcare, may not be as effective when there are further hurdles to taking up this childcare provision that may be associated with being a migrant. For example, the provision may not be available to non-EU migrants, or language or transport barriers may prevent women migrants from accessing the childcare that is available. Similarly, policies aimed at improving migrants' access to the labour force may not be effective for women migrants if such policies do not take into consideration what may be particular about migrant women's ability to benefit from such measures. For example, in the case of large-scale regularisations in Spain in 2005 designed to improve migrants' integration, only those who had been in employment for one year or more were eligible. Therefore, this programme mainly helped integrate those who were already in secure employment, a portion of the population less likely to include migrant women.

With a growing knowledge base, there has been in recent years increasing recognition of the need to commission work that provides the necessary mapping and understanding of the situation of women, as well as of other disadvantaged groups, in many areas such as migration, labour force participation and politics. Improving outcomes in these areas, however, requires integrating evidence from relevant studies into the design of multifaceted policies and programme to build, implement, test and adapt approaches that take account of the complex interrelationships between challenges for different groups.[11]

11. Professor Joni Lovenduski has played an especially pivotal role in teaching generations of researchers about gendering analysis of policy and politics, in her own research on women's representation in politics, and in her ongoing advice and work with those seeking to address the challenges faced by women in politics and in accessing political office.

References

Bacchi, C. and Beasley, C. (2002) 'Citizen bodies: is embodied citizenship a contradiction in terms?', *Critical Social Policy* 22 (2): 324–52.

British Medical Association (2008) *Women in Academic Medicine: Developing equality in governance and management for career progression*, Full Report.

Celis, K., Outshoorn, J., Meier, P. and Motmans, J. (2012) 'Institutionalizing Intersectionality in the Low Countries: Belgium and The Netherlands', in A. Krizsán, H. Skeje and J. Squires (eds) *Institutionalizing Intersectionality: The changing nature of European equality regimes*, Houndmills, Basingstoke: Palgrave Macmillan, pp. 119–148.

Collier, D., LaPorte, J. and Seawright, J. (2008) 'Typologies: Forming concepts and creating categorical variables' in J. Box-Steffensmeir, H. Brady and D. Collier (eds) *The Oxford Handbook of Political Methodology*, Oxford: Oxford University Press, pp. 152–232.

— (2012) Putting typologies to work: concept formation, measurement, and analytical rigor, *Political Research Quarterly* 65 (1): 217–232.

FEMCIT (2007) 'Gendered Citizenship in Multicultural Europe: the Impact of the Contemporary Women's Movements'.

Halsaa, B., Roseneil, S. and Sümer, S. (eds) (2012) *Remaking Citizenship in Multicultural Europe*, Basingstoke: Palgrave Macmillan.

Htun, M. and Weldon, L. (2010) 'When do governments promote women's rights? A framework for the comparative analysis of sex equality policy', *Perspectives on Politics* 8 (1): 207–216.

Kofman, E. (1999) '"Birds of passage" a decade later: gender and immigration in the European Union', *International Migration Review* 33 (2): 269–299.

Krizsán, A., Dombos, T., Kispéter, E., Szabó, L., Dedić, J., Jaigma, M., Kuhar, R., Frank, A., Sauer, B. and Verloo, M. (2010) *Framing Gender Equality in the European Union and its Current and Future Member States*, Final LARG Report, QUING Project, Vienna: Institute for Human Sciences (IWM): http://www.quing.eu/files/results/final_larg_report.pdf

Lovenduski, J. and Randall, V. (1993) *Contemporary Feminist Politics: Women and power in Britain*, Oxford: Oxford University Press.

Lowi, T. (1964) 'American business, public policy, case studies and political theory', *World Politics* 16 (4): 677–715.

— (1972) 'Four systems of policy, politics and choice', *Public Administration Review* 33 (4): 98–310.

— (1998) 'Foreword: New Dimensions in Policy and Politics', in R. Tatalovich and D. Byron (eds) *Social Regulatory Policy: Moral controversies in American politics*, Boulder/London: Westview Press, pp. x-xxii.

McBride, D. and Mazur, A. (eds) (2010) *The Politics of State Feminism*, Philadephia: Temple University Press.

Mazur, A. (2002) *Theorizing Feminist Policy*, Oxford: Oxford University Press.

Mooney, C. (2001) *The Public Clash of Private Values: The politics of morality policy*, New York/London: Chatham House.

Outshoorn, J. (1986) 'The rules of the game: abortion politics in the Netherlands' in J. Lovenduski and J. Outshoorn (eds) *The New Politics of Abortion*, London: Sage, pp. 5–27.

— (1995) 'Administrative accommodation in the Netherlands: The Department for the Coordination of Equality Policies', in D. McBride Stetson and A. Mazur (eds) *Comparative State Feminism*, Thousand Oaks/London/New Delhi: Sage, pp. 168–184.

— (2010) 'Social movements and women's movements', in D. McBride and A. Mazur (eds) *The Politics of State Feminism: Innovations in comparative research*, Philadephia: Temple University Press, pp. 143–164.

Outshoorn, J., Kulawik, T., Dudová, R. and Prata, A. (2012) 'Remaking Bodily Citizenship in Multicultural Europe: The struggle for autonomy and self-determination', in B. Halsaa, S. Roseneil and S. Sümer (eds) *Remaking Citizenship in Multicultural Europe*, Houndmills, Basingstoke: Palgrave Macmillan, pp. 118–141.

Plummer, K. (2003) *Intimate Citizenship: Personal decisions and public dialogues*, Seattle/London: University of Washington Press.

Rose, N. (2007) *The Politics of Life Itself: Biomedicine, power and subjectivity in the twenty-first century*, Princeton/Oxford: Oxford University Press.

Rubery, J. (2002) 'Gender equality and gender mainstreaming in the EU: the impact of the EU employment strategy', *Industrial Relations Journal* 33 (5): 500–522.

Schattschneider, E. (1960) *The Semisovereign People: A realist's view of democracy in America*, New York: Holt, Rinehart and Winston.

Smith, A. 1975) *The Comparative Policy Process*, Santa Barbara, Cal: Clio Books.

Smith, K. (2002) 'Typologies, taxonomies, and the benefits of policy classification', *Policy Studies Journal* 30 (2): 379–395.

Swiebel, J. and Outshoorn, J. (1998) 'Feminism and the State in the Netherlands' in V. Vargas and S. Wieringa (eds) *Women's Movements and Public Policy in Europe*, Latin America and the Caribbean, York/London: Garland, pp. 143–65.

Tatalovich, R. and Daynes, B. (1984) 'Moral controversies and the policymaking process: Lowi's framework applied to the abortion issue, *Policy Studies Review* 3 (2): 207–22.

— (eds) (1998) *Social Regulatory Policy: Moral controversies in American politics*, Boulder/London: Westview Press.

Verloo, M. and Lombardo, E. (2007) 'Contested Gender Equality and Policy Variety in Europe: Introducing a critical frame analysis approach' in M. Verloo (ed.) *Multiple Meanings of Gender Equality: A critical frame analysis of gender policies in Europe*, Budapest/New York: Central European University Press, pp. 21–46.

Vignette – Gendering Policy: The Relationship Between Academia and Policy Campaigns

Mary-Ann Stephenson

Mary-Ann Stephenson is a freelance consultant specialising in gender, participation in decision making and human rights. She has worked in over twenty countries with women politicians, business leaders, civil society activists, youth activists and journalists. Mary-Ann is a former Commissioner of the British Women's National Coalition and former Director of the feminist campaigning organisation, the Fawcett Society. Here she traces the contribution academic feminists made to the Fawcett Society's attempts to influence the policy platforms of political parties.

All too often the links between academic feminism and feminists lobbying for public policy change are weak. Academic feminists can seem out of touch with the public policy agenda and lobbyists and campaigners can fail to take account of the mass of research evidence relating to the issues on which they are working.

The Fawcett Society's origins are in the struggle for votes for women in the nineteenth and early twentieth century. The organisation takes its name from Millicent Garrett Fawcett, leader of the National Union of Women's Suffrage Societies from which the Fawcett Society grew. But Fawcett's founding sisters were always concerned with more than just winning the vote – they wanted to use the power that the vote brought women to bring about broader 'equal citizenship'.

In the mid 1990s with a new Director, Fawcett turned its attention to making the next election all about women. During the previous few elections it seemed like women disappeared through a 'glass trapdoor'. Not only were women politicians and journalists largely absent from media coverage of the campaigns but the concentration on 'Essex man' and his priorities during the 1980s and 1990s had side-lined the concerns of many women. Fawcett wanted to make sure the 1997 election was different to turn the spotlight on women's priorities and to make these central to the election.

We had seen how a high level of political awareness of the 'gender gap' in voting patterns in the US created campaign opportunities for US women's organisations and encouraged politicians to make public appeals to women's voters. We hoped that we could promote something similar in the UK with a focus on women voters and women's political representation.

I started work in 1996 with the task of making the next election all about women and very little idea of how to go about it. Luckily for me Fawcett was able to call on a great many women who did know what we needed to do, and were willing to give their time generously to help make it happen.[1]

The gender gap in voting patterns in the UK differed from the pattern in the US. The US gender gap had favoured the Democrats since 1980 with women more likely to vote Democrat than men. In the UK women voters had historically been more likely than men to vote Conservative. However there were signs that this was changing with a more complex 'gender/generation' gap developing where younger women were more likely to support the Labour party than younger men while older women remained more likely to vote Conservative than older men.

There were women in the Labour party who were using evidence of the gender generation gap to put pressure on the party leadership to focus on the need to win women's votes, including by increasing women's political representation within the party. But the story about the importance of women's votes was still largely untold outside journal articles and internal party briefings. Fawcett wanted to make it front page news.

Fawcett decided to combined academic research on gender and voting with up to date poll data from MORI and focus group findings to produce *Winning Women's Votes*, a report on women's voting patterns and political priorities. The report, and a follow up report on women floating voters did put women's voting patterns firmly on the political agenda – including the front page lead story in the *Daily Mirror*, which claimed that young women voters were likely to be Labour's 'secret weapon' at the next election.

Academic work on women's political representation has been critical to Fawcett campaigns too. All too often discussions within political parties or the media about the low level of women in political life focus on the need to encourage more women to put themselves forward, and to provide support and training for those who did come forward, a 'fix the woman' strategy that places the blame for the lack of women MPs on the lack of good women standing for selection. The British Candidate Survey undertaken by Lovenduski and Norris in 1992 showed that it was the candidate selection process within political parties that needed fixing as much as the women would be candidates. Even when excellent and highly trained women came forward for selection, selection committees in all parties were persistently failing to select them for winnable seats.

Labour's all women shortlist policy, used to select candidates for the 1997 election was adopted in recognition of the discrimination, both direct and indirect, that women faced in getting selected for seats they could win. 1997 saw a historic increase in the number of women MPs, but the all women shortlist policy was abandoned following a challenge at an employment tribunal and in the 2001 general election the number of women Labour MPs fell. In the election's aftermath, Fawcett produced with Lovenduski, a series of snap shot studies of

1. Joni Lovenduski was one of those women who gave generously of her time and shared her research expertise; explaining what the research showed and pointing us towards work by Pippa Norris and others on women's voting patterns.

women's experience of candidate selection in the main political parties. We carried out interviews with women candidates and would be candidates and revealed a depressing culture of discrimination, harassment, and selection systems rigged to benefit 'favoured sons'. This evidence helped support the campaigning by women within the Labour party which led to an amendment to the Sex Discrimination Act in 2002 making positive action, such as all women shortlists, legal.

Chapter Eleven

The Slippery Slope: Measuring Women's Political Interests

Peter Allen, Rosie Campbell and Ana Espírito-Santo

Women's interests?

Even before Virgina Sapiro asked 'when are interests interesting?'(Sapiro 1981), feminist scholars have grappled with the slippery connection between the descriptive and substantive representation of women. Demonstrating a link between descriptive and substantive representation necessitates that there are a set of ideas or interests 'out there' that have particular relevance to either women as a whole, or significant sub-groups of women. Defining women's interests continues to consume feminist scholars' research hours; a special section of *Politics and Gender* was recently dedicated to 'The meaning and measurement of women's interests' (Schwindt-Bayer and Taylor-Robinson 2011). As Chapter Three demonstrates theoretical work on the substantive representation of women has recognised the problems that arise when feminist researchers define what constitutes *women's interests* a priori and then simply assess whether politicians and institutions adequately address these concerns (Saward 2006; 2010). Such an approach tends to depend on an essentialist account of what it is to be a woman and disregards the preferences of women whose views do not sit happily within a feminist frame, perhaps considering them to be the artefacts of false-consciousness (Campbell and Childs 2012). Theoretical researchers have attempted to overcome this problem by first, rejecting the conflation of feminist and women's interests, recognising that different women may well have alternative if not competing conceptions of representation – for example, recognising that feminist women's interests and conservative women's interests may well be distinct – second, by distinguishing between women's interests and women's issues, and third, by recognising creative concepts of representation in which what constitutes women's interests, are constituted as part of the representational process (Celis and Childs 2011). Quantitative empirical research has added to this literature by measuring women's interests, as they are currently constructed, using surveys of public opinion (Campbell 2004; Campbell and Winters 2008; Wängnerud 2000); and asking whether there is a divergence in the political attitudes of men and women and/or sub-groups of men and women (Campbell and Childs (forthcoming); Campbell, Childs and Lovenduski 2010). The most frequent finding in studies of public opinion is that men and women's political attitudes are more similar than they are different, in fact as Lisa Baldez suggests, it might make more sense to talk about 'gender overlap' rather than gender gaps (Baldez 2001).

On occasion this research is used by academics and practitioners to provide evidence to support feminist arguments in public debate (Harman and Mattinson 2000). However, we should be wary of an over-reliance on snapshots of public opinion as a basis for feminist policy demands; political attitudes can change over time and may respond to political leadership. A survey of public opinion conducted in one place and time may simply reflect existing gender norms and practices. Indeed, Virginia Sapiro was careful to distinguish between the claim that women share a common interest, in the form of their different social position from men, and evidence of feminist consciousness (Sapiro 1981). In fact she separated out the normative concept of women's interest from empirically verifiable disagreements between men and women on policy issues (Sapiro 1981: 704). Likewise, in her call for a politics of presence, Anne Phillips argued that women's interests may not be fully articulated until women are fully present in public life and able to have a full debate. She reasoned that interests are realised in the course of deliberation and decision making, as various options, implementation strategies and competing concerns are discussed (Phillips 1995). As a result, empirical research that examines gender differences in public opinion can supply evidence of variation in men and women's attitudes and preferences, and may sometimes even argue that findings are suggestive of women's political interests distinct from men's. But, crucially, the empirical research can only contribute to – and not over-ride – the normative argument for the descriptive and substantive representation of women.

Even so, through time series and comparative analysis, quantitative research can be used in more subtle ways to further a feminist agenda on substantive representation. For example, although women remain less active in politics relative to men, this difference has declined over time and the gap between men and women is larger where women have little access to the public sphere (Andersen 1975; Burns 2001; Hayes and Bean 1993). Thus policy intervention based on the simple fact of women's relative disinterest or relative inactivity may misrepresent the gender difference as immutable and a feature of a 'natural' gender order, rather than a dynamic trend with its roots in patriarchal and exclusionary politics that might decline or disappear over time.

Here we set out what quantitative empirical work *can* tell us about women's political interests, and ask how this may or may not be useful for feminist praxis. The contribution made by studies of political attitudes and behaviour to feminist scholarship and praxis, and the interaction between the two, is its key concern. This chapter highlights the tension between describing the empirical data *as we find it* and modelling the underlying causal processes that generate gender differences. We also consider areas where quantitative analysis of public opinion has added to the resources available to feminist practitioners, whilst acknowledging the academic imperative to play fair with evidence.

Interest in and knowledge of 'politics'

One of the most well-established gender gaps in political attitudes is the one observed within interest in politics (Burns, Schlozman and Verba 2001). Some decades ago, when the gender gap in political interest was first identified, some authors hypothesised that as socio-economic differences between women and men declined, levels of political interest would equalise (Burns, Schlozman and Verba 2001: 62). In Western democracies, although the distribution of resources between the sexes is still far from equal, women now have much better resources (namely higher education and access to paid employment) than in the recent past. Yet the gender gap in political interest has remained fairly stable; women are still less likely to be politically interested, informed, or feel efficacious[1] (Atkeson and Rapoport 2003; Baum and Espírito-Santo 2007; Burns, Schlozman and Verba 2001).

The size of the gender gap in political interest varies depending on how the question is framed. In one British study respondents were asked, 'If you were to open a newspaper and see the following articles how interested would you be in reading each article?' and shown a list of five items relating to education, healthcare, foreign policy, law and order and partisan politics (Campbell and Winters 2008). Women were more likely to say that they would be interested in reading the articles on education and healthcare and men were more likely to say that they would be interested in reading articles on foreign policy and partisan politics. Yet when asked whether they were 'generally interested in politics' (prior to the newspaper articles) the women's self-ratings of political interest were significantly lower than men's. These findings are suggestive of a disconnect between women's high levels of engagement with some policy issues and their conception of what an interest in 'politics' entails and indeed what the researchers think counts as 'politics'.

Nevertheless, the fact remains that women report lower levels of interest in politics than men, even if their underlying interest in some policy domains might be higher, and this is particularly important, as it is likely to have practical consequences. In fact, it has been put forward as one of the main explanations for the persistence of sex differences in some forms of political participation, excluding voting (for example, Burns, Schlozman and Verba 2001). Most importantly, the unequal level of political interest between the sexes can offer a partial explanation for the imbalanced presence of men in political institutions. For example in 1995, Pippa Norris and Joni Lovenduski argued that female underrepresentation might be more the result of a smaller pool of potential women candidates than of gender discrimination (Norris and Lovenduski 1995); although later work demonstrated that direct discrimination against women candidates was a powerful factor restricting their selection (Shepherd-Robinson and Lovenduski 2002).

---

1. Also, the few inferential statistical analyses conducted on explanations for political interest show that ruling out the effect of socio-economic resources, this gender gap remains significant, at least in Spain (*see* Morales 1999).

The gender gap in interest in politics leads to a tendency for young women (Campbell and Wolbrecht 2006; Lawless and Fox 2005; Wolbrecht and Campbell 2007) as well as adult women (Fox and Lawless 2004; Fox and Lawless 2011; Lawless 2012; Lawless and Fox 2005; Lawless and Fox 2010; Norris 1997; Norris and Lovenduski 1995) to have less 'political capital'[2] and to feel less qualified and less motivated to run for office than men. The same applies if we consider both ordinary citizens and the 'candidate eligibility pool', i.e. the group of citizens who are potential candidates.[3] A recent study corroborated this idea using a national survey of more than 2000 'potential candidates' in 2008: 'women are significantly more likely than men to dismiss their qualifications, and significantly less likely than their male counterparts to express self-efficacy to enter the electoral arena' (Fox and Lawless 2011: 70). The only group where no sex disparity in psychological engagement in politics can be found is among those who actually run for office (Fox and Lawless 2004: 275). However, it is also important to take into consideration that women are significantly less likely than men to receive political encouragement to run for office (for example, Fox and Lawless 2004: 275).

The fact that the gender gap in interest in politics has not changed much in the last few decades suggests that education and other socio-economic resources, although important, are not the main explanation for the gender gap in political involvement. What, then, explains it? Much recent scholarship has attributed the gender gap in political activity (in part) to deeply embedded patterns of traditional gender socialisation (Atkeson and Rapoport 2003; Conway, Steuernagel and Ahern 1997; Lawless and Fox 2005; Verba, Schlozman and Burns 2005).

> ...the primary institutions of social and cultural life [...] continue to impress on women and men that traditional gender roles – embodied by heterosexual marriage, in women assume the majority of household labor [sic] and child care responsibilities – constitute a normal, appropriate, and desirable set of life circumstances (Lawless 2012: 58).

In general, boys tend to be better prepared for activities that are potentially better connected to being politically active. However, most of the studies of sex-related political socialisation of adolescents or children are quite old (Greenstein 1961; Owen and Dennis 1988). The rarity of this kind of study is probably due to the fact that it is difficult to prove that whatever differences are observed, between women and men in adult life, are due to having dissimilar experiences during childhood.

2. 'Political capital can be understood to include the resources aspirants bring to the process. This may include not only financial assets but also political connections, party connections, party experience, career flexibility, educational qualification and legislative skills' (Norris 1997: 13).

3. The definition of 'candidate eligibility pool' varies slightly from study to study, but it tends to include all men and women whose professions are most likely to yield political candidacies for legislative office: law, business, education and politics (Fox and Lawless 2004: 275).

Irrespective of the difficulty of unpicking the causes, most social scientists agree that the gender gap in political interest does not have a biological origin. Instead, as Anne Phillips puts it, it is a sign of political inequality.

> This is not to say that everyone must be equally enthralled by the political process: that interest in politics is unevenly distributed, as is the interest in sport or in jazz; and a free society is usually thought to imply a freedom not to engage in politics. [...] But where the levels of participation and involvement have coincided too closely with differences by class or gender or ethnicity, this has been taken as prima facie evidence of political inequality, even without further investigation of where this imbalance might lead (Phillips 1995: 32).

Besides interest in politics (and probably related to it), women tend to do less well than men on measures of political knowledge (Frazer and MacDonald 2003). Furthermore, research has systematically shown that the gender gap in political knowledge has been persistent throughout the years (Delli Carpini and Keeter 2005; Dow 2009); and some are even convinced that it 'will certainly be a fixture in the political landscape for the foreseeable future since only one third of the gap [is] explained by differences between men and women's possession of the attributes that predict political knowledge' (Dow 2009: 133).

That said, some of the most recent research offers a more complex picture. Several authors have, for instance, confirmed the hypothesis that the knowledge gap is partly an artefact of how knowledge is measured (Lizotte and Sidman 2009; Mondak and Anderson 2004). Men are usually more inclined to 'shout out the answers', and in surveys they tend to be more willing to risk being wrong by giving an answer. In contrast, women tend to answer 'don't know' more often, even in domains where they know as much as men do. Similarly, others suggest that knowledge levels are, in part, a reflection of the items employed in the survey (Dolan 2011; Stolle and Gidengil 2010). When political knowledge measures ask for information on the present state of women in American politics, women's traditional disadvantage disappears (Dolan 2011: 105). The same occurs when practical knowledge of government services and benefits are included in the conception of political knowledge (Stolle and Gidengil 2010:100). In addition to gender specific domains of knowledge there is some evidence that women and men learn more in different political environments: a 2011 US study found that partisan conflict was more likely to promote learning during a midterm election campaign among young men, but young women learnt more in contexts of consensus (Wolak and McDevitt 2011).

> Young men gain the most knowledge in environments marked by conflict, such as in debates with friends or by living in communities marked by partisan division. Young women, however, appear to practice a civic or communal style of citizenship, where political learning is greatest for those who discuss politics with family and live in politically homogenous areas (Wolak and McDevitt 2011: 506).

Role models?

Some recent gender and politics research uses quantitative methods to attempt to measure whether women politicians have a role model effect on women in the general population, possibly generating a virtuous circle whereby politically active women raise the ambitions and interests of others. For example, researchers have shown that the gender gap in political knowledge in the United States is reduced to zero in states where women make up twenty per cent or more of state legislators (Schwindt-Bayer and Taylor-Robinson 2011). Others have shown that in societies where women are better represented in leadership roles the gender gap in political interest is reversed (Norris and Krook 2009) or significantly narrowed (Hanes and Thomas 2013) and in their research Christina Wolbrecht and David Campbell have found that where there are higher numbers of women in office, adolescent girls and adult women are more likely to discuss and be interested in participating in politics (Wolbrecht and Campbell 2007). They also find that 'the more that women politicians are made visible by national news coverage, the more likely adolescent girls are to indicate an intention to be politically active' (Campbell and Wolbrecht 2007: 233). Campbell and Wolbrecht argue that the effect on adolescent girls operates through increased levels of political discussion, particularly within the family. Their findings sit comfortably with studies of the social logic of politics which show that the family is a key arena for political socialisation (Zuckerman, Dasovic and Fitzgerald 2007). Alan Zuckerman *et al.* show that wives and mothers' partisanship influences the whole family; a finding that runs counter to early studies of political behaviour, which assumed that women blindly followed the political persuasions of their husbands (Campbell *et al.* 1960). Although the transmission of political information between mothers and other family members is reciprocal, mothers sit at the centre of the network (Zuckerman, Dasovic and Fitzgerald 2007). This research on the family suggests that if mothers can be engaged in politics the potential rewards for society are magnified through their pivotal role in many families.

Perhaps the most exciting contribution that quantitative methods have made to understanding the role model effect is when an experimental method has been applied, the zenith of quantitative methods. Making use of a natural experiment, where leadership positions were reserved for women in Indian villages selected at random, Lori Beaman *et al.* were able to demonstrate that young women's educational attainment and career aspirations were raised in districts with a woman representative (Beaman *et al.* 2012).

Overall, it is clear that there is some evidence that women politicians can have a role model effect on other women, raising their levels of political interest and engagement. However, some argue that, rather than motivating women to participate in politics, higher levels of women's representation might be associated with positive evaluations of the political system itself (Espírito-Santo 2011) and although the studies described here find that the presence of female politicians/candidates has an impact on, at least some indicators of, women's political engagement others find no effect (Dolan 2006; Fox and Lawless 2004).

Political participation and social capital

Quantitative studies of political behaviour in Western democracies have demonstrated that women are no longer less likely to turn out and vote than men; in fact in some states women are more likely to participate in elections.[4] Feminists have been highly critical of outdated measures of political participation that focus only on explicitly partisan activities (Burns, Schlozman and Verba 2001; Norris, Lovenduski and Campbell 2004; Stolle and Micheletti 2006) and overlook protests, boycotting, buycotting[5] and advocacy for pressure groups and the voluntary sector; when these activities are included in studies of political participation it is clear that in many states women are more likely than men to participate in many civic and cause oriented acts. Yet there remains a near universal gap in terms of partisan politics where women are less likely to be members of, or campaign for, political parties (Burns, Schlozman and Verba 2001; Lawless and Fox 2010). Feminists have been troubled by this continuing divide and have sought to explain why women's high levels of civic activism do not translate into an equal presence in partisan politics. Many studies of political participation have used the concept of social capital to help to explain how some people use their social networks to 'get by' whilst other use them to 'get on' (Lowndes 2000; 2004).

The concept of social capital and Robert Putnam's argument that it has a central role in underpinning democracy, has been embraced by political science (Putnam 1995; 2000; Putnam, Leonardi and Nanetti 1993). Feminist reaction to Putnam has followed two tracks, (1) critiquing his failure to consider the gendered dimensions of his claims and (2) highlighting the potential of the concept for explaining continuing inequalities in men and women's political participation. Importantly, when it comes to social capital women are not always worse off than men. Men's greater risk of social isolation, suicide and certain mental health conditions at least partially result from their lower levels of social capital in the form of personal connections and relationships (Halpern 2004). In contrast, women very often have strong personal networks that help them to manage their personal and family lives. But there is a question as to whether women have access to the kind of networks that would generate political connections and participation. We know that men and women join different associations – formal memberships – (Arneil 2006; Burns, Schlozman and Verba 2001; Norris and Inglehart 2006; Norris, Lovenduski and Campbell 2004), and that men and women tend to have different sorts of personal networks – informal memberships – (Lowndes 2000; Norris and Inglehart 2006) but until recently less was known about the political consequences of these differences. Lowndes sets out an important set of questions relating to gender and social capital:

4. In every US presidential election since 1980 a greater proportion of women than men have turned out to vote http://www.cawp.rutgers.edu/fast_facts/voters/documents/genderdiff.pdf

5. Buycotting is deliberately buying goods for ethical or political reasons.

> Are different forms (and levels) of social capital generated in different community settings?
> Are men and women involved in different, gender-specific 'circuits' of social capital? Might these serve to 'capitalize' political engagement in different ways? (Lowndes 2000: 543).

These questions are taken up and explored by a number of researchers in an impressive edited collection (O'Neill and Gidengil 2006). In their chapter, Pippa Norris and Ronald Inglehart (Norris and Inglehart 2006) conduct a comparative study of group membership in fifty societies using the World Values Survey. Their findings corroborate many other studies, showing that men are over-represented in sports, political and professional groups (although the sex differences vary by country), and women are over-represented in voluntary associations, particularly those related to education and religion. Significantly Norris and Inglehart show that time spent with family, as opposed to socialising with networks of colleagues and friends, is negatively associated with participation in formal associations; women's levels of social capital are, notably damaged by this (Norris and Inglehart 2006: 94). These findings are confirmed by Lowndes' chapter in the same volume which shows that women's social capital is more strongly associated with informal local networks than men's (Lowndes 2006). In addition to belonging to different kinds of groups there is some evidence of small differences between men and women in the types of activities they undertake for them, with women more often 'befrienders' and 'footsoldiers' and men more often taking on leadership roles; crucially, undertaking leadership roles for a formal association appears to be more strongly associated with political participation than other kinds of activities (Campbell 2013). Overall, in terms of social capital, there remain small but persistent differences in the nature and quality of men and women's formal and informal networks. Women have better developed informal personal networks but these connections, useful as they are for organising childcare and social support, serve less well as transmitters of political knowledge and participation than other kinds of group memberships.

What difference did the vote make?

Scholars and activists alike are often interested in asking 'what difference did the [women's] vote make?'(Breitenbach and Thane 2010). There are two ways of trying to address this question, one is to look at women's voting behaviour and the other is to look at the behaviour of policy makers.

The welfare state

A broad body of quantitative research has investigated the impact that women's suffrage had on social spending and the creation of the welfare state. One study found that in Switzerland spending on welfare went up by 28 per cent as a result of women getting the vote in 1971 (Abrams and Settle 1999), and a US study found suffrage coincided with increases in state government expenditures, revenue and more liberal voting patterns (Aidt and Dallal 2008). A study of six European countries, between 1869–1960, found that spending on welfare as a percentage of GDP rose by 0.6–1.2 per cent in the short term. In the long term, the effect was three to eight times larger (Aidt and Dallal 2008). Toke Aidt and Bianca Dallal argue that 'women's suffrage not only increased the overall level of social spending, it also shifted the portfolio of spending towards social spending' (Aidt and Dallal 2008: 404). In her analysis of twelve industrialised democracies Catheine Bolzendahl showed that the proportion of women in legislatures influences social spending (Bolzendahl 2009). Together, these studies suggest that women give a priority to spending on social welfare and that women's suffrage translated into real policy change. Of course, the policy makers who increased social spending may have responded to a *perceived* rather than an actual sex difference in policy preferences, but quantitative research of public opinion corroborates the finding that women are to the left of men on social spending.

Women as voters

The study of the international 'gender gap' in attitudes and party of vote has developed in response to the high profile gender gap in US elections; a greater proportion of women than men have voted for every Democratic presidential candidate since 1980 (Box-Steffensmeir, DeBoef and Lin 1997; Burden 2008; Carroll 1999; McBride and Mazur 2002). Using data on the USA from 1972 to 2004, Norrander and Wilcox describe an increasing gender gap in ideology both in magnitude and statistical significance (Norrander and Wilcox 2008). Interest in the subject has spawned a comparative literature that assesses the extent to which the US gender gap can be found elsewhere (Campbell 2006; Gidengil and Harell 2007; Hayes and McAllister 1997; Inglehart and Norris 2000; Norris 1999; Steel 2003; Wängnerud 2000). The research has become ever more nuanced and sophisticated with complex theoretical models employed to explain why men and women might prefer different political parties (Alvarez and McCaffery 2000; Burden 2008; Dolan 2010; Greenberg 2001).

The sources of the US gender gap have been contested. Some researchers have focused on the changing partisanship of men (Mattei and Mattei 1998; Wirls 1986), others on women's movement into paid employment and higher education, or women's predominance in public sector employment and greater dependence on welfare provision (Andersen 1999; Manza and Brooks 1998). And some have argued that women view politics through a more empathetic or care-focused lens due to gendered socialisation processes or the psychological impact of mothering (Box-Steffensmeir, DeBoef and Lin 1997; Lehman *et al.* 1995).

In addition to these apparent aggregate level differences between men and women's vote choice in the US there is also evidence of sub-group variation. In their study of the 1992 US presidential election, Mary Bendyna and Celinda Lake found that US President Bill Clinton constantly won a majority of college-educated women's support, but 'born-again' southern religious women were mainly responsible for the increase in female George Bush supporters during the Republican National Convention in mid-August (Bendyna and Lake 1994).

The study of the gender gap in US elections has expanded to include the influence of candidate sex and candidate gender stereotypes and feminist orientation. Many studies have shown that the electorate is not biased against women candidates (Welch *et al.* 1985) but there is also some, mixed, evidence that women may tend to favour women candidates when making their vote choice in certain circumstances (Cook 1998; Dolan 1998; Dolan 2001; Plutzer and Zipp 1996). Kathleen Dolan found, for example, that candidate sex was a driver of voting behaviour for the US House of Representatives in 1992 (the election framed as 'the year of the woman' by the media where issues of gender equality gained unusual salience in public discourse), but she found no evidence of any impact in 1994 or 1996 (Dolan 1998; 2001; 2004). Others have found that women are more likely to vote for women candidates only when they are perceived as being pro-feminist (Plutzer and Zipp 1996).

The highly developed but contradictory US research on gender and voting behaviour has been used as a springboard for analysis elsewhere. Pippa Norris has summarised the distinct periods apparent in the relationship between sex and vote across Western democracies (Norris 1999). The first period encompasses the 1960s and 1970s, and possibly earlier (Tingsten 1937). In this epoch the traditional gender gap was apparent: in Western democracies women were slightly more likely than men to support parties on the centre right, a pattern highlighted by contemporaneous political scientists (Butler and Stokes 1974; Campbell *et al.* 1960; Duverger 1955). The traditional pattern was replaced in the 1980s by a phenomenon Norris terms gender de-alignment, where any sex differences in vote at the aggregate level were insignificant (Hayes and McAllister 1997; Norris 1999). Norris describes the final phase of gender and vote as gender realignment where a 'modern gender gap is evident' with women voting to the left of men. The drivers of this changing gender pattern in ideology have been identified as largely structural. An historic association – much stronger in the past than the present – between womanhood and religiosity is a key factor, as some scholars were quick to prove (Corbetta and Cavazza 2008). Due to changing demographics other structural factors are also important, such as occupational status, education and marital status; 'Well-educated and single women have always been more liberal than their less educated and married counterparts, and over time they have become more numerous in the population' (Norrander and Wilcox 2008: 521).

It is in the study of gender realignment that Inglehart and Norris extend the analysis of the gender gap in the US to consider the possibility of an international modern gender gap (Inglehart and Norris 2000). They find evidence of the modern gender gap in the 1990s in several advanced industrialised nations: Japan, Ireland, Denmark, Austria, the Netherlands, Norway, Sweden, Switzerland and Canada (Inglehart and Norris 2000). A significant difference between the vote choices of the sexes was absent in West Germany, Italy, Northern Ireland, Portugal, Iceland, Britain, Australia, France, Hungary and Belgium (Inglehart and Norris 2000). In fact, women's propensity to support Left-wing parties increases only when those who participate in the labour market and those who are 'unmarried' are considered (Iversen and Rosenbluth 2006). This explains why 'countries with a traditional family structure and low female labour force participation tend to exhibit small gender gaps' (Iversen *et al.* 2006: 16). 'Feminist consciousness' has been applied as an additional/alternate explanatory factor, with varying success (Bergh 2007; Campbell 2006; Conover 1988; Hayes 1997). According to these scholars, irrespective of the person's sex, having a feminist consciousness can be linked to a preference for Left-wing parties. As having a feminist consciousness is more common among women, this can explain their preference for Left-wing parties. This effect is observable in some countries, such as Britain, the US, and Norway (Hayes 1997; Bergh 2007); however, it is not observable in others, namely the Netherlands (Bergh 2007).

However, Inglehart and Norris also calculated an ideology gap for a number of countries for 1981 and 1990 which showed a clear trend in all of the countries studied, except Spain and South Korea, where women moved from the right of men on the ideological spectrum to the left (Norris and Inglehart 2000: 453). Nathalie Giger has added to the international literature on the gender gap in voting comparing twelve countries over a period of 25 years, from 1974–2000, and concludes that the reversal of the traditional gender gap extends beyond the US to the rest of Western Europe (Giger 2009). One of her strongest findings is that the modern gender gap can be partially explained by increases in women's labour force participation but she acknowledges that the 'causes for differences in gender voting are still under debate' (Giger 2009: 486). In fact she goes on to argue that her analysis suggests that 'explanations not only differ between countries but also over time' (Giger 2009: 88). She suggests that material explanations might provide the best explanation for the decline of the traditional gender gap but that the relationship between gender and voting today might be the result of divergence on issues. She argues that a gender realignment across Western democracies is not necessarily inevitable.

Overall, then, there is evidence that women's political attitudes in Western democracies are more inclined towards social spending and have moved to the left over time. This evidence may be useful to feminist practitioners as they argue that women have distinct political interests/preferences.

Deeds and words?

This chapter opened with a discussion of women's interests and the tension between providing evidence of gender differences in public opinion and the danger of sealing women's preferences for all time in aspic, emphasising the ways in which these change and shift over time and space. It then moved to suggest that in some countries women in public offices of all kinds may consciously or unconsciously provoke a role model effect whereby their presence encourages other women to become more involved in politics. The chapter then considered the role of social capital, and other communal associations, on political interest, before turning to examine the ways in which women and men vote differently.

As one theme of this volume is the interaction between feminist research and praxis, it is appropriate to reflect on the extent to which the research findings presented in this chapter might be employed by feminist activists. We should remember that the differences between men and women's political attitudes and behaviour are small and often diminishing (gender overlaps) and we must avoid making essentialist claims. But there are some differences (gender gaps) that have been highlighted in this chapter that may aid feminists in public debate.

Which came first, the woman politician or the woman activist? As there is some (mixed) evidence of role model effects, advocates of women's greater political presence should use the women we have in politics and public life to mentor and recruit other women, and generate the virtuous circle that might well undermine the gender gap in political interest and participation.[6] Lawless and Fox have shown that women are less likely to be asked to run for office and that women underestimate their skills, so feminist activists are right to continue to protect and create women friendly spaces for political debate and to actively seek out women and encourage them to get involved. At present, women are more often involved in cause oriented activities than men are and these women are obvious targets for party politics.

Moving to women as voters it is evident that women's suffrage had an impact on public policy, and social spending increased across Western democracies as a result. In addition, gender is a factor in electoral politics. Overall quantitative research has set out a clear trend from a traditional gender gap, to dealignment and in some states a realignment to a modern gender gap where women vote to the left of men. The analysis of the modern gender gap is complex and the underlying processes probably multi-causal but there is a significant story about 'women and the vote' available to feminist activists and political party practitioners. The bodies of evidence suggest that policy makers should be aware of the relative left-leaning nature of women on social welfare and the need for political parties to pay attention to women voters for strategic as well as normative reasons. However, we should interject a note of caution. There has been some criticism of the use of the term gender gap in the US. Academic researchers are accused of using the gender gap to further a political read feminist agenda (Greenberg 2001; Seltzer, Newman and Leighton 1997; Steel 2003). This may not be a problem in itself, if the evidence that is employed is reported accurately, but we should be aware that even the US gender gap is not a chasm and academics must be careful not to over-stretch the results for a political cause.

---

6. This volume has been written in honour of an academic who, as many of the contributors of this volume would confirm, is a living embodiment of the role model effect.

References

Abrams, B. and Settle, R. (1999) 'Women's suffrage and the growth of the welfare state', *Public Choice* 100 (3/4):289–300.

Aidt, T. and Dallal, B. (2008) 'Female voting power: the contribution of women's suffrage to the growth of social spending in Western Europe (1869–1960)', *Public Choice* 134 (3/4): 391–417.

Alvarez, R. M. and McCaffery, E. (1999) 'Gender and Tax', in POLMETH Working Papers, http://web.polmeth.ufl.edu/papers.html.

Andersen, K. (1975) 'Working women and political participation, 1952–1972', *American Journal of Political Science* 19 (3): 439–53.

— (1999) 'The gender gap and experiences with the welfare state', PS: *Political Science and Politics* 32 (1): 17–19.

Arneil, B. (2006) 'Just communities: social capital, gender and culture', in B. O'Neill and E. Gidengil (eds) *Gender and Social Capital*, New York: Routledge, pp. 15–44.

Atkeson, L. and Rapoport, R. (2003) 'The more things change the more they stay the same: examining gender differences in political attitude expression, 1952–2000', *Public Opinion Quarterly* 67 (4):495–521.

Baldez, L. (2001) 'The UN Convention to Eliminate All Forms of Discrimination Against Women (CEDAW): a new way to measure women's interests', *Politics and Gender* 7 (3):419–23.

Baum, M. and Espírito-Santo, A. (2007) 'Exploring the Gender Gap in Portugal: Women's political participation', in A. Freire, M. Costa, and P. Magalhaes (eds) *Portugal at the Polls: in 2002*, Plymouth, UK: Lexington Books.

Beaman, L., Duflo, E., Pande, R. and Topalova, P. (2012) 'Female leadership raises aspirations and educational attainment for girls: a policy experiment in India', *Sciencexpress*, 335: 583–586.

Bendyna, M. and Lake, C. (1994) 'Gender and voting in the 92 presidential elections', in A Cook, S Thomas and C. Wilcox (eds) *The Year of the Woman: Myths and realities,* Boulder, San Francisco, and Oxford: Westview Press, pp. 237–54.

Bergh, J. (2007) 'Explaining the gender gap: a cross-national analysis of gender differences in voting', *Journal of Elections, Public Opinion and Parties* 17 (3): 235–61.

Bolzendahl, C. (2009) 'Making the implicit explicit: gender influences on social spending in twelve industrialised democracies, 1980–1999', *Social Politics* 16 (1): 40–81.

Box-Steffensmeir, J., DeBoef, S. and Lin, T.-M. (1997) '*Microideology, Macropartisanship and the Gender Gap*' Paper presented at *American Political Science Association*, Washington, September.

Breitenbach, E. and Thane, P. (eds) (2010) *What Difference did the Vote Make: Women and citizenship in Britain and Ireland in the 20th Century*, London: Continuum.

Burden, B. (2008) 'The social roots of the partisan gender gap', *Public Opinion Quarterly* 72 (1): 55–75.

Burns, N. (2001) 'Gender: Public opinion and political action' in *Political Science: The State of the Discipline*, I. Katznelson and H. Milner (eds) Washington, DC: APSA, pp. 462–87.

Burns, N., Schlozman, K. and Verba, S. (2001) *The Private Roots of Public Action: Gender, equality and political participation*, Cambridge, MA: Harvard University Press.

Butler, D. and Stokes, D. (1974) *Political Change in Britain*, London: Macmillan.

Campbell, A., Converse, P., Miller, W. and Stokes, D. (1960) *The American Voter*, New York: John Wiley & Sons.

Campbell, D. and Wolbrecht, C. (2006) 'See Jane run: women politicians as role models for adolescents', *The Journal of Politics* 68 (2): 233–47.

Campbell, R. (2004) 'Gender, ideology and issue preference: is there such a thing as a political women's interest in Britain?', *British Journal of Politics and International Relations* 6 (1): 20–46.

— (2006) *Gender and the Vote in Britain*, Colchester, Essex: ECPR Press.

— (2013) 'Leaders, footsoldiers and befrienders: the gendered nature of social capital and political participation in Britain', *British Politics* 8 (1): 28–50.

Campbell, R. and Childs, S. (2012) 'To the Left, To the Right', *Representing Conservative Women's Interests* in ECPR Joint Sessions, Antwerp.

— (forthcoming) '"To the left, to the right": Representing Conservative women's interests', *Party Politics*.

Campbell, R., Childs, S. and Lovenduski, J. (2010) 'Do women need women MPs', *British Journal of Political Science* 40 (1): 171–194.

Campbell, R. and Winters, W. (2008) 'Understanding men and women's political interests: evidence from a study of gendered political attitudes', *Journal of Elections, Public Opinion and Parties* 18 (1): 53–74.

Carroll, S. (1999) 'The disempowerment of the gender gap: Soccer Moms and the 1996 Elections', *Political Studies* 32 (1): 7–11.

Celis, K. and Childs, S. (2011) 'The substantive representation of women: what to do with conservative claims?', *Political Studies* 60 (1): 213–25.

Conover, P. (1988) 'Feminists and the gender gap', *Journal of Politics* 50: 985–1010.

Conway, M., Steuernagel, G. and Ahern, D. (1997) *Women and Political Participation: Cultural change in the political arena*, Washington, D.C.: CQ Press.

Cook, E. (1998) 'Voter Reaction to Women Candidates', in S. Thomas and C. Wilcox (eds) *Women and Elective Office: Past, Present and Future*, Wilcox. Oxford: Oxford University Press, pp. 56–72.

Corbetta, P. and Cavazza, N. (2008) 'From the parish to the polling booth: evolution and interpretation of the political gender gap in Italy, 1968–2006', *Electoral Studies* 27 (2): 272–84.

Delli Carpini, M. and Keeter, S. (2005) 'Gender and Political Knowledge', in S. Tolleson-Rinehart and J. J. Josephson (eds) *Gender and American Politics: Women, men and the political process*, New York: M.E. Sharpe.

Dolan, K. (1998) 'Voting for women in the "year of the woman"', *American Journal of Political Science* 42 (1): 272–93.

— (2001) 'Electoral context, issues and voting for women in the 1990s', *Women and Politics* 23 (1): 21–36.

— (2004) *Voting for Women: How the public evaluates women candidates*, Boulder, Colorado: Westview Press.

— (2006) 'Symbolic mobilization? The impact of candidate sex in American elections', *American Politics Research* 36 (6): 687–704.

— (2010) 'The impact of gender stereotyped evaluations on support for women candidates', *Political Behavior* 32 (1): 69–88.

— (2011) 'Do women and men know different things? Measuring gender differences in political knowledge', *The Journal of Politics* 73 (1): 97–107.

Dow, J. (2009) 'Gender differences in political knowledge: distinguishing characteristics-based and returns-based differences', *Political Behavior* 31 (1): 97–107.

Duverger, M. (1955) '*The Political Role of Women*', Paris: UNESCO.

Espírito-Santo, A. (2011) 'The symbolic value of descriptive representation: the case of female representation', *Political and Social Sciences*, Florence European University Institute.

Frazer, E. and MacDonald, K. (2003) 'Sex differences in political knowledge in Britain', *Political Studies* 51 (1): 76–83.

Gidengil, E. and Harell, A. (2007) 'Network diversity and vote choice: women's social ties and left voting in Canada', *Politics and Gender* 3 (2): 151–77.

Giger, N. (2009) 'Towards a modern gender gap in Europe? A comparative analysis of voting behavior in 12 countries', *The Social Science Journal* 46 (3): 474–92.

Greenberg, A. (2001) 'Race, religiosity and the women's vote', *Women and Politics* 22 (3): 59–82.

Halpern, D. (2004) *Social Capital*, Cambridge: Polity Press.

Hanes, D. and Thomas, M. (2013) 'Did feminism really change? Second – and third – wave feminism and the gender gap in political interest' in *ECPG*, Barcelona, Spain.

Harman, H. and Mattinson, D. (2000) *Winning for Women*, Fabian Society.

Hayes, B. (1997) 'Gender, feminism and electoral behaviour in Britain', *Electoral Studies* 16 (2): 203–16.

Hayes, B. and Bean, C. S. (1993) 'Gender and local political interest – some international comparisons', *Political Studies* XLI(4).

Hayes, B. C. and McAllister, I. (1997) 'Gender, party leaders and election outcomes in Australia, Britain and the United States', *Comparative Political Studies* 30: 3–26.

Inglehart, R. and Norris, P. (2000) 'The developmental theory of the gender gap: women and men's voting behaviour in global perspective', *International Political Science Review* 21 (4): 441–62.

Iversen, T. and Rosenbluth, F. (2006) 'The political economy of gender: explaining cross-national variation in the gender division of labor and the gender voting gap', *American Journal of Political Science* 50 (1): 1–19.

Lawless, J. (2012) *Becoming a Candidate: Political ambition and the decision to run for office*, Cambridge: Cambrige University Press.

Lawless, J. and Fox, R. (2005) *It Takes a Candidate: Why women don't run for office*, Cambridge: Cambridge University Press.

— (2010) *It Takes a Candidate: Why women don't run for office*, Cambridge: Cambridge University Press.

Lehman, K., Burns, N., Verba, S. and Donahue, J. (1995) 'Gender and citizenship participation: is there a different voice', *American Journal of Political Science* 39 (2): 267–93.

Lizotte, M.-K. and Sidman, A. (2009) 'Explaining the gender gap in political knowledge', *Politics and Gender* 5 (2):127–51.

Lowndes, V. (2000) 'Women and social capital: a comment on Hall's "Social capital in Britain"', *British Journal of Political Science* 30 (3): 533–40.

— (2004) 'Getting on or getting by? Women, social capital and political participation', *British Journal of Politics and International Relations* 6 (1): 45–64.

— (2006) 'It's not what you've got, but what you do with it', in B. O'Neill and E. Gidengil (eds) *Gender and Social Capital*, New York: Routledge, pp. 213–40.

McBride, D. and Mazur, A. (2002) *The Politics of State Feminism*, Philadephia: Temple University Press.

Manza, J. and Brooks, C. (1998) 'The gender gap in U.S. presidential elections: when? why? implications?', *American Journal of Sociology* 103 (5): 1236–1266.

Mattei, L. and Mattei, F. (1998) 'If men stayed at home: the gender gap and recent congressional elections', *Political Research Quarterly* 5 (2): 411–436.

Mondak, J. and Anderson, M. (2004) 'The knowledge gap: a reexamination of gender based differences in political knowledge', *Journal of Politics* 66 (2): 492–512.

Morales, L. (1999) 'Political participation: exploring the gender gap in Spain', *South European Society and Politics* 4 (2):223–47.

Norrander, B. and Wilcox, C. (2008) 'The gender gap in ideology', *Political Behavior* 30 (4): 503–23.

Norris, P. (ed.) (1997) *Passages to Power*, Cambridge: Cambridge University Press.

— (1999) 'Gender: A gender-generation gap?' in G. Evans and P. Norris (eds) *Critical Elections: British parties and voters in long-term perspective*, London: Sage, pp. 146–63.

Norris, P. and Inglehart, R. (2006) 'Gendering social capital: bowling in women's leagues?' in B. O'Neill and E. Gidengil (eds) *Gender and Social Capital*, New York: Routledge, pp. 73–98.

Norris, P. and Krook, M. (2009) 'One of us: multilevel models examining the impact of descriptive representation on civic engagement', in *HKS Factulty Research Working Paper Series* RWP09-030.

Norris, P. and Lovenduski, J. (1995) *Political Recruitment*, Cambridge: Cambridge University Press.

Norris, P., Lovenduski, J. and Campbell, R. (2004) *Gender and Political Participation*, London: The Electoral Commission.

O'Neill, B. and Gidengil, E. (eds) (2006) *Gender and Social Capital*, New York: Routledge.

Owen, D. and Dennis, J. (1988) 'Gender differences in the politicization of American children', *Women and Politics* 8 (2): 23–43.

Phillips, A. (1995) *The Politics of Presence*, Oxford: Oxford University Press.

Plutzer, E. and Zipp, J. (1996) 'Identity politics, partisanship, and voting for women candidates', *Public Opinion Quarterly* 60 (1): 30–57.

Putnam, R. (1995) 'America's declining social capital', *Journal of Democracy* 6 (1): 65–78.

— (2000) *Bowling Alone: The collapse and revival of American community*, New York: Simon and Schuster.

Putnam, R., Leonardi, R. and Nanetti, R. (1993) *Making Democracy Work: Civic traditions in modern Italy*, Princeton: Princeton University Press.

Sapiro, V. (1981) 'Research frontier essay: when are interests interesting? The problem of political representation of women', *The American Political Science Review* 75 (3): 701–16.

Saward, M. (2006) 'The representative claim', *Contemporary Political Theory* 5 (3): 297–318.

— (2010) *The Representative Claim*, Oxford University Press.

Schwindt-Bayer, L. and Taylor-Robinson, M. (2011) 'The meaning and measurement of women's interests', *Politics and Gender* 7 (3): 417–16.

Seltzer, R., Newman, J. and Leighton, M. (1997) *Sex as a Political Variable: Women as Candidates and Voters in U.S. Elections*, Boulder: Lynne Rienner Publishers, Inc.

Shepherd-Robinson, L. and Lovenduski, J. (2002) *Women and Candidate Selection in British Political Parties*, London: Fawcett.

Steel, G. (2003) 'Class and Gender in British General Elections', Paper prepared for the presentation at the Midwest Political Science Association Annual Meeting, Chicago.

Stolle, D. and Gidengil, E. (2010) 'What do women really know? A gendered analysis of varieties of political knowledge', *Perspectives on Politics* 8 (1): 93–109.

Stolle, D. and Micheletti, M. (2006) 'The Gender Gap Reversed: Political consumerism as a women-friendly form of civic and political engagement' in B. O'Neill and E. Gidengil (eds) *Gender and Social Capital*, New York: Routledge.

Tingsten, H. (1937) *Political Behavior*, Totowa, NJ: Bedminster.

Verba, S., Schlozman, K. and Burns, N. (2005) 'Family Ties: Understanding the intergenerational transmission of participation', in A. Zuckerman (ed.) *The Social Logic of Politics*, Philadelphia: Temple University Press.

Wängnerud, L. (2000) 'Testing the politics of presence: women's representation in the Swedish Riksdag', *Scandinavian Political Studies* 23 (1): 67–91.

Welch, Susan, Margaret Ambrosius, Janet Clark, and Robert Darcy (1985) 'The effect of candidate gender on electoral outcomes in state legislative races', *Western Political Quarterly* 38: 464–75.

Wirls, D. (1986) 'Reinterpreting the gender gap', *Public Opinion Quarterly* 50 (3): 316–30.

Wolak, J. and McDevitt, M. (2011) 'The roots of the gender gap in political knowledge in adolescence', *Political Behavior* 33 (3): 505–33.

Wolbrecht, C. and Campbell, D. (2007) 'Leading by example: female members of parliament as political role models', *American Journal of Political Science* 51 (4): 921–39.

Zuckerman, A., Dasovic, J. and Fitzgerald, J. (2007) *Partisan Families: The social logic of bounded partisanship in Germany and Britain*, Cambridge: Cambridge University Press.

Vignette – Women's Political Interests: How the Women's Vote is Decisive

Deborah Mattinson

Deborah Mattinson is a British pollster and media commentator. She is founder director of research and strategy agency *BritainThinks*. She was formerly a pollster to Gordon Brown, first when he was Chancellor of the Exchequer and then as Prime Minister. Deborah uses her extensive research on the topic of women voters to demonstrate how their behaviour can be pivotal to election outcomes.

'It was the women wot won it'. The Power and Influence of the Women's Vote

The Labour Party's 1997 general election landslide was an enormous achievement – and its wooing of women voters was arguably the greatest success of all. Historically, women voters had been so anti Labour that, had the suffragettes and suffragists failed and women never won the right to vote in 1918, the mathematics of an all male electorate would have resulted in a Labour victory in every election in the UK between 1945 and 1997. Instead, women gifted the power to be in Government to the Conservatives again and again during that period.

However, in 1997, an unprecedented 44 per cent of women voted Labour – up 10 per cent from 1992. Analysis indicated that the toughest sub group within the women's vote was also the most numerically important – women aged over 55. It was this group that shifted disproportionately, the result of more than a decade of internal campaigning by a small number of determined women activists and politicians who sought to change the masculine face of the Labour party and its equally masculine policy offer.

Blair and his babes

Focus groups told us that women's take on politics was different from men's: less motivated by abstract debate, more motivated by issues that affected their immediate family. In this context, women saw Labour as a male dominated talking shop that too often spoke an entirely different language. This was a message that many male politicians found hard to hear.

In the end, however, self-interest won the day and those same male politicians were reluctantly brought on side, persuaded that they simply could not win the election without women's votes. That meant a change of tack: developing policies with women in mind: for example improved childcare and the minimum wage. It also meant having more visible women politicians – although later derided, 'Blair's babes' were, at the time, seen by women voters as a positive symbol of this change. More than both of these, though, winning women voters demanded a different way of doing politics – and political communications – more direct, less adversarial. Tony Blair the leader of the Labour party, himself instinctively 'got' this and personified the fresh approach to Government that lay at the heart of Labour's promise.

From Worcester woman to let down lady

However, just as women had been the first to embrace the positive change that Labour offered, and help Labour to electoral victory, so they were the first to become disillusioned. Their negative mood reached crisis point in the run up to the 2005 General Election. We now saw a new gender gap – not in terms of voting intention but in terms of attitudes. Women were consistently less happy with the Government's performance, especially as the once popular PM turned his attention from more female friendly domestic politics to international affairs post Iraq. As one political commentator wryly observed, 'Worcester Woman had become Let Down Lady'. Women had been so taken with Labour and Blair that their disappointment was acute and deeply personal.

Labour's lead withered away as the 2005 general election drew closer but by March the campaign strategy team had rethought its plans and pushed the economy centre stage, with all campaigning efforts focused on what Labour had achieved, especially for women: nursery provision, working family tax credit, child benefit and flexible working. In the event Labour won again, and, once again women's votes were significant. Indeed, had women not had the vote in 2005, the result would have been a hung parliament. If only women had voted in the election the majority would have almost doubled to more than 100 seats.

The future up for grabs

By the time of Labour's ill-fated general election campaign in 2010 women voters were once again reviewing their allegiance. While Labour strategists agreed that women voters were key, the campaign, led by Gordon Brown, failed to make the emotional connection that was needed to re engage them. The result was that Labour hemorrhaged support amongst women of all ages losing 10 per cent amongst the 18–24s, 6 per cent amongst the 25–34s, 8 per cent amongst the 35–54s and 4 per cent amongst the 55+, where the Conservatives enjoyed a massive 14 per cent rise to 44 per cent. Overall the gender gap still played in Labour's favour but not enough to counter a generally dismal performance amongst men.

At the mid-term point in the 2010 Parliament, all main political parties are looking at women voters with anxiety. Labour's small but consistent lead owed much to women who are significantly less satisfied with the Conservative/Liberal Democrat coalition Government's approach and significantly more supportive of

Labour and its leadership. Women were apparently feeling the effect of the cuts more than men, and were less patient with the Government's long term plan. Yet Labour had not yet successfully set out its new stall in women voters' eyes and continued to be defined by its negative recent past.

It is hard to predict where women's votes will settle in the future – but their significance is now beyond doubt.

Biography of Joni Lovenduski

Judith Squires

Why aren't more people angry about women's political under-representation? This is a question that Joni Lovenduski has posed repeatedly throughout her long and distinguished academic career. As one of the first generation of gender and politics scholars in the UK Joni not only shaped the research field, she has acted as a mentor and inspiration for subsequent generations, both through her ground-breaking research and through her extensive and generous leadership and mentoring contributions to a wide range of professional networks.

Joni was most recently the Anniversary Professor of Politics at Birkbeck, University of London, a post that she has held since 2000. She was previously Professor of Politics and Head of Department at the University of Southampton (1995–2000) and Professor of Comparative Politics at Loughborough University (1993–5). She made a huge contribution to each of these institutions, via her formal and informal leadership roles, acting as an inspiration and mentor for a generation of younger scholars.

Joni has written extensively on gender and politics, British politics, and comparative politics. Her most significant contributions lie in her detailed analysis of the impacts of gender on politics, innovative research into the political representation of women, important new understandings about the selection of candidates for elected office, and the roles of women in political parties, and large-scale comparative analysis of European equality policies.

Her publications on gender and politics include: *Women and European Politics: Contemporary Feminism and Public Policy* (1986), *Contemporary Feminist Politics* with Vicky Randall (1993), *Political Recruitment: Gender, Race and Class in the British Parliament* (1995) (with Pippa Norris), and *High Tide or High Time for Labour Women* (1998) (with Maria Eagle MP), *Feminizing Politics* (2005), *State Feminism and Political Representation* (2005), *The Hansard Report on Women at the Top 2005* (with Sarah Childs and Rosie Campbell), *Gender and Political Participation* (2004) (with Pippa Norris and Rosie Campbell). She was co- editor of *The Politics of the Second Electorate* (1981), *The New Politics of Abortion* (1986), *Gender and Party Politics* (1993) and editor of *Feminism and Politics* (2000) as well as many articles and essays in edited collections on issues of Gender and Politics.

In 2004 she revealed the 'shocking' levels of sexist abuse experienced by women MPs in Westminster at the hands of their male counterparts, with male MPs of all parties engaging in sexist barracking in the Chamber, sexist insults and patronising assumptions about their female colleagues' abilities. Even after the influx of women MPs at the 1997 general election, and greater numbers of women in the Cabinet, female MPs reported that they felt stuck on the edge of a male world. Joni was shocked at the findings:

> We expected a bit of this but nothing like this extent. We expected to find a couple of shocking episodes [...] What I think is shocking to the general public is that these things go on in the House of Commons.

In addition to her writings, Joni has also played a significant role within the discipline as Chair of the Editorial Board of *Political Quarterly* and a member of the editorial boards of *British Politics*, *The British Journal of Political Science*, *The European Political Science Review* and *French Politics*.

Joni played a significant role as European convener of the Research Network on Gender and the State (RNGS), a cross-national collaborative project that investigated the impact of women's movements on public policy. The project was funded by the European Science Foundation, the American National Science Foundation and the ESRC Future Governance Programme. She was also Vice -Chair of the European Consortium for Political Research from 2000–2003 and a member of the Research Council of the European University Institute from 2003–2008. In addition, she has acted as consultant on Gender and Politics for UNECE, the European Commission and the Council of Europe. She directed the European Commission funded investigation of the state of the art of research on Gender and Politics in Europe in 1996 and 1997.

The significance of her contribution was recognised by the European Consortium for Political Research Standing Group on Gender and Politics when they presented Joni with the Gender and Politics Award in 2009. The award recognises the winner's contribution to the scientific development of the field and the development of a scholarly network for gender and politics, and also identified individuals who have furthered the cause and interests of politics and gender scholars. Joni's nominators for this award highlighted her 'pioneering research on the representation of women in politics and public life and her long-standing contribution to women and politics within ECPR'. Her research was celebrated as having altered perceptions of the problem of women's under-representation thereby obliging political parties to take measures to confront the issue of women's legislative recruitment. Joni's work was also recognised by the panel as having led to important inputs to debates on these issues at the European level and through her role as consultant to the European Commission and the Council of Europe. Joni was rightly recognised as a mentor and inspiration for subsequent generations 'actively encouraging and supporting younger researchers'.

The significance of Joni's contribution has also been recognised by mainstream professional associations. In 2007 she was made a Fellow of the British Academy and received the Special Recognition Award from the Political Studies Association of the United Kingdom. The PSA Awards Jury explained their decision to award Joni the prize, saying:

> Her lifelong commitment to improving women's representation at Westminster and her pioneering collaborative work have bridged the gap between the study of British politics and gender. She has been inspirational, especially to female scholars and has mentored many younger scholars.

> CEO of the Political Studies Association, Helena Djurkovic, said:

> Joni Lovenduski has been an inspiration and role model to many young academics working in Britain today. At a time when the casual misogyny of much popular culture is a source of increasing concern, the intellectual case for feminism needs to be heard loud and clear. Joni Lovenduski continues to make that case with energy and passion.

In short, Joni created the intellectual and organisational space for future generations of gender and politics scholars to grow and thrive.

Afterword: Joni Lovenduski's Contribution – Some Personal Impressions

Rosie Campbell and Sarah Childs

> 'I would not be where I am today as a scholar, and as person more generally, without Joni Lovenduski' (Amy Mazur)

Sarah had never heard of a *Festschrift*; and it took us both most of the project to remember how to spell it. But we are most grateful to Judith Squires for suggesting a *Festschrift* for Joni Lovenduski. Joni was one of Rosie's PhD supervisors; she was an informal mentor of Sarah's since she was a PhD student. And she's been an absolute constant in both our lives for nigh on two decades, and we love her dearly: for her pioneering academic contribution it goes without saying; for her immense love of good food and wine, fashion and laughter, as well as her presence when we've needed her personally and professionally; and for taking us to places – geographic and intellectual – that we'd not have got to without her. This is our but small offering of thanks, respect and love.

This is, however, not a traditional *Festschrift*, rather *Deeds and Words* is 'a kind of *Festschrift*'. Whilst it is very much in honour of Joni's work and life, we decided we would produce a Volume that brought together academic research on gender and politics in a tightly edited book, one that presented a coherent set of chapters drawing on contemporary scholarship. We wanted Joni's *Festschrift* to be an informative, intellectually insightful and useful book for students and scholars, as well as the interested public and political actors, alike.

What her friends and colleagues say

It is beyond dispute that Joni Lovenduski is a 'pioneer' (Marila Guadagnini) of gender and politics scholarship or that she is a 'brilliant' scholar of political science (Guadagnini). Her commitment to feminising political science research and political science as a profession clearly runs through her career (Wyn Grant; Dermot Hodson), shaking up the PSA and ECPR, as well as the many departments where she has worked. Joni has also engaged extensively and willingly with political and policy practitioners, challenging insider accounts with her robust research (Dermot Hodson) and transforming political practice.

Though those who do not know her may fear the 'beligerent feminist-oriented professor', this is an outrageous misrepresentation (John Groom). Sure, she does not suffer fools gladly (Dermot Hodson), but an argument (over RCT) is no barrier to friendship (Peter John). Joni is determined and politically shrewd

(Vicky Randall). She can be firm, and is combative when needed (Geraint Parry). Committed to fairness, her judgement is 'sharp acute', very professional (Yves Mény). Joni is also a superb leader, demonstrating great '*maestria*' (Yves Mény). 'Somehow committees with Joni on them work better' (Ken Newton – sentiments shared by Alfio Mastropaolo). Alongside these attributes, Joni is revered too for her professional collegiality even when she is under no obligation (Richard Bellamy); her generosity in support is striking (Clare Dekker).

To younger gender and politics scholars (some who are not so young any more) she has been the most wonderful role model and mentor. A 'rock star' (Amy Mazur), she is the 'godmother' of feminist political science (Fiona Mackay). A Grand Dame, nurturing and inspiring us (Marila Guadagnini; Liz Evans; Fiona Mackay), the very, very opposite of a Queen Bee. Indeed, Joni's generosity feels as if it is unlimited. She gives us faith in our own work; makes us expect more of ourselves; and guides and advises us (Amy Mazur; Liz Evans). In so doing, she has made us want to give back to subsequent generations of gender and politics scholars, in recognition of what she gave to us (Amy Mazur). Our thanks are unbounded.

But to focus on only the academic dimension – is to miss so much of what makes Joni special. It is clear that she is held dear for her person – pretty, bright, and elegant at her 65th birthday party. We notice her beautiful earrings – she appears to have an unlimited collection (Guadagnini and Childs); admire her smooth skin (Guadagnini), her smile and fantastic legs (Childs), and her style (Clare Dekker). Superficial things some might say – not what a feminist academic should be noted for – but this is too limited, for they are the embodiment of who Joni is. And she is 'there' for her friends unconditionally: she might worry about whether we should eat 'scrambled eggs when pregnant' (Vicky Randall); or how we might better balance our work and life –usually this involves a good supper out; and helps us through the difficult personal and professional times.

Key to Joni's personality is her flair for enjoying herself (Vicky Randall), though the coffee had better be good (Fiona Mackay). The immense sense of enjoyment that she brings to so many occasions is richly observed by her many academic friends. She very much enjoys the pleasures of good wine, food and conversation (John Groom), dining out and as well as being the most amazing chef; shopping, for earrings, shoes, and clothes; skiing and walking; and the '*jardin*' (Yves Mény). She adores Italy (Alfio Mastropaolo).

We will informally publish a full 'Friends Book' to accompany this *Festschrift*. Here we have been able to give just a small flavour of the 'difference' Joni has made to the many scholars who have been taught by her, and worked with her, and been befriended by her over the years. Collectively they paint simply an amazing picture of what makes the very best academic and friend. We are supremely confident that Amy Mazur's epithet, which leads this Afterword, holds for us all.

Index

CPSIA information can be obtained
at www.ICGtesting.com
Printed in the USA
LVHW04s2200290818
588519LV00002B/76/P

9 781910 259450